Secretariat

CORRIGENDUM

Ref.: Sales No. E.97.XVII.10
(ST/ESA/STAT/SER.K/14)

18 May 1998
New York

HANDBOOK FOR PRODUCING NATIONAL STATISTICAL REPORTS
ON WOMEN AND MEN

Corrigendum

Page 82, Box, Series A

The denominator of the formula should read

Women (men) in senior positions in all fields

Page 137, Box, Series B

In the formula for 100 read 1,000

Add the following sentence at the end of the box:

This provides a rough estimate of the probability of dying between the
ages of 1 and 5 (expressed per 1,000 children surviving to age 1).

Page 150, Box, Series A

In the formula for 100 read 1,000

Page 165, Box, Series B

The heading should read

Average interval between first, second and subsequent births (in
months)

Page 288, section entitled "Electronic media"

Line 1: For demographic read geographic

- - - - -

Social Statistics and Indicators   Series K, No. 14

Department of Economic and Social Information
Statistics Division

Handbook for Producing National Statistical Reports on Women and Men

UNITED NATIONS • NEW YORK, 1997

DB# 1660776

Note

The designations employed and the presentation of the material in this publication do not imply the expression of any opinion whatsoever on the part of the Secretariat of the United Nations concerning the legal status of any country, territory, city or area, or of its authorities, or concerning the delimitation of its frontiers or boundaries.

The term "country" as used in the text of this publication also refers, as appropriate, to territories or areas.

The designations "developed" and "developing" regions are intended for statistical convenience and do not necessarily express a judgement about the stage reached by a particular country or area in the development process.

ST/ESA/STAT/SER.K/14

United Nations publication
Sales No. E.97.XVII.10
ISBN 92-1-161394-9

UN2
ST/ESA/STAT/SER.K/14

PREFACE

This *Handbook* provides a framework for developing and disseminating, in the form of a publication, a minimum set of statistics and indicators on women's and men's position in society. Since the mid-1980s, many national and regional publications presenting statistical analyses of women and men have been produced. In 1991 *The World's Women 1970–1990: Trends and Statistics* was produced as a collaborative effort of United Nations agencies to present a factual view of progress made globally towards advancing the situation of women relative to men.

Using non-technical language, a carefully designed format and innovative methods of presentation, *The World's Women 1970–1990* became a United Nations best seller and generated demand for gender statistics publications among both technical and non-technical users. As a contribution to the Fourth World Conference on Women, held in Beijing in September 1995, the United Nations published a second edition—*The World's Women 1995*. Several countries and regional institutions also produced and disseminated "World's Women-type" publications and booklets. Yet there are many more countries whose interest in producing similar publications has not been satisfied for varied reasons, among which are lack of knowledge about how such a publication may be produced and a misconception about the amount of resources, financial and human, that an endeavour like this should take.

The present *Handbook* is an operational guide for national statistical offices and gender programmes interested in conducting a statistical analysis on women and men for wide dissemination to users of varied backgrounds and statistical orientations. It emphasizes that the main responsibility for the gender statistics publication lies with the national statistical office but that strong user-producer collaboration and advisory mechanisms are necessary to secure the moral support, technical input and realistic orientation required for the success of the intended publication. The first chapter describes the institutional arrangements and resource requirements for the development of a gender statistics publication as a project that could be either independent or an integral part of a well-established publication programme. The second and third chapters explain how to prepare and use available data and generate indicators on the basis of critical gender issues and concerns identified through user-producer consultations. The fourth provides details on tools for presenting statistics and indicators and on how they are combined to produce a user-oriented publication. The fifth chapter reviews steps in printing a publication and different ways of disseminating it. Other types of statistical outputs, such as wall charts and booklets, are also described.

The *Handbook* is the main output of a project funded by the Gender in Development (GID) Subgroup of the Joint Consultative Group on Policy (JCGP)—comprising the United Nations Development Programme (UNDP), the United Nations Population Fund (UNFPA), the United Nations Children's Fund (UNICEF), the United Nations Development Fund for Women (UNIFEM), the International Fund for Agricultural Development (IFAD) and the World Food Programme (WFP). The major objective of the project, which began in 1993, is to develop national capacities in the production of gender statistics publications. As part of the project activities, the application of the *Handbook* was tested in Mexico, where a national publication was produced in 1995, and by the Economic and Social Commission for Western Asia (ESCWA) in the production of a regional publication in 1997 on Arab women and men. Several sections of earlier drafts of the *Handbook* were also tested in a regional training workshop for eastern, central and southern Africa, held in 1993 in Gaborone, Botswana, and in another workshop for selected countries in Asia, held in 1994 in Bangkok, Thailand.

The Statistics Division of the Department of Economic and Social Affairs of the United Nations Secretariat prepared the *Handbook* with the assistance of Communications Development Incorporated as consultant to the Secretariat. Ms. Mercedes Concepción provided additional draft inputs as consultant to the Secretariat.

CONTENTS

3. Illustrations with selected indicators   41

List of Illustrations

List of tables

USING THE HANDBOOK

Monitoring equal opportunity for individuals and the achievement of their economic, social, political and cultural rights requires an enormous amount of good quality statistical data and innovative skills in communication. Action for change and effective programming depends in large measure on the ability of interest groups to argue and convince policy makers of the need for change. Without facts, no argument, however convincing, can sway the opinion of decision makers and redirect the course of planning. Yet, statistics need to be presented in a logical, concise and compelling format to interest the indifferent, equip the advocate, inform the programmers and indicate possible options.

Economic, social and political development requires the dissemination of information to a wide audience. If information is lacking, inaccurate or outdated, development will be stunted—adversely affecting vulnerable and disenfranchised populations. To be of use, statistical data must be disseminated in a form that is accurate, relevant and accessible.

Gender equity has become a focus of national and international concern, and as programmes and policies directed towards gender equity are considered and implemented, the need has increased for sex disaggregated data. In any nation where equal opportunity for women and men is a goal, comprehensive, reliable and current statistics on the status of women and men can serve to discredit stereotypes and guide national policy towards social, cultural and economic parity.

This *Handbook* aims to help countries respond to this demand by developing a national statistical publication on women and men. It has been developed for use by a broad cross-section of individuals and teams and is aimed at statisticians, demographers and researchers charged with or interested in the task of producing a gender statistics publication. Policy makers, advocates for gender equity, and graphic designers and editors working in gender and development may also find specialized sections of the *Handbook* useful in their work.

The *Handbook* takes users through the steps needed to compile, analyse, produce and disseminate such a publication on the situation of women and men in a country. The goal is to present statistics in a form useful to advocacy groups, non-governmental organizations, national planners, government agencies and the media.

Throughout the *Handbook*, the concept of a special project is only one of several paradigms within which a gender statistics publication can be produced. This sort of publication can as easily be created as part of a programme or activity within a pre-existing unit or office. It need not require the separate funding and structure that the word "project" can imply.

The use of the *Handbook* will depend on the capabilities, resources and intents of its audience. While it provides suggestions, it should be kept in mind that these are not the only viable approaches. Variations in local resources and national issues will dictate different approaches. While the focus is the production of a gender statistics report, the information provided would

be useful in preparing a user-oriented statistical report on any topic or subpopulation.
For those initiating a project to develop a national statistical publication, or for the heads of
statistical bureaus or consultants hired to advise, train or manage a project team, the opening
chapter, "Planning and organizing the work", provides a guide to the process of budgeting
and planning, assembling an advisory group and a production team, managing the team and
monitoring and evaluating their work.

Chapter 2, "Compilation and analysis of statistics", is directed to the statistician who will
identify sources of data and statistics in special fields, select indicators based on the country's
specific development priorities and produce tables and charts that accurately reflect the findings. It also details the relative worth of different data sources and presents their individual
strengths and shortcomings.

Chapter 3, "Illustrations with selected indicators", focuses on preparing indicators from
basic data using a step-by-step process. Policy relevance, likely problems and suggested
presentations are some of the issues discussed for each of 36 sample indicators. The
indicators are divided into six sections: population, families and households; public life and
leadership; education and training; health and child-bearing; housing, human settlements
and environment; and work and the economy.

Chapter 4, "Presenting data and designing the layout", will be of particular interest to statisticians charged with selecting and preparing the publication's charts and tables. It should also
be useful to an editor, designer or graphic artist involved in the project. This chapter offers
effective means of presenting data to clearly show relationships between indicators.

Chapter 5, "Producing and disseminating the book", addresses the writing and editing of the
text for clarity and support of the messages. An editor will want to study the steps to be
taken in building a coherent structure, directing the prose to the audience, keeping focused
on the purpose, establishing an appropriate length and finalizing the text for publication. The
project manager and adviser or trainer should review the end of chapter 5 to prepare an evaluation of the project to improve the efficiency of future publications.

Chapter 5 will also aid in the assessment of the physical format of the book, the print run
and the distribution process. It considers technological aspects that will affect cost and
production quality. Production teams will want to have good data processing and desktop
publishing equipment available. The information and advice provided can be adapted to
many different formats, budgets and constraints.

1. Planning and organizing the work

LAUNCHING THE PROJECT

Gender statistics publications are typically launched by national statistical offices in response to interest and demand from users, and at the urging of organizations concerned with the status of women. These publications differ from most others prepared by national statistical offices in important ways. They are oriented towards a wide and varied audience, including policy makers, researchers and gender equity advocates. Therefore, their statistics and indicators:

- Cover diverse fields.
- Are disaggregated by sex and presented in simplified tables and charts.
- Relate to specific gender issues and policy concerns, and illuminate crucial gender concerns related to unequal access to resources and participation in social, economic and political life.
- Highlight the impact of current or past policies and programmes, especially differentials between women and men and between boys and girls.

Such a publication is generally a product of inter-ministerial and inter-agency cooperation, with the participation of both statisticians and users of statistics. Though this cooperation is achieved through an advisory group, an internal committee within the statistical office should initiate the work. Preliminary decisions must be made and basic parameters defined before the advisory group is convened.

Establish an internal committee

An internal committee within the statistical office should maintain final responsibility for and oversight of the publication. Its preparatory work is to assemble a work team and an advisory group, address budget and timetable details, and define the scope and goals of the publication, the audience and the institutional framework. The committee's work can be made both easier and more comprehensive by inviting inputs from other organizations and individuals involved in gender and development. The committee should also draw on the strengths of the various groups associated with the work, such as the advisory group and subject-matter experts, and consult them for a thorough review and assessment of outputs.

Identify problems and gender issues

The internal committee should first consider the kinds of social and economic inequities that exist in the country. Does a national plan for gender equity exist? If so, where does its focus lie? Here are some possible issues:

- Women's achievements in education and employment lag behind men's. In what geographical regions and subject areas especially?
- HIV infection rates are rising quickly, especially for young women.
- Illiteracy rates remain high, and women are more likely than men to be illiterate.
- Unpaid and informal sector work, mostly done by women, goes unacknowledged in economic policy-making. In what branches of industry is this important?
- Violence hampers people's self-determination and independence. What is the relative importance of domestic violence? Civil violence?
- Representation of women and men remains unequal in elected and appointed political offices.

These are critical issues. The statistics constructed in the publication will help to illustrate the extent of gender inequality within broad fields, such as health, education and economic life. They will also highlight the areas in which more statistical research is needed.

Consider the audience

For whom is the publication being produced? Who can use information on gender statistics?

The audience should be defined in terms of field of work, level of responsibility and ability to understand and use statistics. These parameters determine the characteristics or specifications for the publication being prepared.

Field of work—In general, all sectors of policy-making and programming are targets for the publication, and the primary audience is the government. There should be greater focus, however, on the ministry of planning, which liaises with all other sectors, and on the institution responsible for women's affairs, equal opportunity, or gender and development. In addition to government institutions, international development agencies and non-governmental organizations concerned with social issues, as well as research institutions and the media, are key audiences.

Level of responsibility—While policy makers are an important target for the publication because of the primary goal of influencing policies, programme officers and planners also should be targeted. The position and responsibility of the audience define the publication's potential effectiveness and the impact it is likely to have on the audience.

Ability to understand and use statistics—There should be a good mix among the audience of different levels of familiarity with statistics. Although statistical knowledge facilitates understanding of the statistics and indicators in the tables, the charts are meant to appeal to the less statistically inclined and the simplified form of the text and other tools of presentation are all meant to encourage the non-technical reader.

Agree on goals

What are the goals of the gender statistics publication? Here are some issues to consider:

* Increase awareness about the status of women in relation to men.
* Foster dialogue among women's advocates, beneficiaries and researchers, politicians and programme administrators working on gender issues in development.
* Determine the need for policy reform and for further research, data collection and analysis.
* Provide an objective basis for evaluating progress towards gender equality and achievement of equal opportunity.
* Advance the efforts of advocates for gender equality and improve the situation of women specifically.

Specify the measurable objectives

What are the objectives of the publication? Consider the impression the publication should make in order to reach its goals. How widely ought it to be disseminated? Might it be launched at a specific event or conference? Some of the objectives might be:

* Present data and analyses in a clear, concise and interesting publication that will reach its intended audience, such as key policy makers and the media.
* Create a clear picture of gender roles in society that will influence policy decisions and aid programmes.
* Contribute to the development and improvement of a national database on gender statistics.

Assemble an advisory group

Early in the process—as early as efficient—an advisory group should be assembled. The importance of the advisory group in enabling active and open producer–user communication cannot be overstated. The group should comprise some of the same people who will most benefit from a well-produced gender statistics publication: statisticians, government officials, academics, journalists, women's advocates and professionals from non-governmental organizations. Some members might also represent international organizations working in the country, but the group should consist largely of nationals familiar with local infrastructure, politics and needs.

Try to promote diversity within the advisory group with representatives from a variety of organizations, both governmental and non-governmental, across a broad range of fields with gender concerns. Take care not to let the group grow to an unmanageable size. Six to ten members can usually provide adequate diversity but the group remains small enough to work efficiently.

In assembling the advisory group, the internal committee should decide how many institutions will collaborate on the publication. Although the advisory group can serve as a voice for other institutions, only one institution—usually the national statistics office—should be responsible for the product.

The consultation process is essential and should not be circumvented. The advisory group can identify pressing gender problems, specify desired policies and goals, set objectives, identify additional audiences, create a publication strategy, advise on dissemination and help secure funding. Yet it is important that preliminary decisions about these parameters be made before the group begins discussing them. A good advisory group represents many different points of view. If the discussion of the publication is begun without at least a preliminary structure, the debating of these views will be less constructive.

Formulate a publication strategy

The sponsor and the advisory group should decide on a strategy for the publication. For this exercise to be useful, it is important to have in place general goals, objectives, and targeted audiences and issues.

The example used throughout the present *Handbook* is based on an 80- to 120-page publication illustrating the relative conditions of women and men. Half of the publication will be statistical tables, half will be text, charts, boxes and summary tables. Additional products might include:
- A statistical wall chart or brochure.
- A background informational packet to raise support at the start of the project.
- Two-page information sheets.
- Press releases.
- Summary materials for use in training seminars, lobbying efforts or conventions and conferences on gender and development issues.

Depending on the resources available and time, a smaller and less demanding publication such as a 40- to 72-page booklet may be produced.

See the annex for a description of some of the products mentioned.

The choice of products will determine the scope of the project, the time, staff and financial resources needed. It is a good idea to consider the resource requirements of each additional product when considering the publication strategy.

DEFINING THE SCOPE OF THE PUBLICATION

The essential task of coordinating contributors is made easier if the key users—the primary audience—are targeted. The advisory group will play a key role in coordinating contributors and may in fact comprise the most important contributors.

Decide on the scope

The scope will vary depending on available resources, budget and time constraints. Existing data, data gaps and national issues will also dictate the range of work needed to meet the goals of the publication.

- Consider the aim. Will the focus be on trends or on the current situation?
- Consider the number of institutions collaborating on the production. More institutions can mean a more comprehensive publication—but can also require more time.
- Consider the pros and cons for a big publication. The size of the publication will influence the readership. If the publication is large (e.g., more than 120 pages) the amount of material and cost could put off some people in the targeted audience. In limiting the size of the publication, attention will need to be paid to selecting the most relevant information. A larger publication may contain more information but there is also the danger of not being selective about what is included. A medium-sized publication need not contain less information than a bigger publication. Careful editing can ensure that the relevant information is included even in a medium-sized publication.

The decision on what the size of the publication should be will also be conditioned by availability of resources—human and financial. The publication should be seen as one of the outputs of the national statistics office (or national institution responsible for producing statistical reports). A major part of the resource requirements should therefore be provided internally. Supplementary support could come from the collaborating institutions or from funding agencies.

For present purposes, therefore, a small effort is defined as the minimum level of inputs required to produce the publication.

Staff—Two or more officers should be responsible for producing the publication, one working full-time on the production of the publication, the second responsible primarily for data compilation and preparation of tables and charts. Other staff should be available intermittently to provide the requisite data from their respective statistical fields.

Time requirements—The time span for completion of an average-sized publication will be 18 months to two years. The time could be reduced to one year if there is a team of officers working full-time on the publication.

Cost—There is no standard cost for the publication, since this depends on national situations. However, for a small effort, the cost can be borne almost entirely by the office producing the publication. Minimal external support from collaborators and funders could support some of the processes recommended in the present *Handbook*—meetings with the advisory group, special design and printing requirements (e.g., incorporating colours), and an extensive dissemination plan, including a launch and a workshop.

A larger effort can be defined by the degree to which additional resources are available to contract out for services in order to reduce staff workload; to reduce the time from the start to the completion of the publication; to expand coverage of issues, topics, data sources and the like; and to improve the quality and presentation of the output.

Develop a budget

Every effort should be made to avoid ad hoc planning and budgeting. Planning should always reflect the scope of the project. In addition, the budget should be detailed enough to cover all resources needed for personnel, materials, data processing and the like. Refer to the publication strategy created earlier. That strategy will dictate many aspects of the budget. It should be kept in mind that the strategy may have to be revised once the budget is set.

Budget requirements vary from country to country and publication to publication, depending on existing resources and local costs. First publications often cost more than subsequent issues—start-up costs are often greater than operational costs once the production process is in place.

Developing the budget for the publication should be approached from two angles. The first is to identify the distinct phases of the work and to list the main activities for which resources are required. The second is to determine the type and amount of resources required for the various activities within each phase. Consider the following phases and main activities:

Preliminary work
  Developing a work plan
  Raising support
  Writing the project concept/proposal

Assembling and processing data
Collecting data from published and unpublished sources
Extracting data from administrative records
Tabulating data with electronic storage media
Calculating selected statistics and indicators

Analysis of statistics
Preparing tables for the publication
Producing charts
Analysing the statistics and indicators
Drafting text and other elements of the publication

Presentation of statistics
Combining elements of the publication
Reviewing drafts
Revising tables, charts and text according to accepted format

Production of the book
Editing the text
Design and layout
Typesetting
Printing

Dissemination
Launching the book
Distribution
Meetings and briefings

Evaluation
Budget components include:

Personnel—Salaries and benefits, consultants' fees, travel and related costs. An important consideration is whether consultancy services will be used for very specific tasks, including data processing, data analysis, design and layout.

Subcontracts—These involve all services that are requested from an institution (e.g., a consulting firm) rather than from an individual. One of the activities to be covered under subcontract may be the processing of tables from data that are only accessible to the subcontractor or that require equipment or expertise that the statistical office does not have, or to meet strict deadlines for the publication. Other services that might be subcontracted are editing, design and layout, or typesetting.

Meetings, training and workshops—Many of the meetings of the advisory group are expected to be less than one day in duration and may not entail major expense unless meeting rooms and other facilities cannot be provided by the statistical office. When meetings and workshops that last longer are expected, boarding, transportation and other conference facilities should be envisaged and budgeted.

Equipment (expendable and non-expendable)—To the extent possible, equipment such as computer hardware and software (spreadsheet, graphics, word processing and desktop publishing applications), photocopiers and the like should be provided by the national statistics office. Maintenance and repairs should be covered by the office's budget. If different equipment than that available is needed, the option of renting should be weighed against the cost of purchasing. Resources permitting, buying may be preferred over renting on the basis of long-term considerations. Expendable equipment includes stationery and materials needed to prepare the publication.

Printing—The cost of reproduction of drafts and actual printing of the document should be estimated, taking into account the design specifications—size of the document, number of colours to be used, number of copies, etc. (See chapter 5, on designing the publication.)

Communication (including mailings)—Communication costs are those related to the acquisition of data, calling meetings of the advisory group and other contacts during the preparation of the document. There will probably also be costs involved in the distribution of the final published output.

Contingency—The total budget should include an allowance for price increases, especially if the work is to be completed over a period of more than one year. This could be done by increasing the estimates based on current prices by about 5 per cent.

The preparation of the publication should be supported by the regular budget of the statistics office. If necessary, supplemental funds may be obtained from other government agencies, non-governmental organizations or international donor agencies.

Funding agencies will expect to see that the requesting office is making a major contribution to the publication before they can commit their support. In addition, funding agencies require accountability as part of their conditions for providing financial support.

Whether or not some of the resources are provided by external sources, it is good practice to maintain accurate records of expenditures and to tally these periodically, comparing actual expenditures with the planned budget. This will give a good idea of the cost of the publication and will facilitate pricing of the document. Moreover, it will provide an accurate estimate for subsequent publications and an objective basis from which to seek support for other editions of the publication.

Develop a detailed timetable

As much as possible, the timetable should be closely adhered to. It is expected, however, that some deviations will occur, especially with those activities that run consecutively rather than concurrently. It is advisable to update the timetable to reflect annual periods when activities took place as well as those yet to be undertaken. At the end of the first publication, the updated timetable will give more accurate projections for future publications.

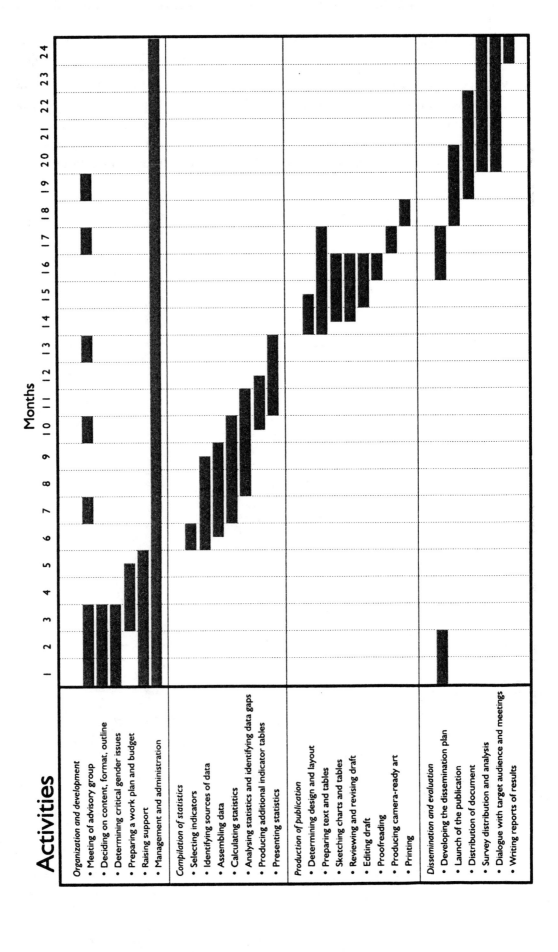

MANAGING THE WORK

The goal of managing the work is to keep abreast of what everyone is doing, to keep track of what has been spent out of the budget and to be sure that members of the team are communicating with each other.

It is important to remember that the major input into the publication is statistical information that must be compiled, analysed and repackaged for non-technical users. The process of selecting and combining sources is crucial to the quality and validity of the publication and therefore requires a great investment of time on the part of the statisticians who produce the data.

Given that gender and development is a specialized and multidisciplinary field, institutions responsible for integrating gender into policy-making might be interested in teaming up with the statistics office on this initiative. But remember, only one institution must ultimately be responsible for the product.

Determine the work plan

Four distinct but often parallel processes are needed to organize and manage the work:

- Planning and management, including production and promotion.
- Data research and analysis.
- Data management, tabulating and charting.
- Rewriting and editing.

Each of these must be considered in the division of labour and the work plan. The plan should indicate the main activities and person(s) or institution(s) responsible, although the overall responsibility for the publication, as mentioned earlier, lies with one institution, most likely the national statistical office. It is important to understand that charting and tabulating are an integral part of the analytical process and should not be left until the end.

It should not take more than one month to develop the publication's work plan. The task of coordinating contributors is made easier if the key users—the primary targeted audience—are involved. The advisory group will play a key role in coordinating contributors and may, in fact, comprise the most important contributors.

Select the publication team

Ideally, there should be a team of staff (or, if organized within the framework of a project, a project team) responsible for specific tasks. This requirement need not be daunting. In many cases, the team can consist of as few as two statisticians. This team should be primarily responsible for the content and format, with support from other statisticians and users such as researchers, gender specialists and gender equity advocates. If substantial external funding is secured (see below), the team may be headed by a project manager responsible for the day-to-day coordination of the work and recruitment of technical people to assist at various stages of the production process.

Identify tasks and assign responsibilities

Once a detailed work plan is established and tasks and responsibilities decided, staff must be assigned to specific jobs. Streamlining and doubling up responsibilities is essential as the budget will probably be limited. For a smaller effort, one person could be responsible for drafting the book and managing the project and another could focus on data processing. For a larger effort, plan for the same staff contingent, with a project manager and either an assistant analyst or a second data processing specialist. Set tasks and responsibilities for each job and then draw up a list of qualifications needed.

The biggest task is ensuring the integrity of the data. This means keeping a log of what has been collected and managing the data that are loaded into the computer (noting the location of back-up files and ensuring that only the latest versions of files are on the computer).

Another task is ensuring that the production process is running smoothly and that all activities are within budget. Someone must approve the selection of a printer and designer and decide on how many copies to print, how to disseminate the book and so on.

RAISING SUPPORT

Support in the context of the publication often has little to do with finances. Because a gender statistics publication can be produced within the pre-existing structure of a statistics office, outside financial support is often of little concern. Government and public support for the project are more important considerations, especially when producing the first issue. Momentum and enthusiasm for a second publication are often easier to create when one has a finished first publication in hand.

Again, members of the advisory group can be key players. As users of the publication, they offer links to donor organizations, government offices and others working in fields of gender concern. Begin thinking about avenues of support early in the production process. Products such as press releases or a background informational packet (listed in the publication strategy) can be disseminated near the outset to provide potential users with information about the upcoming publication. Raising support can also take place at later stages of the production process, especially for those creating the publication within an established programme of work.

Link to broader national and international efforts

A good way to foster interest in the publication and get it onto the policy agendas of key contributors is to link it to national, regional and international programmes and policy goals. At the national level, a good link would be to projects on gender or to an exercise on the formulation of a gender and development policy. At the regional level, an example of a link with a project is the Swedish International Development Agency/Statistics Sweden effort to improve gender statistics in east, central and southern Africa. Eleven countries benefited from training offered through a regional project and a few of these received either technical or financial support in the production of a national gender statistics booklet.

- *Get the word out through the informal network of gender and development to raise support.* This can be done via non-governmental organizations, through the Internet and other electronic information services, through international health programmes and via gender and development programmes.
- *Link the project with other ongoing data collection activities and tap into related sources of technical assistance.* For example, the project could be brought to the attention of regional organizations representing statisticians and demographers, such as the Joint Conference of Planners, Statisticians and Population and Information Specialists of the Economic Commission for Africa.
- *Link data analysis to priority gender concerns at the national, regional and international levels.* This could include contributions to the individual country positions and for the regional agendas to be presented at world conferences on women, social issues and the like.

Involve experts

- *Identify a local specialist already familiar with the data.* Track down the producers of the data you plan to use. Contact the section of the statistical office that compiled the data. Ask the head of that office if a specialist might be available to work on the project.
- *Use local experts from government statistical offices and statisticians from academic institutions to act as reviewers.* A knowledgeable review of the draft data analysis is necessary to ensure the quality of what is produced. Specialists must be convinced that the product is accurate and is relevant to policy makers Since the goal is to produce a country- or region-specific publication, it is essential that the experts have a clear understanding of local, national or regional policy issues.
- *Technical support through expert workshops.* Resources permitting, a series of workshops with experts could be organized to expound on the gender issues in the different sectors, availability of relevant statistics and indicators and data gaps. At the more advanced stages of the process, such workshops could assist with reviewing the concepts, conclusions and any adjustments needed in the form of supplementary information.

MONITORING AND EVALUATING

Reviews should be conducted periodically to ensure that efforts remain focused on the intended audience and that staff are spending their time effectively. Such reviews will supplement the oversight of the project manager, the advisory group and the technical reviewers.

What and when to evaluate

Reviews could consist of staff meetings every two months. At the meetings, the project manager should display the detailed work plan and ask a series of questions about progress on the plan. Questions about the direction of the project and the effectiveness of staff should also be asked, as described below.

The first three project reviews should focus on the quality and relevance of the statistics being compiled. Questions could include:

- Are irrelevant data being weeded out? Is the team satisfied that the selection process was sound?
- What logistical problems have arisen in compiling the data?
- Are procedures for referencing and building a detailed description of sources adequate? Will the footnotes, technical explanations and bibliography be complete?
- Is it easy to find and manage computer files? Do backups of all statistical files exist? Is the file management system effective?
- Are communications with the statistical offices that generated the data well coordinated to avoid duplicated requests?
- Is the office run smoothly with well-maintained equipment and clear work schedules?
- What aspects of the work plan need to be improved?
- How much of the budget has been spent and how much is left?

To evaluate a larger effort, the project manager and office administrator should design programme review forms to be completed at four points in the project cycle—after planning, after the statistics have been identified and compiled, after initial analysis and just prior to publication.

The third and fourth reviews should, in addition to questions about statistics, ask the following questions about preparing the publication and about dissemination:

- Have all recommendations of the expert reviewers and the advisory board been incorporated into the statistical presentation and analyses? Have the main findings changed as a result?

- Is the production schedule realistic? Are activities proceeding on schedule?
- Could production of the tables and charts be streamlined?
- Are there clear procedures for proofing all tables and charts?
- Has the writing and analysis proceeded efficiently? Is it clear who will review the various drafts and what the turnaround will be?
- Is someone in charge of obtaining copyright permission for any special data, photos, drawings or maps to be used in the publication?
- Will the acknowledgements be reviewed by the key contributors?
- Have a designer and a printer been selected who can work within budget constraints and deliver in line with the schedule?
- How are plans for dissemination progressing?

Each evaluation is a good time to consider the publication's original objectives. Are they being met? Are the goals the same as they were at the outset? Have new issues appeared in the data that warrant expanding certain parts of the book?

2. Compilation and analysis of statistics

CONSULTING USERS

Statistics producers are responsible not only for collecting data but for ensuring that the data respond to the needs of users. Consultations with users will ensure that the final product meets those needs in both content and format. The end product of user consideration is increased readership and relevance of publications and greater use of the underlying statistics.

A national statistics publication on gender issues can be a valuable resource for users. It can be a tool for advocacy, an easy-to-read compendium of statistics for training and reference on gender issues, and a source of ready information for both planner and policy maker. The benefit of such a publication for statisticians is the greater use and relevance of national statistics. However, the production of a successful publication requires a level of collaboration with users that is not common in national statistics offices.

Who are the users?

Communication channels need to be established between the statisticians who compile and organize the data and those who can provide analysis and policy direction. These channels must be maintained throughout the production process. The former are usually national statisticians and are referred to as producers of statistics. The latter include planners, managers, researchers, legislators, women's advocates, programme designers, policy and decision makers and the media and are the users of gender statistics. The users must be brought into the publication process in order to produce a successful publication.

Researchers from governmental and non-governmental institutions play a unique role in the consultation process by providing state-of-the-art information about their areas of discipline. They constitute a knowledgeable group of users familiar with policies and the use of statistics in policy analysis. While the team of people commissioned to prepare the publication has the primary responsibility for it, they should be open to substantive recommendations from an advisory group composed of both producers and users of statistics.

Why should they be consulted?

- To obtain an overview of the country's policy goals and gender-specific programmes.
- To make the publication truly user-oriented, put statistics in the hands of users and find out how the publication can best serve their needs.
- To discover the strengths and weaknesses of the information available.

Consultations with users are crucial at the outset to help identify the issues and topics to be addressed. But communication between the production team and the advisory group should be a continuous process, undertaken at each stage of the process. Through consultations with data users:

- Crucial gender issues can be identified.
- Areas of need for policy intervention and formulation of gender goals can be ascertained.
- Deductions from and explanations of statistics and indicators can be verified.
- The clarity and usefulness of the publication's format and presentation can be assessed.

The form of these consultations are apt to vary from informal discussions to workshops or seminars to formal meetings of consultative committees comprising producers and users (including experts in the disciplines covered). Different forms meet different objectives in the production process, and different types of consultation will need to be explained.

In planning these consultations, the producers of statistical data should be responsible for identifying the agencies vital to the development of programmes and policies that address the key issues and topics of the publication.

There are drawbacks to consultations with user groups: they could lengthen the timetable for producing the publication and the statistical team will be confronted with competing demands and conflicting opinions from different user groups. Yet a successful dialogue with users will identify crucial issues and priority areas, and—when the constraints of producers are made clear—help users develop more realistic expectations about the book that can be published. With such open communication, producers can meet user demands to the fullest extent possible.

DEFINING GOALS AND TARGET GROUPS

The goals may be defined broadly: "disseminate statistics on key gender issues to a wide range of the public" or "increase awareness of the general public on the crucial gender issues in society". A more specific goal is to produce a popular publication to provide advocacy groups with facts on the state of gender equity in society.

The goals of the publication to some extent dictate its target groups. While the overall goals can be broad, the target groups should be defined specifically, for example, in terms of professional categories (policy makers, researchers, advocacy groups or general public).

The issues discussed in the publication should focus on gender-specific goals and problems in the country, problems that women or men face by virtue of gender roles in the family or in the economic and social spheres and additional goals needed to solve the problems identified.

Relevant documentation

This process draws on relevant documentation as well as the professional experience of both users and producers. Documents to be consulted include:

- National policy on gender or on women in development (GID/WID).
- National development plan (relevant sections or chapters outlining gender or GID/WID goals).
- National population policy.
- Sectoral policies and/or programme goals (relevant sections), for example, in education, agriculture, health and social affairs.

In addition, documentation on international conventions, strategies and special plans of action are a useful resource to identify areas of policy need. For example:
- Convention on the Elimination of All Forms of Discrimination against Women (1979).[1]
- Global Strategy for Health for All by the Year 2000 (1981).[2]
- Nairobi Forward-looking Strategies for the Advancement of Women(1985).[3]
- Convention on the Rights of the Child (1989).[4]
- World Declaration on Education for All (1990).[5]
- Agenda 21, adopted by the United Nations Conference on Environment and Development (1992).[6]

- Programme of Action of the International Conference on Population and Development (1994).[7]
- Copenhagen Declaration on Social Development and Programme of Action of the World Summit for Social Development (1995).[8]
- Platform for Action of the Fourth World Conference on Women (1995).[9]

Many of the issues, problems and concerns highlighted in these documents (except those specific to gender and development) may not specifically refer to gender differences. However, they provide indications of developmental, social, political and economic problems which are of significance to how women and men, girls and boys participate in, contribute to and benefit from these spheres of activity. A careful reflection on the differences between women and men in the different contexts presented in these documents should lead to specific gender issues in the country.

1. Adopted by the General Assembly in its resolution 34/180 of 18 December 1979.

2. World Health Organization, *Global Strategy for Health for All by the Year 2000*, Health for All Series, No. 3 (Geneva, 1981).

3. See *Report of the World Conference to Review and Appraise the Achievements of the United Nations Decade for Women: Equality, Development and Peace*, Nairobi, 15–26 July 1985 (United Nations publication, Sales No. E.85.IV.10).

4. Adopted by the General Assembly in its resolution 44/25 of 20 November 1989.

5. See *Final Report of the World Conference on Education for All: Meeting Basic Learning Needs*, Jomtien, 5–9 March 1990 (New York, UNICEF, 1990).

6. See *Report of the United Nations Conference on Environment and Development*, Rio de Janeiro, 3–14 June 1992, vol. I, *Resolutions Adopted by the Conference* [United Nations publication, Sales No. E.93.I.8(vol. I)], resolution 1, annex II. See also, *Agenda 21: An Easy Reference to the Specific Recommendations on Women* (New York, UNIFEM).

7. See *Report of the International Conference on Population and Development*, Cairo, 5–13 September 1994 (United Nations publication, Sales No. E.95.XIII.18), chap. I, resolution 1, annex.

8. See *Report of the World Summit for Social Development*, Copenhagen, 6–12 March 1995 (United Nations publication, Sales No. E.96.IV.8), chap. I, resolution 1, annexes I and II.

9. See *Report of the Fourth World Conference on Women*, Beijing, 4–15 September 1995 (United Nations publication, Sales No. E.96.IV.13), chap. I, resolution 1, annex II.

CHOOSING AN ANALYTICAL FRAMEWORK AND TIME-FRAME

The main types of analytical framework are cross-sectional analysis, for a specific period or point in time, and time-series, with several points over a defined period. The choice of framework should be made in consultation with the publication's target audience, but should also be guided by the availability of data, the stated purpose of the publication and the foci of similar publications.

Determine the time-frame

In general, it is useful for a first-time publication on gender statistics to present trends in the comparative situation of women and men, and for subsequent publications to provide updates on the first analysis in the form of a snapshot analysis of current levels (depending on data availability). But there is no rule, and a country may choose to focus its first publication on the situation of women and men at a single point in time (using most recent data) and to devote a second publication to analysing trends.

The decision between these alternatives should be conditioned by the preferences and needs of potential users, the publication's primary and secondary objectives, availability of data, availability of comparable data for various years and resources in the form of time and personnel allocated for production. Analysis of trends is more complex, but is nevertheless a useful start for this type of publication. In reality, the presentation commonly combines both, giving trends for the most important indicators and current information on the others.

Trend analysis

Trend analysis involves several dimensions of comparison: changes in women-men differentials; changes for women compared with changes for men over time; variations between categories of specific variables (such as occupations, educational levels and fields of specialization) among women and men and their changes over time.

Another important decision is the period of time to be covered. Will the analysis be based on all years for which there are data or on a subset of these points? To a larger extent, availability of data will determine the options and choices, but so will the project's resources and user preferences.

Great care should be taken in selecting the data points and the number of points to include in the analyses. Certain indicators cannot easily be analysed in time-series perspective. For most, however, three data points can adequately show a trend.

Trends are best discerned for single variables disaggregated by sex—such as population, economic activity rate, age at marriage, life expectancy and enrollment ratios. When there are variables such as age and residence in addition to the basic variable of interest and years (all disaggregated by sex), the analysis very quickly becomes complex and tedious. Often a multidimensional table can be reduced by selecting one or two categories of each variable to analyse. For example, the combination of age and marital status with sex and years easily leads to several groupings that are difficult to analyse or discern. Among the possible ways of analysing the table are to present the data for only one year, or if the trend is of interest, to select one of two statuses—for example, single or married—and present age- and sex-specific data for one of them for different years. The use of charts may also simplify the presentation and render the pattern more easily discernible.

Choose spatial coverage and levels of aggregation

As a national publication the highest level of aggregation is the country as a whole. It should be decided at an early stage what types of further disaggregation of the national data will be used. The basic and more common level of stratification is by rural and urban residence. Many patterns are differentiated in the two different areas. Therefore generalizations will not always hold for both rural and urban, although depending on the relative shares of rural and urban populations, the national pattern will tend to resemble the area where the majority of the population resides, if the difference in size is substantial (for example, 30 per cent compared with 70 per cent of the population).

There are also administrative divisions to consider—these may be referred to as regions, provinces, states or the like. If some level of stratification is opted for, there should be some consideration given to standardization throughout the publication. The extent to which stratification can be used will depend on how data are made available for analysis. An early decision will help guide the search for data and any additional tabulations that will be requested.

National data are generally more readily available than regional, provincial or other administrative division data. The primary focus may therefore be the country as a whole. Special effort should also be made to present analyses on subnational levels because there are often very marked differences at subregional and district levels. A special study could also focus on region/province or administrative division if the area is of specific policy or programming significance. In such cases a point should be made to compare selected indicators with the national averages.

Highlight special groups

National averages do not tell much about the situation of specific groups or communities (i.e., ethnic and/or linguistic groups, socio-economic and racial groups). Differences in the characteristics of these groups relative to the national averages need to be analysed in order to show any major disadvantage associated with these groups. Of special interest and policy significance is the situation of the disabled, minority ethnic groups, the elderly, the girl child and refugees. The way in which these groups are covered in the publication should be determined by the availability of data and which groups are to be highlighted.

Data on the group(s) of interest can be presented in one or more chapters of the publication. Depending on the extent of coverage desired, the analysis could be presented in "boxes" or a section or a chapter, and may include a mix of tables, charts and text. If it is decided to present the analysis in "sections" or "boxes", they may be included in one or more chapters.

LISTING INDICATORS

Following the identification of crucial gender issues and topics—a result of producer-user consultations—producers of statistics need to identify the statistics and indicators required to study the situation of women and men with respect to individual issues. This process entails listing all statistics related to each issue, irrespective of data availability or accessibility. Some issues may require several indicators from different statistical fields. Because gender concerns are multidisciplinary and cut across several statistical and socio-economic spheres, one indicator can sometimes be used to illustrate several issues.

Suggested topics

It is important that the compilation of statistics and the selection of indicators be based on the topics identified in consultation with users. It is also important to understand that many indicators depend on data availability and suitability, and on policy concerns and gender issues. Users of the *Handbook* will wish to examine a range of feasible indicators, depending on the policies and/or gender goals in national planning. To illustrate, series and indicators for 37 topics have been presented in this *Handbook*.

Six subject-matter fields have been enumerated. This preliminary list is based on topics included in *The World's Women 1970–1990: Trends and Statistics* (United Nations publication, Sales No. E.90.XVII.3). They are:
1. Population, families and households
2. Public life and leadership
3. Education and training
4. Health and child-bearing
5. Housing, human settlements and the environment
6. Work and the economy.

For each category, a set of commonly analysed statistics and indicators is explained. The issues reflected in the statistics and indicators vary from country to country, depending on the level of development, culture, traditions and, to some extent, the degree of inequality existing between women and men. Therefore, no set of indicators should be considered final, but should be seen as illustrative, a starting list to which other statistics can be added.

As will be seen, many different indicators can be derived within a single topic, and only a few of these are illustrated here. Users of the *Handbook* should explore the full range of feasible indicators. The selection of the precise indicators will depend on the policy goals of the country, the availability and suitability of the data and the objectives of the publication.

WHAT KINDS OF SOURCES ARE THERE?

National censuses of population, housing, industry and agriculture are standard sources of data. Others include household surveys, registration systems of births, deaths and marriages, and administrative records dealing with education, health, housing or other social services.

Censuses

Population census data provide information on the demographic, social and economic traits of a nation's human resources. The unit of measure is the individual, and a breakdown by sex is therefore possible in many subjects when the data are tabulated. Such subjects include population size and characteristics such as marital or civil status, education, economic activity, occupation and employment status, and in some cases religion and ethnicity. Some censuses also provide data on fertility, infant death and migration. But such information is not common in censuses. The census is the principal source of data for small areas and for detailed cross-classifications of population characteristics.

National sample surveys

National sample surveys covering a range of subjects generally supplement census data and can potentially provide more current information. Among them are demographic traits of the population; housing characteristics and facilities; population mobility and migration; income; consumption patterns and expenditures; household industries; agricultural enterprises; employment status, occupation and kind of economic activity; and use of time. Because of their adaptability, these household surveys, regardless of type, provide information missing in population censuses.

Registers/administrative records

The registration of vital events, such as births and deaths, produces statistics. So does the record of arrivals and departures at international boundaries and other population registers such as those on voters, aliens, members of the armed forces and employees with social insurance plans. Some registers are completed at a single point in time, others are repeated periodically and still others are cumulative. Cumulative registers may be updated by recording the occurrence of events such as death, migration, naturalization or retirement.

Administrative data come from many sources. Hospital and clinic records can provide health-related statistics, including data on contraceptive use. Various educational agencies collect and maintain statistics on educational institutions. Other organizations are responsible for developing and maintaining data on housing services.

COMBINING DATA FROM VARIOUS SOURCES

Because the proposed publication will be culled from several disciplines and statistical fields, it is inevitable that a number of sources will be combined. Although census data are available for certain fields, they do not cover others. For some statistical fields most data will come from the census; for others, from sample surveys or administrative records; and for still others, from ad hoc or small-scale studies.

Ensure comparable sources

When data from different sources are to be combined, it is essential to ascertain whether they are comparable in terms of the coverage, time period, definitions and concepts. Statistics from different government sources may differ in arrangement, detail and choice of derived figures. Moreover, what appear to be comparable figures may not be, due to errors or variations in classification or data-processing procedures. Lack of comparability can also be a problem with time-series data, if concepts or methods have changed from one period to another.

Check for consistency

Checks for consistency and comparability between different sources should be made any time different sources are to be combined. Obtaining comparable data for the period covered by the study should be a paramount concern. It is most problematic when different sources are used for the same indicator (say, if missing years require supplementary data). Any variation in concepts from different sources and even different years within the same source should be thoroughly checked.

In most cases these checks can be made by reviewing the source's documentation. It is also a good idea to consult specialists in different fields who may themselves supply or use the data. These specialists often have additional information on availability of data (which may not be well publicized). They often understand special considerations of specific types of data, and know of existing evaluations.

Consider the relative worth of data sources

There are limitations and constraints associated with each source of data, which should be taken note of when sources are being identified or selected for the indicators. The general problems relate to spatial coverage, content, frequency of the data, regularity of the information, magnitude of errors and accessibility of the data. The two common sources of data, censuses and surveys, though in contrast to each other, are often used to complement each other.

The census is infrequent. The disadvantage of population censuses for purposes of gender statistics publications is that they are usually taken only once every decade. Although the information available from censuses is a valuable resource, it does not always indicate recent developments, especially when the time lag between the collection and publication of the data is wide. Since the census is a multipurpose statistical undertaking, many different topics are investigated but no single topic can be explored in depth. Nevertheless, it should provide the benchmark figures for the publication. In many countries, it is the primary source of data.

Although all censuses intend to cover the universe (individuals in a population census), the quality of a census is not always as good as the sample surveys, even though the latter contain both sampling and non-sampling errors. Non-sampling errors—such as response and coding errors—tend to be much larger in censuses, and can be more effectively prevented or controlled in surveys.

There are several sources of error in sample surveys. Sample surveys have sampling errors, the magnitude of which can often be computed for the various sample statistics. But there are other types of errors not due to sampling (non-response, reporting bias and so on) that are common to both censuses and surveys. The magnitudes of these errors can rarely be determined precisely.

PREPARING A WORKSHEET

After listing the statistics and indicators, the next step is to identify the sources of data from which they will be compiled. The types of information differ in source, whether primary or secondary; in essence, whether quantitative or qualitative; in nature, whether descriptive or analytical; and in origin, whether basic or derived. This identification process should be limited to the specific indicators previously identified and not cover all available sources, for many may not be relevant for the purpose at hand.

Find tables

Large, detailed tables can be produced from statistics drawn from published reports, unpublished worksheets, magnetic computer tapes and the like, produced by governmental and non-governmental agencies. More simplified tables are available from yearbooks, compendiums of statistics, statistical abstracts, gazetteers and atlases that selectively reproduce statistics. Journals, textbooks and research reports also provide tables that can be useful.

Not all data collected are tabulated or available in readily accessible formats. It is sometimes necessary to examine original questionnaires and survey instruments (or coding manuals for computerized data) to determine what data are potentially available, and to arrange for required tabulations to be prepared, sometimes for a nominal fee.

Classify indicators by source

After taking an inventory of possible indicators, it is helpful to classify them according to availability of data and type of data. The first category includes indicators for which data are available from the main sources with national coverage. These can be from population censuses, national household surveys, administrative records or registers. In the second category are the indicators for which data are available but do not cover the entire country. The data may cover only rural or urban, certain groups of people or establishments, or administrative areas. The third category will include indicators for which there are small research studies that cannot be generalized to the population but nevertheless serve to clarify underlying relationships within the phenomenon considered. The last category contains those indicators for which no data are available.

Most of the publications should be based on the first category of indicators. Within this group, individual indicators can be organized under main and sub-topics. These data may be supplemented with those in the second category, provided that limitations in coverage, concepts and the like are documented and considered in the analyses. The third category of indicators may be included as "boxes" or qualified statements, provided they elucidate the point being made. Although indicators in the fourth category cannot be included in the publication because no data exist, they can be presented to show areas with data gaps that need to be filled. This is an important input to the production of gender statistics as these represent areas of issues and concerns on which relevant information is lacking.

Keep a detailed inventory of sources

An important step in preparing the publication is to make a detailed inventory of available data and relevant references, including how each can be accessed. In so doing, it is essential to list the sources and series available for each statistical field and to describe the coverage in time and space, the concepts used, the techniques employed in the collection of data (whether census or sample survey and, in the case of the latter, its sampling design), the inaccuracies and internal inconsistencies discovered, consistency with other sources and anything else with a bearing on the quality of data or the limits on the interpretations derived. Relevant reports and studies on these sources should also be noted.

The statistics from all these sources must be reorganized and presented in a way that suits the publication's audience. Statistical information from relevant tables must first be extracted from the documentation (these may be transcribed onto worksheets or maintained as photocopies of the basic tables). The sources for the worksheet should rely on and refer to the following (ranked by preference):

- Published data.
- Unpublished tables provided by national statistical agencies or other public agencies.
- Special tabulations prepared by the national statistical agency or other administrative offices.
- Research studies and reports of small-scale surveys by academic, research or other institutions.

Make sure references are complete and correct

All the different sources of information should be well-referenced with full bibliographic citations, including page or table numbers when applicable. Access to the data sources can benefit users who require information beyond that shown in the publication. The reference information should be detailed enough to assist users in accessing original documents should they need to.

Format for referencing sources of data

From a census or survey report
Source: Office (producing the report), *title of report*, volume no., city, publisher, year published, table number(s).

Unpublished tables provided by national statistics agency
Source: "Unpublished tables" from "title of survey or census" available from the statistical office (specify department and unit if applicable), city (of statistical office), year produced.

Special tabulations prepared by the national statistical agency or another institution
Source: "Special tabulations" from "title of census or survey" produced by "name of the institution" for (cite specific purpose, for example, project or programme).

Ad hoc studies or documents
Source: Name of author, title of document or paper, *title of journal, edited book,* or conference/meeting at which paper was presented, city, publisher, year published, pages. (Indicate if it is unpublished.)

Technical notes

Technical notes on compiled statistics should always be included, such as:

- Details on how the original data were collected, data source, the definitions and concepts.
- Formulas used to obtain the indicators.
- Data limitations (any combination of sources used and their overall consistency, period covered, geographical coverage—national, rural or urban, or subnational, and so on).

The use of notations and symbols in the tables should be standardized. Some of the cases requiring notation include: "not applicable", "not available", entries that take the value of zero when rounded off (i.e., less than 5 per cent), insignificant entries or missing data.

DEALING WITH SUBGROUP DIFFERENTIALS

The overriding characteristic of the statistics and indicators to be presented in the publication is that they are compiled separately for women and men or girls and boys. Since gender issues form the basic framework for the proposed publication, the women-men comparison should be maintained, except in such cases as fertility measures and maternal mortality, where statistics are defined exclusively for women. While it is unnecessary to calculate statistics and indicators for both sexes combined, it is useful to present marginal combined totals for indicators such as percentage and sex distributions. The totals in these cases are given in absolute values and allow users to convert percentages to absolute numbers.

Cross-classification by age

In addition to gender, age often produces variations in the statistics. Mortality rates, economic activity rates and marital status all vary by age. Social relationships within a community are affected and often defined by relative ages. Since social and economic characteristics vary with age and since age composition also varies in time and place, populations cannot be meaningfully compared with respect to these other traits until age has been "controlled for"—its effect held constant. Thus it is important to show age differentials.

The experience of different age cohorts (age groups) is also an indication of trends in a specified indicator. For literacy, it is expected that improvements in educational enrolment and attainment over time will result in lower illiteracy rates at younger ages for a given point in time. Indicators compiled for the aggregate female and male populations should thus equally be compiled for women and men in specified age groups. It is important to understand the distinction between controlling for "age", which means the indicator is computed on the basis of the numbers within age groups as the denominator, and "age distribution", where the total (the denominator) sums over the different age groups.

The age of an individual in censuses is commonly defined by the age of the person as of his or her last birthday. In the past, age was defined in terms of the age at the nearest birthday or in some cases even the next birthday, but these definitions are no longer used in national censuses. Care should be taken to ascertain that the years covered in the publication do not reflect two different definitions.

Data on age are most commonly tabulated and published in five-year age groups (0–4, 5–9, 10–14, etc.). These groups should be maintained for indicators known to exhibit patterns associated with the life-cycle variations. For example, it is standard practice to maintain five-year age groups when "age composition" is depicted in the form of an age pyramid. Age-specific fertility, mortality and economic activity rates are also compiled for five-year age groups if presented as line graphs. If not, broader age groups are used.

In most other cases, different standard groupings are used, associated with distinct stages in life, social age groupings or the phenomenon being studied. The classification of indicators by age group must take these into account.

For health and mortality indicators, the lowest age group is further subdivided into below 1 year and 1–4 year age groups.

For education, age groupings correspond to the ages at which children are found in primary level and second level schooling. In some countries the two main groups are ages 6–12 and 13–18, respectively, but these may vary from country to country.

The group classified as "youth" represents ages 15–24, when young people pass from a period of dependency to one of employment and family formation. This broad age group is sometimes subdivided into ages 15–19 and 20–24, to identify more clearly the different stages of transition.

For women, the 15–49 (or 15–44) age group is significant as it corresponds to the reproductive period of life (the child-bearing ages), and ages above this group are the post-reproductive years. Whenever possible, 15–49 is preferred over 15–44.

The most economically active age group is generally 15–59, depending on regulations on legal entry to the labour force and retirement. (In some countries, a lower age limit of 10 or 12 is used in labour force statistics.) The age group 60+ corresponds to the elderly, also sometimes categorized as the post–labour force. For those concerned with issues of the aged, employment and dependency experiences can be shown separately for those aged 60–69, representing a relatively active and self-sufficient period. The age group 70 and over represents the onset of disability, greater ill health and smaller incomes.

Illustration 1. Summary of standard age groupings

Description of group	Ages	Field
Infant	<1	Mortality/health
Child	1–4	
	(5–9)	
Primary level population	6–12[a]	Educational attainment
Secondary level	13–18[b]	
Youth	15–19	
	20–24	
Reproduction age group	15–44 or 49	Fertility
Productive ages	15–59, or 64[c]	Economic activity
Elderly	60+, or 60–69, 70+	

a. The age group for primary level may differ from country to country, depending on the minimum age for enrolment at first level and the number of years required to complete primary school.

b. The age group for secondary level enrolment will depend on the age at which most pupils complete primary school and the minimum years expected for secondary level education.

c. The lower and upper limits for productive age groups are country specific. The lower limit may be set below 15 for some countries and above 15 for others. The upper limit depends largely on the average retirement age.

Cross-classification by geographical area

Other variables reflected in the statistics will relate to geographical locations (such as rural-urban and provinces or regions). Gender roles and disparities are in some cases very differentiated along geographical lines. In this context, three major classifications are (i) urban and rural; (ii) cities and neighbouring urban agglomerations; (iii) localities and other geographical regions.

Since data are more readily available on the country level than for specific regions, provinces or other administrative areas, the focus of study should first be the country as a whole. Time, personnel and financial resources, and data availability permitting, analyses on subnational areas can then be carried out. For example, the most recent census results (1990 or 1991) can be presented to show the number of women and men for the entire country as well as for its rural and urban areas. In addition, the same data may be reported by state, province or region.

Cross-classification by socio-economic grouping

Social class and other socio-economic characteristics are a source of variation in almost all variables of interest. For example, to the extent that customs and traditions affect the distribution of women and men in various spheres of life, ethnic and linguistic groups will reflect these differences. Furthermore, there are traditional practices against women, such as female genital mutilation, early marriages and nutritional taboos, which are tribe specific. Educational attainment and other social characteristics such as socio-economic and marital statuses also affect the way individuals are able to participate in and benefit from development efforts. Statistical series such as economic activity, infant and child mortality, and reproductive health are usually more informative when cross-classified by socio-economic group.

DRAWING CONCLUSIONS FOR POLICY

Analysis and interpretation of the indicators will require:

- A review of relevant studies on the subject. A desirable level or range for the indicator should be established, based on, for example, the average levels in neighbouring countries that have characteristics similar to the country in question, regional averages, urban-rural differentials, past levels in the country concerned and policy goals and targets.
- A comparison of the indicator between women (girls) and men (boys).
- An analysis of the implications of female-male differentials and likely explanations.
- An examination of changes over time between women and men.

The statistical information presented in the publication should aim to improve policy formulation and decision-making on questions and situations relevant to women and men. Hence, whenever possible, policy implications should be drawn from the data presented. The gaps in policies and programmes should be highlighted so that these can be redressed by the appropriate agencies and instruments of government. The publication can then be a useful tool for required policy and programme modifications.

Evaluation of indicators and conclusions

Beyond periodic consultations with producers and users of statistics, it is necessary to consult specialists in the various fields about the validity of conclusions and the adequacy of the indicators analysed.

The specialists consulted should include statisticians in specific areas involved in the collection and processing of the data, researchers who are familiar with the subject or who have undertaken studies on related issues, and policy analysts who are conversant with issues and can draw valid conclusions from statistical information. A thorough understanding of the evolution in women's roles and status, vis-à-vis men's, is a great asset in providing a historical context to the interpretation of data.

Consulting these specialists will help clarify methodological issues and characteristics of data. Their comments on the interpretation of indicators and on policy implications to be deduced should sharpen the analysis presented in the publication, as these specialists are, in general, better placed to point out limitations of the data and therefore constraints in their use and interpretation.

Consultations should continue to take place during each stage of drafting. In particular, the first draft should be subjected to a critical review by a producer-user team before the manuscript is finalized.

The team responsible for the publication should be aware of conflicting interests and be wary of adopting too cautious an attitude in drawing conclusions from the data lest these become too bland or too limited in application. Indicators based on incomplete or controversial data may be presented, provided they are so annotated. It should be emphasized here that the less reliable the data the more important it is to have the commentary and analysis.

References and further reading

Hedman, Birgitta, Francesca Perucci and Pehr Sundström (1996). *Engendering Statistics: A Tool for Change.* Örebro: Statistics Sweden Publications Services.

United Nations (1990). *Handbook for National Statistics Data Bases on Women and Development.* Sales No. E.89.XVII.9.

——— (1992). *Wistat Women's Indicators and Statistics Spreadsheet Database for Microcomputers (Version 2): Users Guide and Reference Manual.* Sales No. E.92.XVII.11.

——— (1995). *The World's Women 1995: Trends and Statistics.* Sales No. E.95.XVII.2.

Wallgren, Anders, Britt Wallgren, Rolf Persson, Ulf Jorner and Jan-Aage Haaland (1996). *Graphing Statistics and Data.* London: SAGE Publications.

3. Illustrations
with selected indicators

INTRODUCTION AND FORMAT OF THE ILLUSTRATIONS

This chapter focuses on preparing indicators step-by-step from basic data. No matter the topic or the indicators, the process and principles are generally the same. The explanation for each topic follows the structure shown below and described in the remainder of the present section:

Selected indicators

Policy relevance

Data sources

Source table

Working tables

Additional indicators or classifications

Likely problems

Interpretation.

The chapter divides the topics covered into six subject-matter sections. These are as follows:

Population, families and households

Public life and leadership

Education and training

Health and child-bearing

Housing, human settlements and environment

Work and the economy.

Each section concludes with a list of references and analytical studies for further research.

Selected indicators

Two indicator series are usually presented for each topic. The first deals with the distribution of a characteristic for each sex, with women's and men's respective totals used as the denominator. Exceptions occur in age-sex composition of the population, which may use the total population as the base for computing the distribution, and life expectancy, which is derived from an entirely different set of principles. Also, all indicators expressed as rates, such as fertility, mortality and economic activity, may have as the denominator the part of the population for which the characteristic is considered relevant; indicators referring to averages, such as age at first marriage, age at first childbirth and income, have as the numerator the sum of the variable in question rather than the simple count of women and men to whom the characteristic related to the indicator applies.

The second indicator is defined as the proportion within each category of the characteristic who are women (or men). In a few cases this is expressed as the ratio of women to men in the category. When the first indicator is defined in terms of rates or averages, no sex-composition indicator is suggested.

An example of the first indicator might be the number of literate women (men) expressed as a percentage of all women (men) above a designated age. The second kind of indicator might be women physicians compared to men physicians, expressed as a percentage of all physicians or as the ratio of women doctors to men doctors.

Each indicator is calculated using an arithmetic expression. For example, the sex ratio of women to men by age group is given as:

$$\frac{\text{Women } (x, x + n)}{\text{Men } (x, x + n)} \times 100$$

where $(x, x + n)$ is the notation for age group: x is the lower limit, $x + n$ is the upper limit of the given age group. This notation implies that a precise age group should be specified each time the formula is used. Formulas may refer to the total population with a given characteristic or may be applied to subsets of the population—such as rural and urban populations or different socio-economic groups—as necessary. Applying the above formula to rural and urban populations gives:

$$\frac{\text{Rural women } (x, x + n)}{\text{Rural men } (x, x + n)} \times 100 \qquad \frac{\text{Urban women } (x, x + n)}{\text{Urban men } (x, x + n)} \times 100$$

The main types of indicators presented in the manual are:

$$\text{Sex ratio} = \frac{\text{Number of women}}{\text{Number of men}} \times 100$$

$$\text{Rate} = \frac{\text{Number of events}}{\text{Number exposed to the event}} \times 100$$

A rate may sometimes be expressed per 1,000 or 100,000 of the population exposed to the occurrence of the event in question.

$$\text{Economic activity rate} = \frac{\text{Economically active population aged } (x, x + n)}{\text{Population of working age } (x, x + n)} \times 100$$

$$\text{Age-specific activity rate} = \frac{\text{Economically active population aged } (x, x + n)}{\text{Population aged } (x, x + n)} \times 100$$

$$\text{Percentage distribution} = \frac{\text{Number in each category}}{\text{Number in all categories}} \times 100$$

$$\text{Occupational distribution} = \frac{\text{Number employed in occupation } i}{\text{Number employed in all occupations}} \times 100$$

$$\text{Sex composition} = \frac{\text{Women (men) in category } i}{\text{Women and men in category } i} \times 100$$

$$\text{Average or mean} = \frac{\text{Sum of values of characteristic } y}{\text{Number of values summed}}$$

Policy relevance

This section explains the significance of the proposed indicators for understanding the situation of women compared with men and developing policies aimed at improving the relative positions of women and men.

Data sources

This section outlines the main data source and any alternate sources. It refers to the different types of data, not to the form in which the data are available (published or unpublished). Discussion for each topic is limited, since the main sources of data—censuses, surveys and administrative records—are presented in more detail in chapter 2. Source problems specific to the topic in question are also briefly mentioned.

Source table

The source table or worksheet is a basic table used for calculating indicators. It may be an actual table taken from a publication, a computer print-out or statistical information compiled from different publications, print-outs or worksheets. The structure of the tables here may differ from those available in national sources. Their main purpose is to serve as the source for calculating the indicators.

Working tables

This section suggests basic elements to consider in preparing and analysing statistical tables. Two types of tables are generally presented: two-way and three-way tables.

Two-way table

An outline of a two-way table, showing one main characteristic or variable cross-tabulated by sex, is given in illustration 2. Descriptions of categories are contained in the row stubs on the left. The three sets of data columns present three different types of indicators:

Illustration 2. Distribution of a characteristic or variable

Categories	Number			Percentage distribution			Sex composition (%)		
	Women	Men	Total	Women	Men	Total	Women	Men	Total
Category 1	x	x	x	x	x	x	x	x	100
Category 2	x	x	x	x	x	x	x	x	100
Category 3	x	x	x	x	x	x	x	x	100
.									
.									
.									
Category n	x	x	x	x	x	x	x	x	100
Total	x	x	x	100	100	100	x	x	100

Source: Compiled from table yy in ... (cite publication in full).

Row stubs: The categories are listed from 1 to n, where n is the last category, plus one row for the total.

Columns 1–3: The first three columns give the number of women and men and the total in each category of the main variable.

Columns 4–6: The second set of three columns gives the percentage distributions of the main variable for women, men, and women and men combined. In each of these columns, the percentages of should sum vertically to 100 per cent.

Columns 7–9: The final set of three columns gives the sex composition within each category as percentages. In each category the percentages of women and men should sum horizontally to 100.

Three-way table

A sample outline for a three-way table is given in illustration 3. There are usually fewer categories used for the second characteristic in a three-way table than for the first, primarily to keep the table easy to interpret.

A three-way table is generally constructed in two steps. The first step is to construct a two-way table with the main characteristic cross-tabulated with sex. A second characteristic ("B") is then chosen, which helps to highlight and clarify some of the differences between women and men shown by the distribution of characteristic "A". Characteristic A is cross-classified

Illustration 3. Distribution of characteristic A by characteristic B

	Categories of B																	
	Category 1						Category 2						Total					
	Women		Men		Total		Women		Men		Total		Women		Men		Total	
Category A	No.	%	No.	%	No.	%	No.	%	No.	%	No.	%	No.	%	No.	%	No.	%
Category 1	x	x	x	x	x	x	x	x	x	x	x	x	x	x	x	x	x	x
Category 2	x	x	x	x	x	x	x	x	x	x	x	x	x	x	x	x	x	x
Category 3	x	x	x	x	x	x	x	x	x	x	x	x	x	x	x	x	x	x
.																		
.																		
.																		
Category n	x	x	x	x	x	x	x	x	x	x	x	x	x	x	x	x	x	x
Total	x	100	x	100	x	100	x	100	x	100	x	100	x	100	x	100	x	100

Source: Compiled from table yy in ... (cite publication in full).

Illustration 4. Sex composition within characteristic A by characteristic B

	Categories of B																	
	Category 1						Category 2						Total					
	Women		Men		Total		Women		Men		Total		Women		Men		Total	
Category A	No.	%	No.	%	No.	%	No.	%	No.	%	No.	%	No.	%	No.	%	No.	%
Category 1	x	x	x	x	x	100	x	x	x	x	x	100	x	x	x	x	x	100
Category 2	x	x	x	x	x	100	x	x	x	x	x	100	x	x	x	x	x	100
Category 3	x	x	x	x	x	100	x	x	x	x	x	100	x	x	x	x	x	100
.																		
.																		
.																		
Category n	x	x	x	x	x	100	x	x	x	x	x	100	x	x	x	x	x	100
Total	x	x	x	x	x	100	x	x	x	x	x	100	x	x	x	x	x	100

Source: Compiled from table yy in ... (cite publication in full).

with B. A typical example is rural and urban. Age groups are also used as a second characteristic for analyses such as marital status.

Two or more working tables are presented under each suggested indicator or subtopic in the present *Handbook*. For simplification, there is in general one working table per indicator series. Illustrations 3 and 4 are outlines of working tables presented in the *Handbook*. The last set of six columns of illustration 3 corresponds to the first six columns in illustration 2, which presents percentage distributions across categories of the first characteristic. In illustration 4, the series dealing with sex composition is presented, showing the total of 100 per cent for women and men in each row.

Using the basic data presented in the table, other types of indicators such as rates, ratios and averages can be prepared in addition to percentage distribution and sex composition.

Illustrations 5 to 9 are examples of how two-way and three-way working tables are generated from a source table. Illustration 5 gives the absolute numbers of employment classified by broad industry groups and status in employment. The first variable of interest is industry. In illustration 6, the two-way table showing employment distribution by industry and sex is illustrated. This table is derived from illustration 5 (taking the first two data columns—women and men under "all categories") and shows two indicator series, percentage distribution and sex composition. The total number employed is also presented to give an idea of the magnitude of the different categories.

Illustrations 7, 8 and 9 show different indicators that can be compiled in a three-way working table. Illustration 7 gives the percentage distributions across categories of characteristic "A" (industry) in each group of characteristic "B" (status in employment) for women and men; while illustration 9 gives the percentage distributions across categories of characteristic "B" (status in employment) in each group of characteristic "A" (industry) for women and men. Illustration 8 presents the sex composition within each industry/status-in-employment pair.

Illustration 5. Employment by industry, by status in employment and by sex, Botswana 1991

Industry	All categories		Employers and own account workers		Employees		Unpaid family workers	
	Women	Men	Women	Men	Women	Men	Women	Men
Agriculture, hunting, forestry and fishing	27 665	72 781	956	2 454	4 357	25 347	22 352	44 980
Mining and quarrying	767	12 520	8	30	752	12 426	7	64
Manufacturing	13 337	13 298	4 419	2 144	8 078	10 933	840	221
Electricity, gas and water	781	5 644	4	64	776	5 553	1	27
Construction	7 501	49 500	411	3 657	6 914	45 503	176	340
Wholesale/retail trade, restaurants and hotels	20 734	13 588	6 806	2 574	12 993	10 625	935	389
Transport, storage and communication	1 790	8 304	20	365	1 763	7 882	7	57
Financing, insurance, real estate and business service	4 634	8 758	182	460	4 399	8 255	53	43
Community, social and personal services	57 243	45 802	412	2 023	56 610	43 441	221	338
Activities not adequately defined	6 384	10 786	711	1 049	3 803	6 541	1 870	3 196
Unemployed	29 504	32 134						
Total	140 836	240 981	13 929	14 820	100 445	176 506	26 462	49 655

Source: International Labour Office, Year Book of Labour Statistics 1993 (Geneva, 1993) table 2C.
Note: A hyphen (–) indicates that the item is not applicable.

Illustration 6. Employment by industry, by status in employment and by sex, Botswana 1991

Industry	Total employed[a]	Percentage distribution		Sex composition (%)	
		Women	Men	Women	Men
Agriculture, hunting, forestry and fishing	100 446	20	30	28	72
Mining and quarrying	13 287	1	5	6	94
Manufacturing	26 635	9	6	50	50
Electricity, gas and water	6 425	1	2	12	88
Construction	57 001	5	21	13	87
Wholesale/retail trade, restaurants and hotels	34 322	15	6	60	40
Transport, storage and communication	10 094	1	3	18	82
Financing, insurance, real estate and business service	13 392	3	4	35	65
Community, social and personal services	103 045	41	19	56	44
Activities not adequately defined	17 170	5	4	37	63
Total	381 817	100	100	37	63

Source: International Labour Office, *Year Book of Labour Statistics 1993* (Geneva, 1993), table 2C.

Note: Excluding the unemployed.

a. Totals are presented to give an idea of the magnitude and also to facilitate further analysis.

Illustration 7. Industrial distribution of the employed by status in employment and by sex, Botswana 1991

Industry	All categories		Employers and own account workers		Employees		Unpaid family workers	
	Women	Men	Women	Men	Women	Men	Women	Men
Agriculture, hunting, forestry and fishing	20	30	7	17	4	14	84	91
Mining and quarrying	1	5	0	0	1	7	0	0
Manufacturing	9	6	32	14	8	6	3	0
Electricity, gas and water	1	2	0	0	1	3	0	0
Construction	5	21	3	25	7	26	1	1
Wholesale/retail trade, restaurants and hotels	5	6	49	17	13	6	4	1
Transport, storage and communication	1	3	0	2	2	4	0	0
Financing, insurance, real estate and business service	3	4	1	3	4	5	0	0
Community, social and personal services	41	19	3	14	56	25	1	1
Activities not adequately defined	5	4	5	7	4	4	7	6
Total (%)	100	100	100	100	100	100	100	100
All employed[a]	140 836	240 981	13 929	14 820	100 445	176 506	26 462	49 655

Source: International Labour Office, 1993. *Year Book of Labour Statistics 1993* (Geneva, 1993), table 2C.

Note: Excluding the unemployed.

a. Total numbers are presented to give an idea of the magnitude and for derivation of numbers in the respective rows and columns.

**Illustration 8. Sex composition of the employed within industry group
by status in employment and by sex, Botswana 1991** (*percentage*)

Industry	All categories		Employers and own account workers		Employees		Unpaid family workers	
	Women	Men	Women	Men	Women	Men	Women	Men
Agriculture, hunting, forestry and fishing	28	72	28	72	15	85	33	67
Mining and quarrying	6	94	21	79	6	94	10	90
Manufacturing	50	50	67	33	42	58	79	21
Electricity, gas and water	12	88	6	94	12	88	4	96
Construction	13	87	10	90	13	87	34	66
Wholesale/retail trade, restaurants and hotels	60	40	73	27	55	45	71	29
Transport, storage and communication	18	82	5	95	18	82	11	89
Financing, insurance, real estate and business service	35	65	28	72	35	65	55	45
Community, social and personal services	56	44	17	83	57	43	40	60
Activities not adequately defined	37	63	40	60	37	63	37	63
Total	37	63	48	52	36	64	35	65

Source: International Labour Office, *Year Book of Labour Statistics 1993* (Geneva, 1993) table 2C.
Note: Excluding the unemployed.

Illustration 9. Employment status distribution within industry group and by sex, Botswana 1991
(*percentage*)

Industry	All categories		Employers and own account workers		Employees		Unpaid family workers	
	Women	Men	Women	Men	Women	Men	Women	Men
Agriculture, hunting, forestry and fishing	100	100	3	3	16	35	81	62
Mining and quarrying	100	100	1	0	98	99	1	1
Manufacturing	100	100	33	16	61	82	6	2
Electricity, gas and water	100	100	1	1	99	98	0	0
Construction	100	100	5	7	92	92	2	1
Wholesale/retail trade, restaurants and hotels	100	100	33	19	63	78	5	3
Transport, storage and communication	100	100	1	4	98	95	0	1
Financing, insurance, real estate and business service	100	100	4	5	95	94	1	0
Community, social and personal services	100	100	1	4	99	95	0	1
Activities not adequately defined	100	100	11	10	60	61	29	30
Total	100	100	10	6	71	73	19	21

Source: International Labour Office, *Year Book of Labour Statistics 1993* (Geneva, 1993) table 2C.
Note: Excluding the unemployed.

Additional indicators or classifications

This section suggests additional statistics, indicators, classifications or alternative presentations of data that can be used. In some cases, alternative formulas can be used to reach similar conclusions. In others, a third characteristic greatly enhances the analysis.

Likely problems

Data quality problems and definition issues that may affect interpretation and conclusions are discussed in this section. The section is necessarily relatively general. Data quality is specific to national practices, which often vary from one census to another, one survey to another or one time period to another. Relevant documents on the specific data sources should be reviewed and, if necessary, experts familiar with the data consulted.

Interpretation

This section describes what the statistics say and mean. Such interpretation also entails describing conclusions and exploring implications or explanations for the findings. The interpretation should address certain basic issues:

• The general significance of the characteristic or indicator.
• Acceptable or expected levels of the indicator and any gender differentials shown by the data.
• Specific types of variation to look for and what a variation might mean.
• Whether observed patterns are similar or differ markedly across all categories of the characteristics being analysed.
• Recent trends indicated by the results.

The first attempts to interpret the series may lead to further exploration of data, such as cross-classifications with other variables that are postulated to be associated with the variations or differentials in the indicators being analysed. Interpretation of the statistics and indicators may be facilitated or guided by other related studies, policy documents or similar publications, such as the United Nations publications *The World's Women 1970–1990: Trends and Statistics* and *The World's Women 1995: Trends and Statistics* (Sales Nos. E.90.XVII.3 and E.95.XVII.2).

Regional gender statistics publications produced in 1995 are also useful to review:

• *Women and Men in East, Central and Southern Africa: Facts and Figures 1995.*[1]
• *Gender Indicators of Developing Asian and Pacific Countries.*[2]
• *Latin American Women: Compared Figures.*[3]
• *Women and Men in Europe and North America 1995.*[4]
• *Women and Men in the Nordic Countries: Facts and Figures 1994.*[5]

These publications are a source of information on the relevant gender issues in the region and present a basis for comparing achievements at the national level with those of neighbouring countries or countries in other regions. In addition, it will be useful to consult national gender statistics publications from other countries for ideas on indicators to be compiled, their presentation in the form of tables and charts, and ways of interpreting the results.

A note on presentation of tables

As can be seen from the examples of working tables presented above, there is a need to further simplify the presentation of statistics if the gender statistics publication is to reach the intended audience. The different ways of simplifying tables and other forms of presentation of data are discussed in chapter 4. However, a few points need emphasizing at this stage of data compilation.

The next stage after the working tables is to extract the statistics that would be presented in a small table within the text or as a larger annex table. This step is highly dependent on the results that are to be highlighted and may change at different stages of the analysis and drafting. Therefore no suggestions for presentation are provided, but there are a few considerations that should be borne in mind.

In the final presentation of a two-way table, some of the columns might be dropped and some of the categories shown in greater or lesser detail and with subtotals, depending on the findings of the analysis as to the most interesting groups and the most striking differences between men and women. However, in the first stage of the analysis it is important to show the complete set of numbers and distributions to facilitate the analysis and comparisons with other data.

- Present the relative situation of women and men. Regardless of the number of characteristics or whether the statistics are for one or several points in time, the primary comparison should be between women and men.

- For ease of comparison, present the statistics for women and men side by side, in columns. The categories of characteristics should be presented in rows. The main analytical table should be concise. Its message should be clear. The numbers of columns and rows should be limited and excess data excluded. Categories or characteristics can be combined, but only if patterns of variation are not then compromised. In the case of age groups, many different classifications are possible. The main ones are five-year age groups and broad age groups corresponding to children, youth, productive or reproductive ages, post-retirement and elder years.

• When dealing with three-way tables (that is, two characteristics plus sex), the main characteristic and women and men remain where they are in a two-way table and the secondary characteristic sits either side by side or within each category of the main characteristic, depending on the number of categories. In some cases it might be necessary to present separate two-way tables for each category of the secondary characteristic.

---

1. Kenya, Central Bureau of Statistics, Women and Men in East, Central and Southern Africa: Facts and Figures 1995 (Nairobi, 1995).

2. Asian Development Bank, Center for International Research, Gender Indicators of Developing Asian and Pacific Countries (Manila, 1993).

3. FLACSO, Latin American Women: Compared Figures (Santiago, Instituto de la Mujer, 1995).

4. United Nations Economic Commission for Europe and others, Women and Men in Europe and North America 1995 (United Nations publication, Sales No. GV.E.95.0.12).

5. Nordic Council of Ministers, Women and Men in the Nordic Countries: Facts and Figures 1994 (Copenhagen, 1994).

POPULATION, FAMILIES AND HOUSEHOLDS

Age-sex composition of the population

SERIES A	Population of women and men in five-year age groups expressed as a percentage of the total population

Formula

$$\frac{\text{Women } (x, x + n)}{\text{Total population}} \times 100 \qquad\qquad \frac{\text{Men } (x, x + n)}{\text{Total population}} \times 100$$

SERIES B Ratio of female to male population in selected age groups

Formula

$$\frac{\text{Women } (x, x + n)}{\text{Men } (x, x + n)} \times 100$$

Policy relevance

Statistics and indicators on the age composition of the population can help assess the needs of the population as a whole and of specific age groups, such as care for preschool-aged children, education for the young, employment for adolescents and working age adults, and social security benefits for the elderly. In countries where persistent imbalances exist in the overall sex ratio and across age groups such that the ratio of women to men is low ("missing women"), excess female mortality should be an area of policy concern. High male mortality may also be a concern in the young adult and elderly years.

Data sources

The population census should be the main source of data for calculating the age-sex composition of the population. Use of different data sources to derive the age distributions for different years should be avoided. Other sources of data, such as sample surveys and administrative records and registers, should be used only to complement census data, unless they are the only source for the period to be analysed. Because the latter surveys are based on samples, variations in the computed ratios can be attributed not only to changes in the ratios between periods but also to differences in the samples (for example, a sample containing more men than women). When survey data must be used, it is best to use data from the national statistical office unless a national survey of acceptable quality is available only from other institutions.

Source table

Table 1.1. Population by age group and sex, for total, urban and rural areas, 1970–1990

Age groups	1970		1980		1990	
	Women	Men	Women	Men	Women	Men
Total						
0–4						
5–9						
10–14						
15–19						
.						
.						
.						
80–84						
85–89						
90+						
All ages						
Urban						
Same age groups as above						
Rural						
Same age groups as above						

Source: Give full citation for census report used.
Note: The open-ended age group may be at an earlier age in some countries.

Working table

Table 1.2. Percentage distribution of the population by age group for each sex, and women per 100 men in each age group, for total, urban and rural areas

Age group	Population		Percentage distribution		Women per 100 men
	Women	Men	Women	Men	
Total (urban and rural)					
0–4					
5–9					
10–14					
15–19					
.					
.					
.					
80–84					
85–89					
90+					
All ages	Nw	Nm	100	100	Rw/m
Urban					
Same age groups as above					
Rural					
Same age groups as above					

Technical note: Nw and Nm correspond to the total female and male populations. Rw/m is the number of women per 100 men in the total population.

Source: Compiled from table yy in (cite publication in full).

Note: The open-ended age group could be at an earlier age in some countries. Broader age groups can be constructed based on substantive and demographic relevance.

Additional indicators or classifications

The percentage distribution of the population by age and sex is often presented in an age pyramid (see chapter 4). For an effective chart, group intervals should be narrow (for example, five-year age groups, although one-year age groups may be shown when data are available and the quality of age reporting is high).

For policy analysis it may be useful to present a simplified table showing the age composition and sex ratios in broad age groups depicting children, youth, adult (or reproductive) and elderly.

The following variations may be introduced in the definition and presentation of the indicators:

• The age composition can be calculated using female and male population totals as the denominators.

• The sex composition within each age group can be presented instead of the sex ratio. A summary indicator, the child-to-woman ratio, can be used as a rough indicator of the child-care burden for women in a specific age group. The usual formula is

$$\frac{\text{Children 0–4}}{\text{Women aged 15–44}} \times 100$$

The formula can cover wider age groups, for example, ages 0–9 or 0–14 for children and ages 15–59 for women's economically active years. The different age groups, however, have particular significance for special care: ages 0–4 are the most care-intensive years, when infants make many competing demands on mothers' time, as do the elderly aged 60 and over. At ages 10–14 children need less care and in some cultures even lend support, reducing women's work in child and household care.

In addition to rural-urban breakdowns, sex ratios can be compiled for the different provinces and regions. This level of analysis is needed if, for example, there is sex-selective migration between provinces and regions. It is sometimes useful to make comparisons with neighbouring countries or to compare with regional averages.

Likely problems

Age reporting in any census or survey is subject to errors, such as failure to record age and age misreporting. There is a tendency for the errors in age data to offset one another in broader age-groups as errors are more likely to average out. The extent to which this occurs depends not only on the nature and magnitude of the errors but also on the grouping of the data. Reports may be available on the degree of accuracy of age reporting in each census. The demographers who have produced the data or researchers who have evaluated age errors in census or survey enumerations should be consulted on how best to adjust the data, if need be.

Interpretation

These indicators describe the age composition of the population, the distribution of women and men in the population, and the relative numbers of women and men at all ages. Analyses of these indicators may seek to answer the following questions:

• Is the population young or aging?

• Is there a balanced ratio of women to men or is there significantly more of one sex?

• At what ages are deficits of women or men substantial and what are the likely causes?

The proportion of the total population that is less than 15 years old is a good indicator of an ageing or youthful population. If the proportion is more than 40 per cent, the population may be described as young. A proportion of 25 per cent or less is associated with an old population. A proportion of at least 10 per cent of a population in the age category of 65 years and over can also be a good indication of an ageing population.

The sex ratios reveal an excess or deficit of one sex in the population. Worldwide, there are approximately 1 per cent fewer women than men but the ratios vary significantly from country to country and from region to region.

According to the United Nations projections and estimates for 1995, the ratios at the country level can be as low as 52 women per 100 men (e.g., the United Arab Emirates, where there is a large male immigrant population) and as high as 117 women per 100 men (Ukraine). At the regional level, women outnumber men in the developed regions (with ratios of 105 in Europe, 103 in other developed regions) as well as in sub-Saharan Africa (102), in the Caribbean (103) and in central Asia (104). In some of the other regions, women are outnumbered by men—by a ratio of 97 women to 100 men in northern Africa and eastern Asia, 95 in southern Asia and Oceania and 92 in western Asia. Latin America and south-eastern Asia show an equal balance of women and men (United Nations, 1995a).

The women-to-men ratio is influenced by three factors: the sex ratio at birth, age-sex differentials in migration, and differences in mortality (Coale, 1991). An interpretation of the women/men ratios (and of the age-sex structure of the population) would include examining the ratio at birth (if available) and for each age group, taking the following into account:

- There are usually 93 to 96 girls born for every 100 boys. If there is under-reporting of female births, the reported ratio will be lower.

- Biologically, women have lower mortality, especially as infants and after age 40, and thus tend to live longer than men if they receive similar nutrition and medical attention. Therefore the ratio of women to men should increase with age. Extreme deviations from expected age-mortality patterns are indicative of marked differential mortality at those ages or of sex-selective migration, and should be examined more closely. In some developing countries, mortality of women is higher than for men. This difference may have several possible explanations, including sex discrimination in nutrition and health care, which increases girls' vulnerability to infectious diseases (Waldron, 1987), high maternal mortality rates during child-bearing ages, cultural practices such as widow burning, killing of women for unpaid or insufficient dowries, induced abortions of female foetuses and infanticide.

- Differences in female and male migration (international as well as rural-to-urban if available) could have significant effect on the sex ratios and age-sex composition of the population when there are large organized streams either to or from the country, which are age and/or sex specific.

Marital status

SERIES A   **Percentage distribution by marital status in age groups**

Formula

$$\frac{\text{Women (men) aged } (x, x + n) \text{ in marital status category } i}{\text{Women (men) in age group } (x, x + n)} \times 100$$

SERIES B   **Sex-distribution within marital status categories by age groups**

Formula

$$\frac{\text{Women (men) aged } (x, x + n) \text{ in marital status category } i}{\text{Person aged } (x, x + n) \text{ in marital status category } i} \times 100$$

Policy relevance

Early marriage interferes with the educational and career development of women to a much higher degree than for men, especially when early marriage is associated with early pregnancy. Women's risk of dependency and poverty is also greater in countries where early marriage and marital dissolutions are highly prevalent. Moreover, widows are particularly vulnerable because they often have little support from their husband's family and few property rights. Women who are discouraged from taking paid work and thus have little means to support themselves without relying on family members are also most vulnerable in case of divorce or widowhood.

Data sources

The main source for these indicators is the national population census. Sample survey data can be used as a supplementary source if marital status information has been obtained for all members of the household. Many countries have special fertility or demographic surveys, which are relatively good sources of data provided they cover both women and men 15 years and over, independent of their marital status. Many of the fertility and demographic surveys use samples restricted to women of child-bearing ages and their husbands. These data should not be combined with other more broad-based sample and census data unless noted.

Source table

Table 2.1. Population aged 15 and older by marital status, age group and sex, for total, urban and rural areas

	Marital status													
	Single		Married		Widowed		Divorced		Separated		Not stated		Total	
	W	M	W	M	W	M	W	M	W	M	W	M	W	M
Total (urban and rural)														
15–19														
20–24														
.														
.														
65–69														
70+														
All ages														
Urban														
Same age groups as above														
Rural														
Same age groups as above														

Technical note: Note any changes in concepts and definitions or limitations to the series. Separated may be combined with married or divorced in some countries.

Source: Compiled from table yy in (cite publication in full).

Note: This table will have to be compiled separately for each year covered by the analysis.

Working table

Table 2.2. Percentage distribution of women and men aged 15 and older by marital status and age group, for total, urban and rural areas

| | Marital status | | | | | | | | | | | | Total | |
| | Single | | Married | | Widowed | | Divorced | | Separated | | Not stated | | | |
	W	M	W	M	W	M	W	M	W	M	W	M	W	M
Total (urban and rural)														
15–19													100	100
20–24													100	100
.													.	.
.													.	.
65–69													100	100
70+													100	100
All ages													100	100
Urban														
Same age groups as above														
Rural														
Same age groups as above														

Technical note: Note any changes in concepts and definitions or limitations to the series. Separated may be combined with married or divorced in some countries.

Source: Compiled from table yy in (cite publication in full).

Note: This table will have to be constructed separately for each year covered by the analysis.

Additional indicators or classifications

The final presentation could show selected age groups or combinations of age groups of particular importance to the country. The marital status for particular age groups is also important, such as divorced or separated for ages 25–49 or widowed for age 50+. For fertility analysis, it is important to show the percentage of women 25 years and older who are currently married and women 50 years and older who have never married.

Another way to assess the prevalence of early marriage is to examine the mean age at first marriage for women and men. If data on age at first marriage are unavailable, the marital status data presented above will give a proxy indicator called singulate mean age at marriage. The formula for the singulate mean age at marriage can be obtained from a demography text or by consulting a demographer. To analyse trends in the age at first marriage, the average or median age at marriage for women and men of different age groups can be compiled. If the age at marriage is lower for those of older age groups compared to those of younger age groups, it can be deduced that the age at marriage is rising.

There are variations in the timing of marriage with respect to educational attainment, rural/urban residence, ethnic groups or regions, which can be illustrated by using cross-tabulation.

Polygamous unions have important implications for women's status and the welfare of their children. The percentage of women living in polygamous unions by their rank, or by number of husband's other wives, is a good indicator to analyse. The percentage of polygamous men can also be classified by the number of wives they have.

The situations of individuals after the dissolution of marriage vary considerably. Some live alone, others stay with their children, some enter into long-term relationships and remarry. These varying circumstances pose different problems for women and men. Women who are not currently married often face a high risk of poverty. Women's activity status, income and the presence of supplementary earners cross-tabulated by marital status is used to assess the relationships among household composition, marital status and women's economic standing.

Likely problems

Consensual unions have long been prevalent in some cultures and cohabitation is becoming increasingly common in many developed countries. In such cases another category should be included to cover these groups, or a decision should be made as to whether to combine them with the married group.

There is a tendency to under-report married girls or boys who are below the legal age. There are also problems associated with misreporting of other statistics, especially where consensual unions are prevalent or where there is a stigma on unwed mothers. The separated may also be wrongly classified as divorced or married. Polygamy is prevalent in some societies and has implications for the status of women. An attempt should be made to obtain data on women in polygamous unions, which are sometimes collected in general household surveys or fertility surveys.

Interpretation

Most women and men marry at least once in their life, though women marry at younger ages than men. The proportion of women aged 45 and older who have never married varies from 1.9 per cent (eastern and southern Asia) to 26 per cent (Caribbean). In many developing countries, women marry at very young ages, often before age 18. Men generally marry four or more years later. The lowest proportion of women aged 15–19 who are currently married is 2 per cent in eastern Asia compared to 1 per cent for men. The highest proportions are found in western Africa, where most countries show more than 50 per cent of women aged 15–19 are married but less than 10 per cent of men in the same age group are married (United Nations, 1995a). In Latin America, the proportions of married women aged 12–24 years are twice as high as married men in the same age group; but there are almost equal proportions of women and men aged 25–44 who are married (FLACSO, 1995). In developed regions, although both women and men marry later, women still marry earlier than men. Hence, women's parental roles start at an earlier age; they manage a family, divorce, separate and are widowed at much younger ages than men. Early marriage and child-bearing can deprive women of the opportunity to complete secondary school or to work outside the home. With less education and paid work experience, women are more likely to become dependent on their spouses or their children or to require social services.

In interpreting trends in marital status, it is important to take into account the timing of marriage, life expectancy and the rates of marriage and family dissolution.

Differences in women's and men's ages at marriage can be analysed from the proportion of never-married women and men and of married women and men in each age group. Comparisons can be made both within and across age groups. Some questions to ask include:

- What proportions of women and men aged 15–19 or 20–24 are married?

- What proportion of women and men aged 60+ are never married?

- In which age groups are less than one quarter of women or men never married?

- In which age groups are one third or two thirds of women or men married?

- How are these indicators changing from one period to another?

Patterns to look for include:

• Whether the proportions of women and men who are divorced, separated or widowed decrease or increase.

• Whether the proportions of married women and men in the age groups decrease or increase.

Cultural practices that affect women's and men's marital status such as treatment of widows, laws on inheritance and the legal age for marriage, and the degree of compliance with these laws should be taken into consideration. The legal age at marriage is particularly important in preventing girls from marrying early and thus avoiding the attendant consequences. Compliance with these laws can be tested by examining the proportions married within the age group of the legal age or, if available, the proportion that are married by the legal age and how these are changing over time.

Fertility

SERIES A   Age-specific fertility rate

Formula
$$\frac{\text{Births during the year to women aged } (x, x + n)}{\text{Women aged } (x, x + n) \text{ at mid-year}} \times 1000$$

SERIES B   Total fertility rate

Formula
$$\frac{\text{Sum of ASFRs for } 15\text{--}19 \text{ through } 45\text{--}49}{1000} \times 5$$

Policy relevance

Early and repeated child-bearing influences women's health and often keeps them from obtaining sufficient education or training to ensure a secure future for themselves and their children. It also interferes with their employment in at least two ways. First, when educational experience is truncated the opportunities for employment are limited. Second, women are the ones who tend to withdraw, for long or short periods, from the labour market in order to attend to family and child-care responsibilities, thereby jeopardizing their career development. By contrast, men's careers and educational opportunities are less affected by the number of their children or by poorly planned child-bearing.

Data sources

Age-specific fertility rates are often available from demographic reports produced by the national statistics office. If not readily available, age-specific fertility rates can be calculated using the formula given below. Two types of data are required: number of births by age of the woman and the mid-year population of women in the reproductive age groups, in a given year.

In general, birth data come from the civil registration system while the mid-year population of women comes from censuses and population projections. Because the quality of vital registration systems in many developing countries is low, fertility or demographic surveys are the main alternative source.

Source table

Table 3.1. Births to women aged 15-49 by age group, for total, urban and rural areas, 1970–1995

Age group	1970		1995	
	Births	Number of women	Births	Number of women
Total (urban and rural)				
15–19				
20–24				
.				
.				
.				
45–49				
All ages				
Urban Same age groups as above				
Rural Same age groups as above				

Technical note: State whether vital registration system or fertility surveys were used and indicate completeness of coverage.
Source: Compiled from table yy in (cite publication in full).

Working table

Table 3.2. Age-specific fertility rates (per 1000 women) and total fertility rate, for total, urban and rural areas, 1970–1995

Age group	1970	1995
Total (urban and rural)		
Age-specific fertility rate		
15–19		
20–24		
25–29		
30–34		
35–39		
40–44		
45–49		
Total fertility rate		
Number of women		
Urban Same categories as above		
Rural Same categories as above		

Technical note: If rates are computed from a sample survey, also give the number of women in the sample.
Source: Give full citation for survey reports or studies from which the statistics were compiled.

Additional indicators or classifications

In the absence of a total fertility rate, the mean number of children ever born to women aged 50–54 or 45–49 (depending on the age limit applied to the end of the reproductive period, 49 years or 44 years, respectively). The age-specific rates can also be presented in a table and chart showing the pattern of child-bearing over women's life spans. In general, births are concentrated between ages 20 and 35.

Residence and educational attainment are important sources of variation for fertility rates and also need to be examined. If there are reasons for expecting ethnic differences in fertility level, these should be presented.

The age at first birth indicates how early women begin child-bearing and its responsibilities. It is useful to look at mean age at first birth for different age groups in order to view trends towards delay of childbirth, which leads to lower fertility. This is evidenced by higher ages at first birth among successively younger age groups. The data needed for this indicator are not often readily available and must be obtained by processing the original data sets, unless this indicator was the focus of a previous study.

Likely problems

Indicators may be affected by the quality of birth registration data or by recall errors on the part of the respondent and by errors with maternal birth date and age at the time of birth (if census or survey data on births occurring within a specified year are used). The quality of the data should be ascertained from relevant documentation as well as from data producers and researchers who are in a position to help evaluate the information.

Interpretation

In most countries in Latin America and the Caribbean and in Asia and the Pacific, women had fewer children in 1990–1995 compared with 20 years prior. In almost all of sub-Saharan Africa, the fertility rate remained unchanged. The average number of children per woman in 1990–1995 ranges from fewer than two in the more developed regions to around six in sub-Saharan Africa, with wide intercountry differences (United Nations, 1995a).

Regional patterns and levels of fertility indicate that differences in total fertility rates do not necessarily mean differences in levels of age-specific fertility. For example, while the average sub-Saharan African woman has six children, Latin American and Caribbean women have three to four children and Asian women four children, the age patterns are similar. Average fertility peaks at ages 25–29 for women in all three regions, as in most countries in the more developed regions. However, in high-fertility countries age-specific fertility declines much more slowly with older age groups than in low-fertility countries (United Nations, 1987).

Women's child-bearing is determined by direct factors such as age at marriage, contraceptive use, abortion, breastfeeding, prevalence of infertility and sexually transmitted diseases, as well as indirect factors such as education, urbanization, government policies, infant mortality rate and the social and economic environment.

A partial explanation for the persistence of high fertility, especially at older ages, can be obtained from data on women's and men's family-size preferences. Analysis of the 1993 Demographic and Health Survey data for the United Republic of Tanzania shows that though on average both women and men desire additional children, at higher ages proportionately more men than women would like additional children, and of those who would like additional children, men want the children sooner (i.e., at shorter intervals) than do women (United Republic of Tanzania, Bureau of the Census, 1995).

Analysis of data should examine the following questions:

- What is the current level of total fertility and what has been the trend over the years? What factors (including policies or programmes) may have contributed to this trend? For example, has mean age at first marriage or mean age at first birth increased or decreased? (Total fertility is supposed to decrease as the mean age at first marriage increases.)

- What are the age patterns of fertility? Special attention should be given to adolescent women, since childbirth poses greater health risks to young mothers and their children. Further analysis of adolescent fertility could entail expressing births to women aged 15–19 as a proportion of all births and, data permitting, the distribution of births in this age interval.

Headship and composition of households

SERIES A	Distribution of female- and male-headed households by size
Formula	$\dfrac{\text{Number of women (men)-headed households with y members}}{\text{Total number of women (men)-headed households}} \times 100$
SERIES B	Sex-composition of the heads of households with each size category of the household
	$\dfrac{\text{Number of women (men)-headed households with y members}}{\text{Total number of heads of households with y members}} \times 100$

Policy relevance

Data on the household provide the basis for studying issues of great policy concern, specifically patterns and changes in the family and economic well-being. Statistics on household headship, size and composition are useful indicators of the living arrangements of families, the number of wage earners and the overall economic needs that have to be provided for within the household.

Data sources

The national population and housing census is the main data source for these indicators. These data are also usually available from household sample surveys, which may be used as supplementary sources. The accuracy and reliability of the estimates will depend on the sample size and whether it is large enough to produce significant numbers in the detailed cross-national and subnational tabulations needed for the analyses.

Source table

Table 4.1. Number of households by size and by age and sex of head, for total, urban and rural areas

	Age and sex of household head									
	15–24		25–44		45–59		60+		All ages	
Size of household	W	M	W	M	W	M	W	M	W	M
Total (urban and rural)										
1										
2										
3										
.										
.										
.										
10+										
Total (all sizes)										
Urban										
Same household sizes as above										
Rural										
Same household sizes as above										

Technical note: Note definitions or concepts used in data collection and differences in classification or definitions used.

Source: Give full citation for census publications from which data have been extracted.

Note: This table will have to be compiled separately for each year covered by the analysis.

Working tables

Table 4.2. Percentage distribution of women-headed and men-headed households by size, for total, urban and rural areas

| | Percentage distribution | |
Household size	Women-headed households	Men-headed households
Total (urban and rural)		
1		
2		
3		
.		
.		
.		
10+		
Total (all sizes)	100	100
Urban		
Same household sizes as above		
Rural		
Same household sizes as above		

Technical note: Note definitions or concepts used in data collection and differences in classification or definitions used.

Source: Give full citation for census publications from which data have been extracted.

Note: This table will have to be constructed separately for each year covered by the analysis. Selection for final presentation should be guided by findings to be highlighted.

**Table 4.3. Percentage of households headed by women and by men,
by size of household, for total, urban and rural areas**

	Percentage women-headed	Percentage men-headed	Total
Total (urban and rural)			100
1			100
2			100
3			100
.			
.			
.			
10+			100
Total (all sizes)			100
Urban			
Same household sizes as above			
Rural			
Same household sizes as above			

Technical note: Note definitions or concepts used in data collection and differences in classification or definitions used.

Source: Give full citation for census publications from which data have been extracted.

Notes: While the above table summarizes data for all ages, sometimes it is of interest to do the analysis for each broad age group to determine if female headship increases with age, for example. Selection for final presentation should be guided by findings to be highlighted.

This table will have to be constructed separately for each year covered by the analysis.

Additional indicators or classifications

It may be of interest to show proportions of the population living in particular types of households in a specific year or over several years. In addition, one could look at:

- Proportion of women- and men-headed households by size of household for selected age groups (for example, ages 15–24, 25–44, 45–59, and 60+).

- Average household size by sex and age of household head.

- Proportion of women- and men-headed households by presence (or absence) of children and spouse.

- Marital status distribution of women and men heads.

- Sex composition of heads of household in different marital status categories.

For social policy, two types of households are of special interest:

- One-person households.

- Single-parent households with children, by marital status (important where male labour migration is common).

Likely problems

The term head of household is used in censuses and surveys to identify a reference through whom information is obtained on the individuals and characteristics of the household and on household structure. Thus the definition used for data collection does not necessarily correspond with the concept of headship as the decision-making authority within the household. Furthermore, the designation of head within the household is often biased by cultural beliefs and customs that assign authority to the male, regardless of age. In some cases, the head person may not even reside in the household. And in cultures that practice polygamy, one man may be the nominal head of more than one household.

In general, therefore the proportion of women heads will tend to be an underestimation. There should be a closer examination of the data to ascertain any biases that may exist. Cross-tabulations of headship with age and activity status can give an indication of sex-based bias in recording of heads of household.

Thus, determining which households are headed by women can be difficult. Moreover, the procedures followed in applying the concept may themselves be biased: in some cases, instructions to enumerators may state that a woman can be recorded as head only in the absence of a man above a specified age; in others, enumerators assume that no woman can be head of a household in which an adult man is present.

Interpretation

A majority of the women household heads in developing countries do not have a spouse but do have children and other household members; and a vast majority of their households have at least two members. In the developed regions, households headed by women are more closely divided between one-person households and those of two or more persons (United Nations, 1991).

Average household size ranges from about three members in the developed regions to around five in Asia and the Pacific. About 8 per cent of households in Asia and the Pacific consist of one person; of these, 45 per cent are women and 55 per cent men. Households in developing regions are much more likely to have children than those in the developed regions (United Nations, 1991).

Around the world, more and more households are headed by women.
There is considerable diversity in the prevalence of women-headed households across regions and across countries. The highest proportion of women-headed households is 35 per cent for the Caribbean, and the lowest is 12–13 per cent in northern Africa, western Asia and southern Asia. Within regions, for example in sub-Saharan Africa, where the average is 20 per cent women-headed households, the national averages range from 10 per cent in the Niger and Burkina Faso to 46 per cent in Botswana (United Nations, 1995a).

Female headship is very much associated with marital dissolution by widowhood, divorce or separation. Women heads are therefore more likely to be without a spouse. It is important to examine in more detail differences in the characteristics of households headed by women and by men:

• Examine the relative structure of both women- and men-headed households: proportions that are one-person; head without a spouse and head with a spouse; proportion of women and men heads of household under age 15 and aged 15–19; also the marital status of the heads of household.

The following statistics can be used to ascertain whether boys with no major economic responsibility in the household are being designated as head:

• Examine the activity status of those designated as heads: age-specific activity rates for heads of households—that is, are non-economically active men more likely than their women counterparts to be designated as heads?

• What proportion of the women- and men-headed households have two to four members, or more than five?

References and further reading

Bruce, Judith, Cynthia Lloyd and Ann Leonard (1995). *Families in Focus: New Perspectives on Mothers, Fathers and Children.* New York: The Population Council.

Bruce, Judith and Cynthia Lloyd (1992). *Finding the Ties That Bind: Beyond Headship and Household.* Working Papers No. 4. New York: The Population Council.

Coale, Ansley (1991). Excess female mortality and the balance of the sexes in the population: An estimate of the number of missing females. *Population and Development Review* (New York), vol. 17, No. 3, pp. 517–523.

FLACSO (1995). *Latin American Women: Compared Figures.* Santiago: Instituto da la Mujer.

Hajnal, J. (1953). Age at marriage and proportions marrying. *Population Studies,* vol. 7, No. 2.

United Nations (1987). *Fertility Behaviour in the Context of Development: Evidence from the World Fertility Survey.* Sales No. E.86.XIII.5.

_____ (1988a). *Adolescent Reproductive Behaviour, vol.I, Evidence from Developed Countries.* Sales No. E.88.XIII.8.

_____ (1988b). *Adolescent Reproductive Behaviour, vol.II Evidence from Developing Countries.* Sales No. E.89.XIII.10.

_____ (1988c). *First Marriage: Patterns and Determinants.* ST/ESA/SER.R/76.

_____ (1988d). *World Population Trends and Policies:1987 Monitoring Report.* Sales No. E.88.XIII.3.

_____ (1990). *Patterns of First Marriage: Timing and Prevalence.* ST/ESA/SER.R/111.

_____ (1991). *The World's Women 1970–1990: Trends and Statistics.* Sales No. E.90.XVII.3.

_____ (1995a). *The World's Women 1995: Trends and Statistics.* Sales No. E.95.XVII.2.

_____ (1995b). *Living Arrangements of Women and Their Children in Developing Countries: A Demographic Profile.* Sales No. E.90.XIII.5.

United Republic of Tanzania, Bureau of the Census (1995). *Analysis of Women and Men: The Tanzanian Case.* Dar es Salaam.

Waldron, Ingrid (1987). Patterns and causes of excess female mortality among children in developing countries. *World Health Statistics Quarterly,* vol. 40, Geneva: World Health Organization.

PUBLIC LIFE AND LEADERSHIP

Leadership in legislative assemblies

SERIES A: Percentage distribution of elected/appointed officials by level of political leadership (national, municipal and so on)

Formula

$$\frac{\text{Number of elected/appointed women (men) officials at level } i}{\text{Total number of elected/appointed women (men) officials}} \times 100$$

SERIES B: Sex-composition of elected and appointed officials at various levels of government (national, municipal and so on)

Formula

$$\frac{\text{Number of elected/appointed women (men) officials at level } i}{\text{Total number of elected/appointed officials at a level } i} \times 100$$

Policy relevance

In a democratic political system, women and men ought to be represented equally in political posts to reinforce both the legitimacy and quality of government. Moreover, having women in political posts is more likely to lead to the broader objectives of equal opportunities policy being accomplished (Netherlands, Ministries of Social Affairs and Employment and Home Affairs, 1993, p. 1).

Data sources

The numbers of women and men in parliament are based on data provided by national authorities. They may be available in published form or they may need to be compiled from listings. Data for representatives at the state, provincial or regional level and at the municipal or district council level may be more difficult to obtain. Such data may need to be compiled from any available lists.

Source table

Table 5.1. Number of elected and appointed positions occupied by women and men, for three periods

	1970–1974			1980–1984			1990–1994		
	Women	Men	Total	Women	Men	Total	Women	Men	Total
Parliament									
Upper house (chamber)									
Lower house (chamber)									
State/provincial level									
...									
Local/district level									
...									
Total elected/appointed									

Technical note: Note definitions of parliamentary participation.
Source: Compiled from unpublished registries in Ministry of ...; and/or give full citations for publications used.

Working tables

Table 5.2. Percentage of elected and appointed positions occupied by women and men, for three periods

	1970–1974			1980–1984			1990–1994		
	Women	Men	Total	Women	Men	Total	Women	Men	Total
Parliament									
Upper house (chamber)									
Lower house (chamber)									
State/provincial level									
...									
Local/district level									
...									
Total elected/appointed									

Technical note: Note definitions of parliamentary participation.
Source: Compiled from unpublished registries in Ministry of ...; and/or give full citations for publications used.

Table 5.3. Percentage distribution of elected and appointed women and men by level of political leadership, for three periods

	1970–1974		1980–1984		1990–1994	
	Women	Men	Women	Men	Women	Men
Parliament						
Upper house (chamber)						
Lower house (chamber)						
State/provincial level						
...						
Local/district level						
...						
Total elected/appointed	100	100	100	100	100	100

Technical note: Note definitions of parliamentary participation.
Source: Compiled from unpublished registries in Ministry of ...; and/or give full citations for publications used.

Additional indicators or classifications

Some countries have a single chamber of parliament, which is elected. Others have a bicameral parliament, which may be either elected or appointed. It is important to maintain this distinction since different factors can account for the numbers of women and men in the two chambers. If there is a quota established for women to be appointed into political positions, this needs to be noted and the numbers of women who benefit from this policy should also be presented.

In countries where the role of chief is prominent, a table on district-level chiefs is also relevant.

Where there are data on candidates who contested for parliamentary elections, the proportion of women and men contestants who are elected may be included, as well as the proportion of women and men among all of the candidates.

The percentage of women and men in political parties and in leadership positions in these parties (e.g., national executive committee, regional/provincial and local chapters or cells) may also be presented.

Information pertaining to the history of women's political advancement (such as the year women were allowed to vote and to stand for election, the first woman voted president, governor, mayor, or to parliament) may also be presented.

Likely problems

Since the data usually come from various national authorities or individual government departments, the completeness of coverage and reporting will vary. Also, it is sometimes difficult to determine if the name refers to a woman or a man. The listings should be checked for completeness and accuracy.

Data may not be available for all areas at the provincial and local levels. In such cases, present those areas with complete data and explain that they are illustrative examples and not intended to be representative of all areas.

Interpretation

Factors that may be important in interpreting the data include the existence of quota systems or reserved seats and the length of the parliamentary system in a country. In most countries of more recent parliamentary tradition, the access of women to parliament has often coincided with the founding of the parliamentary institution (Inter-Parliamentary Union, 1995).

In 1994 women represented 20 per cent or more of the members of parliament (in a unicameral or lower chamber) in only 25 countries. Progress for women in parliaments over the past 10 years has been mixed and varies widely among regions. Women's membership in parliaments has declined in eastern and western Asia. It dropped sharply in eastern Europe after 1987 but turned up in some of these countries in recent elections. It increased slightly in Africa and Latin America and somewhat more so in developed regions outside eastern Europe (United Nations, 1995).

At the high extreme, five countries (Denmark, Finland, the Netherlands, Norway and Sweden) have women comprising 30 to 40 per cent of the single/popular chamber of national parliament. At the low extreme, there are no women in the assemblies of 12 countries and in 46 countries women account for 0 to 5 per cent (Inter-Parliamentary Union, 1995).

Parliamentary seats are reserved for women in a few countries. In 1995 these included Bangladesh (30 out of 330 seats), Eritrea (10 out of 105 seats) and the United Republic of Tanzania (15 out of 255 seats) (Inter-Parliamentary Union, 1995).

Questions that need to be addressed are, for example:

- What is the share of women compared with men at national, at provincial and at local level politics?

- How is women's election or appointment to political positions changing over time?

- Are greater increases in women's political representation occurring at the national, provincial or local levels?

- In the history of the country, how many women, if any, have held the position of president, prime minister, head of state, head of parliament or speaker of the house?

Decision-making in government

SERIES A: Percentage distribution of senior officials (minister to level of deputy director of a department) by field, for each sex.

Formula

$$\frac{\text{Women (men) in senior positions in field } j}{\text{Women (men) in senior positions in field}} \times 100$$

SERIES B: Sex composition of senior level positions below deputy permanent secretary level by field

Formula

$$\frac{\text{Women (men) in senior positions at level } i \text{ in field } j}{\text{Total senior positions at level } i \text{ in field } j} \times 100$$

The fields may be classified as follows: office of chief of state or office of prime minister; political ministries (foreign affairs, defence and internal/home affairs); economic ministries (finance, industry, agriculture and trade); law and justice ministries (including the court system and institutions such as ombudsman); social ministries (education, health, culture, social welfare, community development, youth, women's affairs, etc.). (United Nations, 1992, p. 6 and United Nations, 1995, pp.151–152).

Policy relevance

An equal sharing of jobs among women and men in government is important to make full use of human resources. In addition, because women often have different interests and needs, they are in a better position than men to articulate and defend these interests when placed in positions of authority.

Data sources

Data on women and men in executive positions should come from administrative sources such as the office responsible for government employment, or the civil service commission. The data may also be available in published form in statistical abstracts produced by the national statistical office. If neither of these sources provides the necessary information, the data will need to be collected from primary sources, compiled from listings of personnel that can be obtained from relevant government offices.

Posts of top governmental officials include ministers, deputy ministers, permanent and principal secretaries and their deputies, directors and deputy directors of departments, etc.

Source table

Table 6.1. Appointees to senior-level positions in political and civil service by field, level and sex

	President's office		Prime minister's office		Political		Economic		Law and justice		Social affairs		All fields	
	Women	Men	Women	Men	Women	Men	Women	Men	Women	Men	Women	Men	Women	Men
Ministers														
Deputy ministers														
Principal/ permanent secretaries														
Deputy secretaries														
Commissioners														
Directors														
Deputy directors														
Total														

Technical note: Note completeness of coverage and reporting, and frequency of changes, as well as period in a year to which this refers.

Source: Compiled from unpublished registries in Ministry of ...; and/or give full citations for publications used.

Note: This table will have to be compiled separately for each year covered by the analysis.

Working tables

Table 6.2. Percentage distribution of senior-level officials by field and sex

Field	Percentage distribution	
	Women	Men
President's office		
Prime minister's office		
Political		
Economic		
Law and justice		
Social affairs		
All senior positions	100	100

Technical note: Note completeness of coverage and reporting, and frequency of changes, as well as period in a year to which this refers.

Source: Compiled from unpublished registries in Ministry of ...; and/or give full citations for publications used.

Note: This table will have to be constructed separately for each year covered by the analysis.

Table 6.3. Percentage of women among senior-level officials by level and field

Level	President's office	Prime minister's office	Political	Economic	Law and justice	Social affairs	All fields
Ministers							
Deputy ministers							
Principal/permanent secretaries							
Deputy secretaries							
Commissioners							
Directors							
Deputy directors							
All senior positions							

Technical note: Note completeness of coverage and reporting, and frequency of changes, as well as period in a year to which this refers.

Sources: Compiled from unpublished registries in Ministry of ...; and/or give full citations for publications used.

Note: This table will have to be constructed separately for each year covered by the analysis.

Additional indicators or classifications

Percentage distribution and sex composition of senior officials may also be classified by level for all fields combined.

Sex composition of members of advisory bodies to the government and interdepartmental committees could be compiled, and classified by field.

Likely problems

If data must be collected from primary sources, that is, from the different government institutions or offices, a complete list of the government offices should first be compiled and the different classifications of top positions ascertained. The appropriate cut-off point for the executive posts will also need to be decided upon. Specialists on this subject should be consulted for the interpretation of the data. One problem is high turnover in the ministerial and deputy ministerial posts in some countries. A position may have been held by different people during the reference period, which can affect the sex distribution. A decision will need to be made as to which month of the year the data should refer to (such as the beginning or end of the calendar year or of the fiscal year).

Interpretation

Women are poorly represented at the top echelons of government, but there are some signs of progress. Between 1987 and 1994 the number of countries where women held no ministerial positions dropped from 93 to 59. Only 5.7 per cent of the world's cabinet ministers were women in 1994, but that was an increase from 3.3 per cent in 1987. In 1987 women held more than 15 per cent of ministerial positions in only eight countries—in 1994, in 16 countries. Six countries—Denmark, Finland, the Netherlands, Norway, Sweden and the Seychelles—have around one third women ministers. And in Sweden after the 1994 election, women increased from about one third to parity with men (52 per cent) in ministerial posts (United Nations, 1995).

Women are only slightly better represented at subministerial levels, in such posts as permanent secretary, deputy secretary and director.

Women's higher representation at ministerial and subministerial levels is usually tenuous, however. Most countries with women in top ministerial positions do not have comparable representation at the subministerial level. And where significant numbers of women are found at subministerial levels, very few are at the top (United Nations, 1992 and 1995).

Given that there are so few women relative to men at the decision-making level, using other neighbouring countries as an indication of the goal or standard for comparison serves very little purpose.

It is therefore advisable to set objective standards of comparison on the basis of the sex composition in categories such as: all those employed; managerial and administrative personnel either in the labour force or in the civil service; professional staff in the civil service, etc.

- How does the sex composition of the civil service professional compare with the sex composition at progressively higher levels of decision-making? Are women more or less likely to be appointed to ministerial positions relative to subministerial positions?

- Another dimension of the analysis is to examine the distribution of women and men among the different fields of decision-making. Does the balance of sexes become better or worse with the more prestigious fields such as foreign affairs, legal affairs, trade, etc.? Or are women more likely to be represented in the social ministries, such as health, education, housing and welfare?

- Are women as likely to be directors of department as deputy directors? In which fields are women deputy directors and in which are the women directors? How different is this from the patterns for men?

Decision-making in public and private enterprises

> **SERIES A:** Percentage distribution of managers of public and private enterprises by type of establishment, each sex
>
> Formula
> $$\frac{\text{Women (men) managers in enterprise type } i}{\text{Women (men) managers in all public and private enterprises}} \times 100$$
>
> **SERIES B:** Shares of women and men among managers in public enterprises and in private sector enterprises by type of establishment
>
> Formula
> $$\frac{\text{Women (men) managers in enterprise type } i}{\text{All managers in enterprise type } i} \times 100$$
>
> Where type of enterprise i is according to national classifications used—for example, public, joint public/private, private corporation, and other private.

Policy relevance

Enterprise development, in both the public and private sectors, is essential for the expansion of countries' industrial base and employment. Effective linkages with other sectors of development can be realized only with top quality management that draws fully from the pool of human resources, women as well as men.

Data sources

The primary source of data is statistical inquiries on employment in public and private enterprises, which many national statistical offices conduct on a regular basis for national accounts purposes, such as industrial censuses and establishment surveys. These data may not be published on a regular basis but are generally available at the statistical office or published in statistical abstracts. Other sources are population censuses and labour force surveys that obtain information on the institutional sector of those employed as well as their occupation. A cross-classification of these two characteristics will provide the requisite statistics, limiting the tabulation to managers in the following groups—administrative and managerial workers, sales workers, and service workers (according to the 1968 Revision of the International Standard Classification of Occupations (ISCO)) or corporate managers and managing supervisors (in the 1988 Revision of ISCO) in public and private institutions.

Source table

Table 7.1. Number of managers in public and private enterprises by sex, 1970–1990

Type of enterprise	1970			1980			1990		
	Women	Men	Total	Women	Men	Total	Women	Men	Total
Public									
Joint public/private									
Private									
Corporation									
Non-corporation									
Large									
Medium									
Small									
Total									

Technical note: Define the sizes that correspond to categories of large, medium and small.

Source: Give full citations for publications used and any other sources of data.

Working tables

Table 7.2. Percentage distribution of women and men managers by type of enterprise managed, 1970–1990

Type of enterprise	1970		1980		1990	
	Women	Men	Women	Men	Women	Men
Public						
Joint public/private						
Private						
Corporation						
Non-corporation						
Large						
Medium						
Small						
Total	100	100	100	100	100	100

Technical note: Define the sizes that correspond to large, medium and small.
Source: Compiled from table yy in (cite publication in full).

Table 7.3. Percentage of women among managers in selected types of enterprises, 1970–1990

Type of enterprise	1970	1980	1990
Public			
Joint public/private			
Private			
Corporation			
Non-corporation			
Large			
Medium			
Small			
Total			

Technical note: Define the sizes that correspond to large, medium and small.
Source: Compiled from table yy in (cite publication in full).

Additional indicators or classifications

The classification of type of enterprise may be further defined according to size, such as large, medium, etc. following national definitions (or expressed in terms of number of employees—for example, 200 or more, 100 to 199, 50 to 99, 20 to 49).

Other decision-making executives in enterprises—such as president and vice-president, director, deputy director (or equivalent), board of directors—may also be presented.

If the available data do not allow for cross-tabulations of occupations with type of establishment, sex-composition indicators can be presented for managers and working proprietors separately for administrative and managerial workers, sales workers, and service workers, or by branch of activity (excluding agriculture).

Likely problems

Published data may not be disaggregated by sex, in which case the statistics would have to be compiled from unpublished sources. There is also the problem of completeness of reporting and coverage of the enquiries, which should be noted. Reports will generally indicate the non-response rate. Due to the introduction of a newly revised International Standard Classification of Occupations, a careful review of occupational codes for different census periods will be necessary to ensure that representation of managers is not significantly different across censuses or surveys.

When unpublished or administrative sources are used, it should be noted that job titles may also differ between private and public sector enterprises. Where differences can not easily be reconciled, both classifications should be presented in separate tables.

Interpretation

Women constitute a small and growing pool of middle managers in the private sector but men maintain a stronghold on the top executive positions. For example, in the Nordic countries' 100 largest private enterprises, almost no women were managing directors. And at other levels of management and on corporate boards, there are very few women (Nordic Council of Ministers, 1994).

Women are still the minority in administrative and management jobs overall, but their participation increased in every region but one from 1980 to 1990. In the developed regions outside Europe it jumped from 16 to 33 per cent. Women now constitute as much as 40 per cent of administrators and managers in Australia, Canada, Hungary, Sweden and the United States. Latin America and the Caribbean continues to have a high proportion of women in management and administration (25 per cent, up from 18 per cent in 1980). Increases from a lower base were also seen in western Europe (from 12 to

18 per cent) and in sub-Saharan Africa (from 8 to 14 per cent) (United Nations, 1995, p.153).

More specific issues that can be addressed are:

- Which types of establishments have proportionately more women than men in administrative and management positions?

- How are managers distributed across the different types of establishments? Is the distribution very different between women and men?

- What, if any, are the changes in the composition by sex of the managers over the years?

- Compare the proportion of women in management in public sector enterprises and private sector enterprises. Which of the sectors have proportionately more women?

Public order and safety

SERIES A: Sex composition within public order and public safety occupations

Formula
$$\frac{\text{Number of women (men) in public safety occupation } i}{\text{Total employed in public safety occupation } i} \times 100$$

Judges, magistrates, public prosecutors and lawyers/attorneys would be classified by level of jurisdiction (i.e., national, regional or district level courts). The first series could also be computed using total numbers of women and men employees in the labour force as the denominators for women and men, respectively, and expressed in per 1,000 (or higher) instead of 100. The hierarchical structure of the attorney-general's office could also be analysed with respect to the distribution of women and men and the sex composition within the different categories of professionals.

Policy relevance

Persons working with the law—judges and lawyers, the police, prison guards and other administrative personnel—have an important role in advancing gender equality. Judges and lawyers affect the development and interpretation of gender-sensitive legislation, and the police and other administrative personnel affect the treatment of victims, particularly women who are the victims of violence. The presence of women among public order and safety personnel has policy relevance for both equality of opportunity in employment and also for a gender-sensitive approach to the law.

Data sources

Population censuses and household surveys are the usual sources of statistics on the economically active population by occupation and by sex. Information on public order and safety officials requires the detailed level of classification (i.e., the three-digit level). Administrative data can also be used to compile data on services provided for victims of violence against "women only", such as special facilities in police stations and shelters for battered women.

Source table

Table 8.1. Number of women and men in selected public order and safety occupations, 1970–1990

Occupation	1970			1980			1990		
	Women	Men	Total	Women	Men	Total	Women	Men	Total
Judges									
Magistrates									
Public prosecutors									
Lawyers/attorneys									
Police officers									
Prison officers									
Total									

Source: Give full citations for publications and any other sources used.

Working table

Table 8.2. Percentage of women in selected public order and safety occupations, 1970–1990

Occupation	1970	1980	1990
Judges			
Magistrates			
Public prosecutors			
Lawyers/attorneys			
Police officers			
Prison officers			

Source: Give full citation for publications and any other sources used.

Additional indicators or classifications

The percentage distributions of women and men judges could be presented by the court of their jurisdiction (for example, supreme court, appeals court and trial court). Also, percentage distributions of women and men lawyers (attorneys) classified by their field of practice (such as criminal, family, business, etc.) may be presented.

Likely problems

Occupational data, especially those obtained from labour force and general household surveys, may not be available in the required detail. Furthermore, when they are available a careful study of the classification and coding is necessary in order to extract all the relevant information. It should be noted that the occupational classification may have changed over the years. Prior to 1990 most national data collection classified occupations on the basis of the 1968 Revision of the International Standard Classification of Occupations (ISCO) with some adaptation. The new international classification (1988 Revision) has been adopted and may now be in use. Where the classifications are not to the required detail, administrative sources such as the Ministry of Internal Affairs, Ministry of Justice or relevant departments or offices may be able to provide some information. Problems of timeliness and confidentiality are usually encountered with administrative data.

Interpretation

In 1980, few countries reported data disaggregated by sex on criminal justice prosecutors. The proportion of women in this profession was less than 10 per cent in most of these countries (the former Czechoslovakia, Madagascar, Morocco, Senegal and Uruguay). The proportions ranged from 54 to 23 per cent (United Nations, 1995).

In very few countries in Latin America have women reached the highest court. In general, the lower in the hierarchy the court is, the higher the number of women (FLACSO, 1995). For example, in Venezuela 4 out of 15 (27 per cent) supreme court judges are women, while women's share in trial courts is more than 50 per cent.

Specific questions for investigation could include:

• When was the first woman appointed to the supreme court (or higher court) or appeals court, or to the highest levels of the police or prison force? How many women have been appointed as judges to the supreme court?

• In which occupations of the judiciary system do women outnumber men? Do these occupations have a high level responsibility, middle level or low level?

- How have these patterns of distribution changed over time? Is there a definite trend towards higher or lower participation of women in any of the occupations; or has their participation not changed?

Crime and violence

SERIES A: Percentage distribution of convicted women and men by type of offence

Formula

$$\frac{\text{Number of women (men) convicted of crime } i}{\text{Total number of offenders convicted}} \times 100$$

SERIES B: Share of women and men among those convicted of offence

Formula

$$\frac{\text{Number of women (men) convicted of crime } i}{\text{Total number of offenders convicted of crime } i} \times 100$$

Examples of specific types of offences are crimes against persons—homicide, aggravated assault, robbery, rape; crimes against property—burglary, larceny/theft, motor-vehicle theft, arson; crimes without victims—gambling, prostitution, vagrancy, illicit drug use; and white-collar crime—tax evasion, corruption of public officials, embezzlement and fraud.

SERIES C: Percentage of women (or girls) who have been victims of violence

Formula

$$\frac{\text{Number of women (or girls) who have been victims of violence } i}{\text{Total number of women (or girls) included in the survey or study}} \times 100$$

Specific types of violence against women include rape, wife beating, physical assault by an intimate partner, molestation, kidnapping/abduction, etc.

Policy relevance

The prevalence of crime and violence restricts the freedom of individuals in society, infringes on their standard of living and can result in bodily harm and death. The problem is compounded when the violence is perpetrated by members of the victim's family, as in the case of spouse abuse, childhood sexual abuse, rape, etc. Many women are vulnerable to assault and battery, while many girls are exposed to rape and incest within the family.

Data sources

Crimes involve both offenders and victims. Basic statistics on offenders are normally derived from records of the criminal justice institutions, but these are rarely available in tabulated form. It is usually necessary to compile the data from official records and case histories. To the extent that there are survey data on the topic, these can also be used. Each of the sources have distinct disadvantages that will affect the quality of the data. There is even less data on victims of crimes and it is this dimension of crime that is of particular importance to women. Currently the only quantitative data that most governments regularly collect on violence against women are reports of crime statistics on rape, assault and a few other sex crimes. These have serious limitations and should be complemented with data from other sources. Most data on violence against women are from small ad hoc studies, but several countries have recently conducted national surveys on aspects of violence against women.

Data on violence against women and national actions in response to violence against women are difficult to find, but every effort must be made to investigate additional sources of data. Administrative data may be available, for example, in the ministries dealing with women's affairs, health or the judiciary. Specialized shelters for victims may also compile data on the number of non-governmental organizations working on violence against women.

Source table

Table 9.1. Number of women and men convicted, by type of offence, 1970–1990

Type of offence	1970			1980			1990		
	Women	Men	Total	Women	Men	Total	Women	Men	Total
Crimes against persons									
Homicide									
Aggravated assault									
Robbery									
Rape									
Crimes against property									
Burglary									
Larceny-theft									
Motor-vehicle theft									
Arson									
Crimes without victims									
Gambling									
Prostitution									
Vagrancy									
Illicit drug use									
White-collar crime									
Tax evasion									
Bribery and corruption									
Embezzlement									
Fraud									
Total									

Source: Compiled from table yy in (cite publication in full).

Working tables

Table 9.2. Victims of violence, by sex, age group and type of violence inflicted

	Total pop.[a]		Homicide		Assault/battery		Rape		Other(specify)	
	Women	Men	Women	Men	Women	Men	Women	Men	Women	Men
0–9										
10–14										
15–24										
25–49										
50–59										
60+										
All ages										

Source: Compiled from table yy in (cite publication in full).

a. Refers to the population in the sample survey or data source.

Note: This table will have to be compiled separately for each year covered by the analysis.

Table 9.3. Percentage distribution of convicted women and men by type of offence, 1970–1990

	1970		1980		1990	
Type of offence	Women	Men	Women	Men	Women	Men
Crimes against persons						
Homicide						
Aggravated assault						
Robbery						
Rape						
Crimes against property						
Burglary						
Larceny-theft						
Motor-vehicle theft						
Arson						
Crimes without victims						
Gambling						
Prostitution						
Vagrancy						
Illicit drug use						
White-collar crime						
Tax evasion						
Bribery/corruption						
Embezzlement						
Fraud						
Total	100	100	100	100	100	100

Source: Compiled from table yy in (cite publication in full).

Table 9.4. Percentage of women among persons convicted, by type of offence, 1970–1990

Type of offence	1970	1980	1990
Crimes against persons			
Homicide			
Aggravated assault			
Robbery			
Rape			
Crimes against property			
Burglary			
Larceny-theft			
Motor-vehicle theft			
Arson			
Crimes without victims			
Gambling			
Prostitution			
Vagrancy			
Illicit drug use			
White-collar crime			
Tax evasion			
Bribery/corruption			
Embezzlement			
Fraud			
Total			

Source: Compiled from table yy in (cite publication in full).

Table 9.5. Victims of violence as a percentage of the population by sex, age group and type of violence inflicted

Age group	Homicide		Assault/battery		Rape	
	Women	Men	Women	Men	Women	Men
0–9						
10–14						
15–24						
25–49						
50–59						
60+						
All ages						

Source: Compiled from table yy in (cite publication in full).
Note: This table will have to be constructed separately for each year covered by the analysis.

Additional indicators or classifications

These indicators may be presented for specific age groups, corresponding to, for example, juveniles, youth and adults.

Another set of indicators could be developed with a focus on victims (of crimes against persons) classified by age and sex of the victim.

Likely problems

Reliance on case histories or official records alone will lead to understatement of the problem, since only a proportion of the incidence of crime is reported and only a fraction of reported cases are tried in court. While survey data are particularly useful and potentially more complete, there may be under-reporting of the incidence of crime by perpetrators as well as by the victims who wish to avoid being stigmatized. When using such survey data, it is important to describe the sources and limitations of the data. It is desirable to provide specific information about response rates for each survey cited and to exclude from the analysis those surveys that either do not provide such information or do not attain some reasonable level of response. The special problem of classifications, concepts and definitions of the different types of crimes needs to be dealt with as well.

Statistics on victims of violence are often available in small-scale surveys or studies, and increasingly from small national samples. Most of these are given in the study reports in terms of percentages or rates (per 1,000), with an indication of the sample size. In such cases, the calculation step can be skipped and the reported percentage or rate adopted, after ascertaining the validity and quality of the data.

Interpretation

Data on the proportions apprehended and the prison population by sex reveal an overwhelming proportion of male offenders and prisoners. For example, in the Philippines crimes committed by women were 13 times lower than those committed by men in 1991, and in 1990 there were 43 men inmates per 100,000 male population compared with one woman inmate per 100,000 female population (Philippines, National Statistics Office, 1992). In Chile women comprised 7 per cent of all convicted persons in 1994 (Chile, National Statistics Institute, 1995).

Theft was the predominant crime for both women and men in Zambia over the period 1979–1988. Ninety-seven per cent of convictions among women were for theft, 3 per cent more than for male convictions. Drugs were a far second (2 per cent each for women and men) and fraud came last (Zambia, Central Statistics Office, 1991).

The most pervasive form of gender-based violence against women is reported to be abuse by a husband or intimate partner. National studies in 10 countries estimate that between 17 and 38 per cent of women have been physically assaulted by an intimate partner. More limited studies in Africa, Latin America and Asia report even higher rates of physical abuse among the population studied—up to 60 per cent or more of women (United Nations, 1995).

Sexual assault is also common, but only a small fraction of rapes are reported to the police, making police-based crime statistics of limited use for evaluating the magnitude of the problem. In the United States more than 100,000 attempted and completed rapes of women and girls were reported to the police in 1990. But a national survey found the rate was more than six times greater, even when considering only adult women and completed rapes. In the Republic of Korea fewer than 2 per cent of women rape victims ever contacted the police (United Nations, 1995).

Some of the questions to consider are:

- How do women compare with men in convictions of crimes?
- Which crimes do convicted women tend to be responsible for? And which crimes do men tend to be convicted for?
- How are patterns of conviction of women and men changing?
- Are there shifts from one category of crime to another for women, men or both?
- Reviewing the indicators on victims of violence, which kinds of violence are women and girls subjected to the most? Are these different with respect to age groups?

References and further reading

Chile, National Statistics Institute (1995). *Women and Men in Chile: Figures and Reality 1995.* Santiago.

FLACSO (1995). *Latin American Women: Compared Figures.* Santiago: Instituto de la Mujer.

Heise, Lori, Kristen Moore and Nahid Toubia (1995). *Sexual Coercion and Reproductive Health: A Focus on Research.* New York: The Population Council.

Heise, Lori (1993). Violence against women: the hidden health burden. *World Health Statistics Quarterly,* vol. 46, No. 1. Geneva: World Health Organization.

International Centre for Public Enterprises in Developing Countries (1986). *The Role of Women in Developing Countries: A Study.* Ljubljana.

Inter-Parliamentary Union (1995). *Women in Parliaments 1945–1995: A World Statistical Survey.* Geneva.

Netherlands, Ministries of Social Affairs and Employment and Home Affairs (1993). *Facts about Women in Politics and Public Administration in the Netherlands.* Randstad, Aalsmeer.

Nordic Council of Ministers (1994). *Women and Men in the Nordic Countries: Facts and Figures 1994.* Copenhagen.

Philippines, National Statistics Office (1992). *Statistics on Filipino Women.* Manila.

United Nations (1989). *Violence Against Women in the Family.* Sales No. E.89.IV.5.

_____ (1991). *The World's Women 1970–1990: Trends and Statistics.* Sales No. E.90.XVII.3.

_____ (1992). *Women in Politics and Decision-Making in the Late Twentieth Century: A United Nations Study.* Dordrecht, The Netherlands: Martinus Nijhoff Publishers. United Nations publication, Sales No. E.91.IV.3.

_____ (1995). *The World's Women 1995: Trends and Statistics.* Sales No. E.95.XVII.2.

Zambia, Central Statistics Office (1991). *Women and Men in Zambia.* Lusaka.

EDUCATION AND TRAINING

Literacy

SERIES A: Illiteracy rates for specific age groups

Formula: $$\dfrac{\text{Illiterate women (men) in age group } (x, x + n)}{\text{Total women (men) in age group } (x, x + n)} \times 100$$

SERIES B: Percentage of illiterate population in specific age groups who are women/men

Formula: $$\dfrac{\text{Illiterate women (men) in age group } (x, x + n)}{\text{Total illiterates in age group } (x, x + n)} \times 100$$

Age groups $(x, x + n)$ are defined for groups of constant or variable intervals such as 15–19, 20–24, 25–34, 35–44, 45–59, 60+.

Policy relevance

Literacy is a vital skill by which individuals can expect to fulfil the social, economic and political demands of life and to cope with basic routines of mainstream contemporary society. It is a critical factor in improving conditions of life as it ensures access to knowledge. Special priority is placed on advancing women's literacy and education as these have clear effects on fertility and on the health and economic welfare of women and their children.

Data sources

The main source of data is the population census. Other sources are household surveys, which ask questions about educational characteristics, and ad hoc surveys dealing with educational topics, usually carried out by university or other independent survey organizations, or in some cases by local governments.

Source table

Table 10.1 Percentage of the population aged 15 and older by literacy status, sex and age group, for total, urban and rural areas, 1970–1990

Age group	1970		1980		1990	
	Women	Men	Women	Men	Women	Men
Total (urban and rural)						
Population						
15–19						
20–24						
25–44						
45–60						
60+						
Total 15+						
Literate						
15–19						
20–24						
25–44						
45–60						
60+						
Total 15+						
Illiterate						
15–19						
20–24						
25–44						
45–60						
60+						
Total 15+						
Urban						
Same categories as above						
Rural						
Same categories as above						

Technical note: Any comments relating to the data should be included, such as changes in concepts, definitions and classifications from one census or survey to the next.
Source: Give full citations for publications and any other sources used.

Working tables

Table 10.2. Illiteracy rates by sex and broad age group, for total, urban and rural areas, 1970–1990

Age group	1970		1980		1990	
	Women	Men	Women	Men	Women	Men
Total (urban and rural)						
15–24						
25–44						
45–60						
60+						
Total 15+						
Urban						
Same age groups as above						
Rural						
Same age groups as above						

Source: Calculated from table yy in (cite publication in full).

Table 10.3. Sex composition of the illiterate population by age group, for total, urban and rural areas, 1970–1990 *(percentage)*

Age group	1970		1980		1990	
	Women	Men	Women	Men	Women	Men
Total (urban and rural)						
15–24						
25–44						
45–60						
60+						
Total 15+						
Urban						
Same age groups as above						
Rural						
Same age groups as above						

Source: Calculated from table yy in (cite publication in full).

Additional indicators or classifications

Detailed breakdown by age groups (five-year age groups) can be used, in which case it is more useful to present illiteracy rates in a chart. The rates can alternatively be compiled for broad age groups such as youth, reproductive ages, elderly population or for ages 15+, 25+, 45+. If broad age groups are used, it is useful to compare these rates with illiteracy rates in other neighbouring countries, especially when time-series data are not available. Comparisons may also be made between rural and urban.

Likely problems

The data from population censuses and household surveys will largely be derived from information on literacy, which is usually either self-reported or reported by the head of household. Because of the reluctance of some persons to admit illiteracy and the difficulties of applying a test of literacy during a census investigation, the data may be inaccurate. When grade completion is used as a proxy criterion of literacy, it should be noted that the validity of the responses depends on uniformity in the nature and quality of different schools. This approach also ignores the fact that some learning is done through informal means.

Interpretation

Despite marked progress in literacy, a high proportion of women in some developing countries remain illiterate, especially in rural areas. High illiteracy among women is a reflection not only of the considerable historical deficit in women's education but also of their limited access to today's education and literacy programmes.

In most of Latin America and the Caribbean, and eastern and south-eastern Asia, less than 25 per cent of women aged 15 and over are illiterate. However, illiteracy rates remain high in much of northern and sub-Saharan Africa and south Asia as well as a few countries in other developing regions (United Nations, 1995a).

There are large differences in rates between women and men in countries where illiteracy rates are high. Illiteracy rates for women over 45 years of age in the late 1980s were usually at least 50 per cent in developing regions and often exceeded 70 per cent in Africa and Asia (United Nations, 1995a).

Illiteracy rates are particularly high for rural women. The illiteracy rate for rural women aged 15–24 is often two to three times that for urban women (United Nations, 1995a).

Some ways of analysing the data are:

• Compare female and male rates with a standard. The standard could be the levels in neighbouring countries, except that when the situation in other countries is as unfavourable or less favourable, it gives a more positive picture than the actual situation. Therefore the gap between the rates for women and men gives a better idea of the discrepancy. Consider the direction of the difference (whether positive or negative) and the magnitude of difference.

- Compare the gaps for rural and urban areas. Do these change in favour of women or of men over time?

- Examine the difference between female and male illiteracy rates and changes in these differences over time. The trend in literacy can be indirectly deduced from comparisons in the rates and in the proportion of women of the different age groups among the literate population. The proportions can be compared with the sex composition of the given population subgroup (age group) or with an expected value, such as a range. For example, if 10 per cent is deemed an acceptable gap between women and men, the comparison should be made on the basis of how close the proportions are to 45 or 55 per cent for either sex.

- Examine the percentage of illiterate population in each age group who are women and men and the changes across age groups. If the proportion of women in the illiterate population decreases for younger age groups, it shows a favourable trend in literacy of women, while a decrease for younger men only shows that there is an unfavourable trend in female literacy.

- How many times higher is the illiteracy rate for rural and urban women aged 60+ compared to those aged 15–24? How is this different for men?

Educational attainment

SERIES A: Percentage distribution of the population by level of schooling completed in selected age groups

Formula
$$\frac{\text{Women (men) aged } x, x + n \text{ who have completed level } i}{\text{Women (men) aged } x, x + n} \times 100$$

SERIES B: Sex-composition within levels of schooling completed by selected age groups

Formula
$$\frac{\text{Women (men) aged } x, x + n \text{ who have completed level } i}{\text{Population aged } x, x + n \text{ who have completed level } i} \times 100$$

Where levels of schooling are defined as: no schooling, incomplete first level/primary, completed first-level primary, second-level /primary, second-level first cycle (junior high school), second-level second cycle (senior high school), and higher education.

Policy relevance

The educational attainment levels of the population give an overview of the distribution of skills and the extent of preparedness for the labour force. Education opens up specific opportunities and changes values. Benefits also accrue to non-market work, which has significant and positive economic value for families and the economy as a whole. An indication of the competitiveness of women as compared with men for access to specialized training and jobs is seen in differences in their levels of educational attainment.

Data sources

Population censuses provide statistics on educational attainment for all of the population and reflect both past and present school attendance. Sample surveys based on households also ask questions about the educational status of those covered, and because they are more frequent than censuses, provide more up-to-date data on educational characteristics.

Source table

Table 11.1. Percentage of the population aged 15 and older by sex, age group and level of schooling completed, for total, urban and rural areas

Age group	No Schooling		First level incomplete		First level completed		Second level, first cycle[a]		Second level, second cycle[b]		Third level		Total	
	W	M	W	M	W	M	W	M	W	M	W	M	W	M
Total (urban and rural)														
15–19														
20–24														
.														
.														
55–59														
60+														
Total 15+														
Urban														
Same age groups as above														
Rural														
Same age groups as above														

Technical note: The levels of education are classified in accordance with the International Standard Classification of Education (ISCED).

Source: Give full citations for publications and any other sources used.

a. Corresponds to junior secondary or high school.

b. Corresponds to senior secondary or high school.

Note: This table will have to be compiled separately for each year covered by the analysis.

Working table

Table 11.2. Percentage distribution of the population aged 20 and older by sex, age group and level of schooling completed, for total, urban and rural areas

Age group	No Schooling		First level incomplete		First level completed		Second level, first cycle[a]		Second level, second cycle[b]		Third level		Total	
	W	M	W	M	W	M	W	M	W	M	W	M	W	M
Total (urban and rural)														
20–24													100	100
.													.	.
.														
.													.	.
55–59													100	100
60+													100	100
Total 20+													100	100
Urban														
Same age groups as above														
Rural														
Same age groups as above														

Technical note: The levels of education are classified in accordance with the International Standard Classification of Education (ISCED).

Source: Calculated from table yy in (cite publication or administrative source in full).

a. Corresponds to junior secondary or high school.

b. Corresponds to senior secondary or high school.

Note: This table will have to be constructed separately for each year covered by the analysis.

Additional indicators or classifications

The age groups can also be constructed to correspond with the ages at which a majority of the population are expected to have completed a certain level of schooling (e.g., 15–24 for primary and secondary; 25–34 for post-secondary; and 35+). The average years of schooling completed for selected age groups also indicates the extent of schooling of the population. This can be computed for the regions and provinces and for rural and urban residence. When this indicator is used it should be noted that years may be overstated because of repetitions. It might also be of interest to examine the percentage distribution of women and men who have completed specific grades in primary or secondary (high school), especially for those who have not completed either primary or secondary.

Likely problems

Computations of the percentage of persons who achieve a particular level of education must be limited to those above the age when that level would normally be completed. This depends on the school-going age, the number of years required for preceding levels and the prevalence of repetitions in the school system.

Educational attainment varies between rural and urban areas, and therefore these indicators should be presented also for these areas if data are available.

When average years of schooling is used, it is important to ascertain that repetitions are not reflected as additional years of schooling; rather the grade completed should be converted into years taking into account the type of educational system that is applicable.

Interpretation

A statistical analysis of women and men in eastern and southern Africa indicates that, in general, the number of women decreases at higher levels of education (Kenya, Central Bureau of Statistics, 1995). In Asia and the Pacific, the percentage of women 20 years and over who had completed secondary school varied from 15 to 25 per cent in China, Hong Kong, the Philippines and the Republic of Korea, but was much lower in the other developing countries in the region. The proportions of men were universally higher (Asian Development Bank, Center for International Research, 1993). The difference between the proportions of women and men aged 25 to 44 who have completed lower secondary (compulsory level) varies from 2 to 21 percentage points; and for those aged 45 to 64, from 1 to 27 percentage points (but 45 percentage points for Iceland) (United Nations, Economic Commission for Europe, 1995).

Disparities in the educational attainment of women and men are manifested in different ways. For the total population as well as for each age group, the following questions need to be addressed:

- At what levels of schooling do we find at least a third, half or three quarters of women and men of specified age groups?

- What is the general pattern of variation in the percentages for women and for men? Do the percentages increase or decrease at higher levels of schooling?

- How do the percentages of women at each level of schooling compare with those of men? Does the gap converge or diverge with increasing levels of schooling?

- Comparing across age groups for specific levels of schooling, are the percentages of women and men higher or lower for younger age groups relative to older age groups? Higher proportions imply more favourable trends for educational attainment while lower proportions show the opposite. Trends are, however, more directly discerned from comparing indicators over different periods, if these are available.

School enrolment and retention

SERIES A: Gross enrolment ratio at primary and secondary levels

Formula
$$\frac{\text{Number enrolled in primary school}}{\text{Population aged } (x, x + n)} \times 100$$

$$\frac{\text{Number enrolled in secondary school}}{\text{Population aged } (y, y + n)} \times 100$$

SERIES B: Ratio of female to male enrolment at various grades in primary and secondary levels

Formula
$$\frac{\text{Girls enrolled in school at level } i}{\text{Boys enrolled in schools at level } i} \times 100$$

SERIES C: Sex-composition of the primary and secondary school drop-outs

Formula
$$\frac{\text{Girls (boys) dropping out of level } i}{\text{Number dropping out of level } i} \times 100$$

The age groups $(x, x + n)$ and $(y, y + n)$ are defined according to national regulations, corresponding to the ages of those who should be enrolled at primary and secondary levels respectively.

Policy relevance

Enrolment data offer an easy way to compare numbers of girls and boys registered in schools each year. The enrolment ratios of girls and boys indicate the accuracy of educational resources to achieve the goal of universal education for both girls and boys. High levels of drop-outs are a serious obstacle to the attainment of national goals such as universal primary education, eradication of illiteracy and equality of educational opportunities.

Data sources

Data on school enrolment, completion and drop-outs are derived mainly from the administrative records of educational institutions. In general, these records are maintained by sex. Census data and special surveys on school enrolment and retention may also be available. These are particularly useful as they provide the data for both the numerator and the denominator of enrolment ratios. They may also provide information on why pupils have dropped out of the school system. When administrative records and census or survey data are presented in the same table or compared, the differences in the concepts should be carefully noted.

Source table

Table 12.1. School enrolment, drop-outs and population by sex and level of education, 1970–1990

Level of education	Enrolment		Drop-outs		Population[a]	
	Girls	Boys	Girls	Boys	Girls	Boys
1970						
First level						
Second level						
First cycle[b]						
Second cycle[c]						
1980						
Same levels as above						
1990						
Same levels as above						

Technical note: The levels of education are classified in accordance with the International Standard Classification of Education (ISCED).

Source: Give full citations for administrative records and any other sources used.

a. Population corresponding to ages of those who should be enrolled at the specified level, according to national regulations.

b. Corresponds to junior secondary or high school.

c. Corresponds to senior secondary or high school.

Working tables

Table 12.2. Gross enrolment ratio at primary and secondary levels of education by sex, 1970–1990

Level of education	1970			1980			1990	
	Girls	Boys		Girls	Boys		Girls	Boys
First level								
Second level								
First cycle[a]								
Second cycle[b]								

Technical note: The levels of education are classified in accordance with the International Standard Classification of Education (ISCED).

Source: Compiled from table yy in (cite publication or administrative source in full).

a. Corresponds to junior secondary or high school.

b. Corresponds to senior secondary or high school.

Table 12.3. Girls enrolled per 100 boys and percentage of girls among drop-outs by level of education, 1970–1990

Level of education	Girls enrolled per 100 boys				Percentage of girls among drop-outs		
	1970	1980	1990		1970	1980	1990
First level							
Second level							
First cycle[a]							
Second cycle[b]							

Technical note: The levels of education are classified in accordance with the International Standard Classification of Education (ISCED).

Source: Compiled from table yy in (cite publication or administrative source in full).

a. Corresponds to junior secondary or high school.

b. Corresponds to senior secondary or high school.

Additional indicators or classifications

Indicators of enrolment can also be expressed as a combined primary-secondary ratio defined as the ratio of girl (boy) enrollees at both levels to the relevant age group.

Two other indicators that can be presented are (i) the proportions of girls and boys enrolled at the different levels of schooling and (ii) the sex composition at each level of schooling expressed respectively as:

$$\frac{\text{Girls (boys) enrolled in school at level } i}{\text{Girls (boys) enrolled in primary and secondary}} \times 100$$

$$\frac{\text{Girls (boys) enrolled in school at grade } i \text{ level } j}{\text{Total enrolled in grade } i \text{ level } j} \times 100$$

Vocational education is an important part of secondary education through which practical skills, attitudes, understanding and knowledge relating to occupations in various sectors of economic and social life are acquired. Secondary education may be classified into (a) general; (b) teacher training; (c) vocational.

Important indicators to compute are (a) percentages of secondary education by type for women and men; (b) percentage distribution of women and men in vocational training by field of study; (c) sex composition within each category of secondary education and field of vocational study.

Likely problems

Since some of the pupils or students may be outside the expected age range for their respective levels, it would not be unusual for the ratios to exceed 100.

Over-reporting of school enrolment, mostly at the first grade of the primary level, is a potential problem when administrative records are used. Registers may include names of children who, though enrolled, do not attend school. It is important to ascertain how these figures have been compiled. Furthermore, the statistics may not cover all schools, since some schools may not provide the requisite information at all or on time. Variations in coverage from one year to the next will lead to distortions in the enrolment trends.

Interpretation

Girls' enrolments at the first and second levels have caught up with those of boys in most of the developed regions and in Latin America and the Caribbean. But in southern Asia and in sub-Saharan Africa, enrolment of girls lags far behind that of boys (United Nations, 1991).

By 1980, most countries had in place a vigorous policy to promote education. This resulted in substantial increases in the enrolment at primary level, but for most developing countries universal primary education has still not been attained and wide variations in girls' and boys' enrolment persists. Sex differences in enrolment ratios are greater at the secondary school level than at primary level. Girls' enrolment lags farther behind boys' in sub-Saharan Africa (68 girls to 100 boys) and is lowest in south Asia (60 girls to 100 boys) (United Nations, 1995a). The ratio of girls to 100 boys enrolled in primary school in the 1980s was as high as 125 in Lesotho and as low as 22 in Yemen. At the secondary level the ratios ranged from 18 girls per 100 boys in Chad to 208 girls per 100 boys in Nicaragua (United Nations, 1991).

Bearing in mind that enrolment and enrolment rates are often overstated and may include drop-outs and repeaters, the level of enrolment ratios should be as high as 100 or above. Comparisons can be made in the following:

• The ratios for girls and for boys, compared with the expected ratio of at least 100, which represents universal education at the primary level.

• The gap between girls and boys in enrolment ratios.

• Differences between the female to male enrolment at each level (primary and secondary).

• The gap between girls' and boys' enrolment ratios at primary and secondary levels and changes over time.

• The proportion of girls and of boys among drop-outs in primary and secondary levels, and from primary to secondary.

• If possible, differences in the distributions of girls and boys should be explained by reason for dropping out.

Specialization at the third level

Series A: **Percentage of enrolment in tertiary education in specific fields of study**

Formula

$$\frac{\text{Women (men) enrolled in field of study } i}{\text{Women (men) enrolled in tertiary education}} \times 100$$

Series B: **Female and male shares in field of tertiary education**

Formula

$$\frac{\text{Female students in field of study } i}{\text{Students in field of study } i} \times 100$$

Policy relevance

Higher education is vital for communicating with the scientific and intellectual community of the world and defines the extent to which women have equal opportunity with men with respect to educational programmes, options and standards. It also enhances employment opportunities within fields generally dominated by men.

Women will continue to be excluded from employment in technical and scientific areas if tradition, stereotypes or family constraints prevent them from having greater access to these areas.

Data sources

The preferred source of information on both enrolment and fields of study is administrative records. These data may or may not be available in published form. Data can also be obtained from population censuses and household surveys, which provide information on school attendance and attainment. Unless there was a special form given to education in these sources, the fields of specialization may not be available.

Source table

Table 13.1. Students in third level education by sex and field of study, 1970–1990

Field of study	1970		1980		1990	
	Women	Men	Women	Men	Women	Men
Education science						
Humanities and religion						
Fine and applied arts						
Law						
Social and behavioural sciences						
Commercial and business admin.						
Mass comm. and documentation						
Home economics						
Service trades						
Natural science						
Mathematics and computer science						
Medical and health-related						
Engineering						
Architecture and town planning						
Trade, craft & industrial programmes						
Transport and communications						
Agriculture						
Other and not specified						
Total						

Technical note: The fields of study are classified in accordance with the International Standard Classification of Education (ISCED).

Source: Give full citations for publications used. If administrative records are used, indicate the kind, year and whether or not the data are published.

Working tables

Table 13.2. Percentage distribution of students in third level education by sex and field of study, 1970–1990

Field of study	1970		1980		1990	
	Women	Men	Women	Men	Women	Men
Education science						
Humanities and religion						
Fine and applied arts						
Law						
Social and behavioural sciences						
Commercial and business admin.						
Mass comm. and documentation						
Home economics						
Service trades						
Natural science						
Mathematics and computer science						
Medical and health-related						
Engineering						
Architecture and town planning						
Trade, craft & industrial programmes						
Transport and communications						
Agriculture						
Other and not specified						
Total	100	100	100	100	100	100

Technical note: The fields of study are classified in accordance with ISCED. They may be aggregated to combine science and engineering; law and business; and liberal arts, social sciences and education.
Source: Table yy in (cite publication in full).

Table 13.3. Percentage of females among third level students by field of study, 1970–1990

Field of study	1970	1980	1990
Education science			
Humanities and religion			
Fine and applied arts			
Law			
Social and behavioural sciences			
Commercial and business admin.			
Mass comm. and documentation			
Home economics			
Service trades			
Natural science			
Mathematics and computer science			
Medical and health-related			
Engineering			
Architecture and town planning			
Trade, craft & industrial programmes			
Transport and communications			
Agriculture			
Other and not specified			
Total			

Technical note: The fields of study are classified in accordance with ISCED. They may be aggregated to combine science and engineering; law and business; and liberal arts, social sciences and education.

Source: Table yy in (cite publication in full).

Additional indicators or classifications

There are three further classifications within the third level that can be used: (i) education that ends in awards not equivalent to a first university degree; (ii) education that leads to a first university degree or equivalent; (iii) education that leads to a postgraduate degree or equivalent.

The sex-composition indicator may be presented as sex ratios within each field and all fields combined. In addition, these other indicators may be presented:

- The tertiary enrolment ratios defined as the percentage of women and men aged 18+ enrolled in tertiary education is obtained by taking the entry under the column for women (men).

- The percentage distribution of women and men graduates by field of study, in the given years. Where available, the percentages of women and men in the population who have completed tertiary education by field. This gives an idea of the type of skilled workforce available.

Likely problems

Data on enrolment at third level may have to be compiled from the different institutions if they are not compiled by the administrative body responsible for education.

The classification of fields may differ from one college to another, or from one degree to another. When census or survey data are used, the fields are likely to be misreported.

Interpretation

While most women's enrolments at the tertiary level are increasing, considerable disparities remain. In sub-Saharan Africa and in southern Asia in 1990, only 30 and 38 women, respectively, were enrolled in higher education per 100 men compared with 63 in northern Africa and 71 in eastern Asia. In Latin America and the Caribbean and in western Asia, however, women outnumber men in higher education (United Nations, 1995a).

In the developed regions and in Latin America and the Caribbean, more women have entered male-dominated fields of study (engineering, law, business, science) in the last two decades. In Africa, however, fewer women than men enrol in all fields, even in the so-called female-dominated fields such as liberal arts, social sciences and education. Although women can make a substantial contribution if they are trained in agriculture, forestry or fishing, the ratio was still 1 to 5 in 1984 in Africa and in Asia and the Pacific. In law and business, of those enrolled, women comprised only 26 per cent in Africa and 38 per cent in Asia and the Pacific.

Women have made significant gains in science and engineering, representing at least 30 per cent of all persons training in these fields in all regions except Africa (United Nations, 1991).

- How does the proportion of women among all third-level students compare with the proportion of women in each field of study?

- In which fields are women predominantly enrolled?

- How do these differences in distribution compare with the apparent job segregation?

- Which fields have more than one quarter, a third or half of the women or men students? Which fields have less than a tenth of the women or men students?

- Are the fields with the highest percentage of women/men those that have a small or big intake of students?

Teachers by school level

Series A: **Percentage distribution of teachers by level**

Formula
$$\frac{\text{Women (men) teachers at level } i}{\text{Women (men) teachers at all levels}} \times 100$$

Series B: **Sex composition of teachers by level**

Formula
$$\frac{\text{Women (men) teachers at level } i}{\text{All teachers at level } i} \times 100$$

Policy relevance

Teaching, at least at primary-school level, has traditionally been open to women and thus an important source of their employment in most countries. To have the number and quality of teachers needed to advance educational levels (especially with a rapidly growing child population), it is essential that women have equal access to teaching positions at all levels within the educational system. Moreover, women teachers serve as influential role models for young girls, particularly in those societies where girls' education is discouraged or unsupported or where the teaching of girls by men is not permitted.

Data sources

Although information on teachers may be obtained from population censuses, more detailed information is certain to be found in administrative records of educational institutions. Such information is often compiled on a regular basis by the ministry of education and may be available in published form. Wherever possible, administrative sources should be used and supplemented with census or survey information.

Source table

Table 14.1. Number of teachers by sex and educational level taught, for total, urban and rural areas, 1970–1990

Educational level	1970			1980			1990		
	Women	Men	Total	Women	Men	Total	Women	Men	Total
Total (urban and rural)									
Pre-school									
Primary level									
Secondary level									
Tertiary level									
All levels									
Urban									
Same categories as above									
Rural									
Same categories as above									

Technical note: Note concepts, definitions and classifications used in the collection of the data.

Source: Give full citations for publications used. If administrative records are used, indicate the kind, year and whether the data are published.

Working tables

Table 14.2. Percentage distribution of teachers by sex and educational level taught, for total, urban and rural areas, 1970–1990

Educational level	1970		1980		1990	
	Women	Men	Women	Men	Women	Men
Total (urban and rural)						
Pre-school						
Primary level						
Secondary level						
Tertiary level						
All levels	100	100	100	100	100	100
Urban						
Same categories as above						
Rural						
Same categories as above						

Technical note: Note concepts, definitions and classifications used in the collection of the data.
Source: Give full citations for publications used. If administrative records are used, indicate the kind, year and whether the data are published.

Table 14.3. Percentage of women among teachers by educational level taught, for total, urban and rural areas, 1970–1990

Educational level	1970	1980	1990
Total (urban and rural)			
Pre-school			
Primary level			
Secondary level			
Tertiary level			
All levels			
Urban			
Same categories as above			
Rural			
Same categories as above			

Technical note: Note concepts, definitions and classifications used in the collection of the data.
Source: Give full citations for publications used. If administrative records are used, indicate the kind, year and whether the data are published.

Additional indicators or classifications

The breakdown of levels can also include types of schools, especially at secondary and tertiary levels. Analysis can be made by comparing not only rural and urban but also indicators for major cities. The qualifications of teachers are also very important if pupils are to derive maximum benefit from their educational experience. In addition to the above indicators, the percentage distribution of teachers at each level by type of training and qualification could also be compiled.

Likely problems

Census and survey data may not be detailed enough to show the levels of teaching. When administrative sources are used, statistics related to the educational system are often available only for the formal system, specifically the public sector. Informal, private and other non-governmental educational activities are not generally covered, due to the difficulty of collecting the necessary information.

Administrative records of educational institutions, both public and private, and any ad hoc educational surveys, should be consulted for the information needed.

Interpretation

In most of the developed world and in Latin America and the Caribbean, female primary school teachers outnumber their male counterparts. Even in those countries where employment opportunities for women are scarce, the number of women engaged in first-level teaching is significant. In Latin America, nearly all the preschool teachers are women and at primary level more than two thirds of the teachers are women (FLACSO, 1995).

The proportion of women teachers declines at higher levels of education. More men than women are secondary-school teachers everywhere except in the developed regions, Latin America and the Caribbean and south-eastern Asia, where the numbers are equal. In sub-Saharan Africa, only 1 out of 4 secondary school teachers is a woman (United Nations, 1995a).

• Examine the percentage distributions by level of education for women and men to determine at which levels women are concentrated. Does women's participation as teachers decline in relation to men's at higher levels? Comparisons of the sex composition also show the levels at which women dominate and those at which men dominate.

• Compare the distributions for either sex over time to determine the trends. Are proportions of women increasing/decreasing or unchanged over time?

Scientific, technical and professional training and personnel

Series A:	**Percentage of women and men in specific fields of training and employment within science and technology**
Formula	$$\frac{\text{Women (men) trained in specified field } i}{\text{Total women (men) trained in all fields}} \times 100$$
	$$\frac{\text{Women (men) working in specified field } i}{\text{Total women (men) working in all fields}} \times 100$$
Series B:	**Shares of women and men in fields of training and employed in science and technology**
Formula	$$\frac{\text{Women (men) trained in specified field } i}{\text{Total women and men trained in the field } i} \times 100$$
	$$\frac{\text{Women (men) employed in specified field } i}{\text{Total women and men employed in field } i} \times 100$$

The fields in science include scientists, agronomists, technicians and technologists.

Policy relevance

Women and men can make substantial contributions to development if they gain advanced education and training, but access to higher education and specialized training is still greatly limited to men, particularly in the scientific and technological areas. Within scientific and technical fields, women are better represented in positions at the bottom levels of the status and wage hierarchy than they are in positions at higher levels.

Data sources

Data on training and personnel in the science and technology fields are generally obtained from population censuses and surveys of households, by examining the educational characteristics and detailed classification of occupations.

Source table

Table 15.1. Graduates and professionals in science and technology, by sex and field of specialization

| Field of specialization | Graduates of tertiary programmes | | | | | | | | Professionals in science/technology | | | | | |
| | Level 5 | | Level 6 | | Level 7 | | Total | | Tertiary inst. | | Research/ dev. | | Other | |
	W	M	W	M	W	M	W	M	W	M	W	M	W	M
Scientists														
Medicine/health sciences														
Natural sciences														
Mathematics and computer sciences														
Engineering														
Agriculture/agronomy														
Technicians														
Technologists														
Total														

Technical note: Note concepts, definitions and classifications used in the data source.
Source: Give full citations for publications and any other sources used.
Note: This table will have to be compiled separately for each year covered by the analysis.

Working tables

Table 15.2. Percentage distribution of graduates and professionals in science and technology by sex and field of specialization

Field of specialization	Graduates of tertiary programmes								Professionals in science/technology					
	Level 5		Level 6		Level 7		Total		Tertiary inst.		Research/ dev.		Other	
	W	M	W	M	W	M	W	M	W	M	W	M	W	M
Scientists														
Medicine/health sciences														
Natural sciences														
Mathematics and computer sciences														
Engineering														
Agriculture/agronomy														
Technicians														
Technologists														
Total	100	100	100	100	100	100	100	100	100	100	100	100	100	100

Technical note: Note concepts, definitions and classifications used in the data source.
Source: Give full citations for publications and any other sources used.
Note: This table will have to be constructed separately for each year covered by the analysis.

Table 15.3. Percentage of women among graduates and professionals in science and technology by field of specialization

Field of specialization	Graduates of tertiary programmes				Professionals in science/technology		
	Level 5	Level 6	Level 7	Total	Tertiary inst.	Research/ dev.	Other
Scientists							
Medicine/health sciences							
Natural sciences							
Mathematics and computer sciences							
Engineering							
Agriculture/agronomy							
Technicians							
Technologists							
Total							

Technical note: Note concepts, definitions and classifications used in the data source.
Source: Give full citations for publications and any other sources used.
Note: This table will have to be constructed separately for each year covered by the analysis.

Additional indicators or classifications

More detailed breakdowns may be presented for the natural sciences (e.g., physics, chemistry, biology, geology). To determine the extent to which training matches with employment, the proportion of trained scientists and technicians working in their respective fields can also be compiled. Special tabulations from census and survey data may need to be prepared for this purpose. If possible, subcategories corresponding with ranks in the different professional disciplines should also be presented.

Likely problems

Data on this topic are not readily available in many countries except to those working in universities. However, where the population census collects such data, the information may be in the form of educational qualifications (degrees, diplomas, certificates and the like) and may not indicate whether the individual is currently engaged in such work. Specialists from the education department should be consulted on this matter. Tabulations on detailed occupations should also be used.

Interpretation

Although significant gains have been made by women in science and engineering, their number and proportion still lag behind those of men. Among engineering graduates, even 20 per cent representation of women is found in only very few countries. Further disaggregation shows that with some exceptions, women are in general represented among scientists and engineers at about half the rate they are among technicians (United Nations, 1995a).

- Examine the representation of women in specific science and technology disciplines compared with men.

- Compare levels of representation with the overall representation of graduates of tertiary-level programmes.

- Within each category, assess whether the distributions according to training are the same, slightly or significantly different from the distributions among those employed. Are the differentials to the same degree for women as for men? Or are women (men) more or less likely to remain in their fields of training?

References and further reading

Asian Development Bank, Center for International Research (1993). *Gender Indicators of Developing Asian and Pacific Countries.* Manila.

FLACSO (1995). *Latin American Women: Compared Figures.* Santiago: Instituto de la Mujer.

Kenya, Central Bureau of Statistics (1995). *Women and Men in East, Central and Southern Africa: Facts and Figures 1995.* Nairobi.

United Nations (1989). *Measuring Literacy through Household Surveys: A Technical Study of Literacy Assessment and Related Educational Topics through Household Surveys.* National Household Survey Capability Programme. DP/UN/INT-88-X01/10.

_____ (1991). *The World's Women 1970–1990: Trends and Statistics.* Sales No. E.90.XVII.3.

_____ (1995a). *The World's Women 1995: Trends and Statistics.* Sales No. E.95.XVII.2.

_____ (1995b). *Women in a Changing Global Economy: 1994 World Survey on the Role of Women in Development.* Sales No. E.95.IV.1.

_____ Economic Commission for Europe (1995). *Women and Men in Europe and North America, 1995.* Sales No. GV.E.95.0.12.

United Nations Educational, Scientific and Cultural Organization (1980a). *Comparative Analysis of Male and Female Enrolment and Illiteracy.* Current Studies and Research in Statistics, CSR-E-36. Paris.

_____ (1980b). *Wastage in Primary and General Secondary Education: A Statistical Study of Trends and Patterns in Repetition and Drop-out.* Current Studies and Research in Statistics, CSR-E-37. Paris.

_____ (1983a). *Technical and Vocational Education in the World 1970-1980.* Current Studies and Research in Statistics, CSR-E-47. Paris.

_____ (1983b). *Trends and Projections of Enrolment by Level of Education and by Age, 1960-2000 (as assessed in 1982).* Current Studies and Research in Statistics, CSR-E-46. Paris.

_____ (1992). *Literacy Assessment and Implications for Statistical Measurement.* Current Studies and Research in Statistics, CSR-E-62. Paris.

_____ (1993). *World Education Report.* Paris.

HEALTH AND CHILD-BEARING

Life expectancy

SERIES A	**Life expectancy at birth and at selected ages (women and men)**
Formula	See life tables published by responsible authority in the country.

Policy relevance

Life expectancy is the most comprehensive measure of health, which is an important component of well-being. Women generally live longer than men, but in a few countries men live longer and in some others the difference is small. Trends in the life expectancy of women and men, the gap between their life expectancies and its changes provide basic indicators of health and living conditions and the relative status of women and men.

Data sources

Life expectancy figures are one of the main outputs of a life table. They are based on age-specific mortality rates, usually disaggregated by sex. Life table parameters are available in most countries and from international organizations such as the United Nations that compile these statistics. When mortality rates are not available, indirect estimates can be made from child survival reports from population censuses and demographic surveys. At the international level, life expectancy estimates are compiled in the United Nations Demographic Yearbook and Women's Indicators and Statistics Database (Wistat).

Source table

Table 16.1. Abridged life table for each sex

Age[a] (x)	Central death rate for the age interval (x, x + n) ($_nm_x$)	Probability of dying[b] ($_nq_x$)	Of 100,000 born alive — Number living at age x (l_x)	Of 100,000 born alive — Number dying during age (x, x + n) ($_nd_x$)	Number of person-years lived — In age interval (x, x + n) ($_nL_x$)	Number of person-years lived — At ages x and older (T_x)	Expectation of life at age x (e_x)
Female							
0							
1							
5							
10							
.							
.							
80							
85							
Male							
Same ages as above							

Source: Give full citations for publications used.

a. The initial age of the age interval (x,x+n), where x is the initial age and n is the length of the interval. The interval n equals 5 years with the exception of the first interval (1 year), second interval (4 years) and last interval (open-ended).

b. Probability of an individual of age x dying before the end of the age interval (x,x+n).

Note: This table will have to be compiled separately for each year covered by the analysis.

Working table

Table 16.2. Life expectancy at birth and at selected ages for each sex, selected years

Age	Year 1 Women	Year 1 Men	Year 2 Women	Year 2 Men	Year 3 Women	Year 3 Men	Year 4 Women	Year 4 Men
0								
5								
15								
25								
50								
60								

Source: Give full citations for publications used or national authority from which statistics were compiled; if not available from national published sources, estimates can be obtained from the United Nations *Demographic Yearbook* or the Women's Indicators and Statistics Database (Wistat).

Additional indicators or classifications

The life expectancy of women in relation to men may be expressed in the form of a ratio (female life expectancy as a ratio of male life expectancy) or a gender-gap (the difference in years between women's life expectancy and men's). For a better indication of the trend, it is useful to present in a chart the life expectancies at birth (or at other ages) at more than three points in time, spanning several decades.

Likely problems

This indicator is not always available by sex, especially when based on indirect estimates from censuses and surveys. The accuracy of the estimates depends on the quality of age-specific mortality rates in the case of direct estimates and on accurate reporting of child deaths and survival when indirect methods are used. The assistance of a demographer should be sought to obtain indirect estimates or research studies on the subject.

Interpretation

Girls and women have a biological advantage in survival and this is especially true during infancy and childhood.

In all major regions women live longer than men but the margin of difference varies substantially between regions as well as between countries within a given region. In the developed regions, girls' life expectancy is seven years longer than boys (77 years compared with 70), whereas in developing regions the difference is only three years (62 years compared with 59). The longest life expectancies are found in developed countries (82 years for women in Japan) and the biggest gap between women's and men's life expectancies (12 years) is found in the Russian Federation. In some developing countries (Bangladesh, Maldives and Nepal), men have slightly higher life expectancies than women (United Nations, 1995b).

Significant gains in life expectancy have occurred over the last two decades in every region except eastern Europe. Also the spread of AIDS is now reversing gains in some countries, particularly in sub-Saharan Africa (United Nations, 1995b).

• For a better indication of the trend, it is useful to compare life expectancies and sex differentials with those of countries of similar socio-economic backgrounds (neighbouring countries, other developing countries and more developed countries).

• Have the life expectancies of women and men improved over time? Is the life expectancy increasing faster for women than for men? Or is it changing at the same pace?

- Examine the ages at which the differences between women's and men's life expectancy are highest. At what ages is the life expectancy of women lower than men's, an indication of women's mortality disadvantage?

- At what ages does the gap between women's and men's life expectancies change over the life course? At what ages does the gap become smaller or wider relative to the gap in life expectancies at birth?

Infant and child mortality

SERIES A: Infant mortality rate (per 1,000 live births)

Formula
$$\frac{\text{Deaths of girls (boys) under age 1 in year } t}{\text{Number of girl (boy) live births in year } t} \times 1{,}000$$

SERIES B   Child mortality (per 1,000)

Formula
$$\frac{\text{Deaths of girls (boys) aged 1–4 years}}{\text{Population of girls (boys) aged 1 years}} \times 100$$

Policy relevance

Infant and child mortality rates provide comprehensive measures of child well-being and trends. Trend rates are the result of a wide variety of inputs: the nutritional health and the health knowledge of mothers, level of immunization and the use of oral rehydration therapy, availability of maternal and child health services, income and food availability in the family, the availability of clean water and safe sanitation and the overall safety of the child's environment (UNICEF, 1996, p. 95).

Deaths among girls and boys between the ages of 1 and 4 are largely preventable, so high mortality of young children is an indication of a significant health problem. Further, mortality rates for girls and boys at these early ages should not differ substantially. But in countries where son preference is strong, the mortality of girls is higher than that of boys, pointing to the need for policy intervention.

Data sources

National measures of infant and child mortality are generally derived from birth and death registration and population censuses (for estimates of child population). Indirect estimates can also be derived using retrospective questions in censuses or household surveys on deaths of household members over a specified period or on the aggregate numbers of children born and now dead. If estimates are not already available, experts in this field should be consulted to develop indirect estimates.

Source table

Table 17.1. Deaths and population under age 5 by sex and age group, for total, urban and rural areas, selected years

| | Year 1 | | | | Year 2 | | | | Year 3 | | | |
| | Population | | Deaths | | Population | | Deaths | | Population | | Deaths | |
Age group	Girls	Boys	Girls	Boys	Girls	Boys	Girls	Boys	Girls	Boys	Girls	Boys
Total (urban and rural)												
0–1												
1–4												
Under 5												
Urban												
Same age groups as above												
Rural												
Same age groups as above												

Technical note: If population figures do not correspond to the mid-year population, adjustments should be made to them and noted here.

Source: Give full citations for vital statistics reports or other sources used.

Working table

Table 17.2. Mortality rates by sex for specified age groups, for total, urban and rural areas, selected years

| | Year 1 | | Year 2 | | Year 3 | |
Age group	Girls	Boys	Girls	Boys	Girls	Boys
Total (urban and rural)						
0–1						
1–4						
Under 5						
Urban						
Same age groups as above						
Rural						
Same age groups as above						

Technical note: Note any incompleteness in the recording of births and deaths. Imputations or indirect estimates made should also be documented.

Source: Calculated from table yy in (cite publication in full).

Additional indicators or classifications

A detailed distribution of deaths during the first year of life (i.e. early neonatal, late neonatal and postnatal) can produce striking results, as can the proportion of deaths to children under age 5 among all deaths. Neonatal mortality rates are expressed as deaths to girls (boys) aged under one week, 1-4 weeks, and 4-52 weeks per 1,000 live births. Mortality rates can also be presented for older children, say, in the 5-9 year age group. Where cross-tabulations with other variables are available, especially from surveys, mortality of children can be compiled for different characteristics of the mother and father, such as education and socio-economic status or occupation.

Likely problems

Data on birth and death registration are often not readily available due to a time lag between registration and compilation and dissemination. In addition, delays in the registration of events can lead to their being recorded in subsequent years. Indicators may also be affected by the completeness of reporting. In cases where census or survey data are used, events may be under-reported due to recall lapses. Mortality data are also often incomplete; newborn and infant deaths often go unrecorded, especially in countries where a newborn is only considered a person and given a name after surviving a certain number of days. The distinction between stillbirth and neonatal death may not be clearly defined or may be influenced by traditional beliefs. Infant deaths tend to be under-reported and deaths often cluster around certain ages due to preferences for certain numbers by those who report on children's deaths. To ascertain the quality of the data to be used in the interpretation of these indicators, the data producers and researchers who assessed the information should be consulted.

A special problem for gender analysis on this topic is that although data are often registered or collected by sex, they are not compiled or disseminated by sex.

Interpretation

Women usually have lower mortality rates than men. This advantage is most evident in the first month of life, when deaths are predominantly due to endogenous factors and a baby boy is more likely to die before his first month than a baby girl simply because of the biological disadvantage of boys. As age increases, however, the physical and social environment obscures the effects of biological factors, in some cases producing a disadvantage for girls relative to boys and an excess mortality for girls under age 5 (Gómez, 1993).

In developing countries where the population is young and mortality levels relatively high, 30 per cent of all deaths in 1990-1995 occurred to children under age 5. In contrast, deaths among this group form only 2 per cent of all deaths in developed countries, with their older population age structures and lower overall mortality (United Nations, 1995a).

In many developing countries, more girls than boys die between the ages of 1 and 4, indicating sex-biased treatment of children. This is in contrast with developed countries, where deaths of boys typically surpass those of girls by 25 per cent. In 17 of 38 developing countries where death rates were sex disaggregated, girls experienced a higher mortality than boys between ages 1 and 4 (United Nations, 1995b). In some countries or areas the mortality rates for girls are higher than for boys by 20 per cent (north-eastern Brazil, Cameroon and Togo), by 40 per cent (Egypt) or by as much as 60 per cent (Pakistan) (United Nations, 1995b).

Additional specific questions should be considered:

• Examine the rates and probabilities of dying over the past 10 to 20 years. How has mortality changed for infants and in the early childhood years? Is the pace of change slower or faster in recent years?

• Considering the gap between girls' and boys' mortality experience in the age ranges under 1 and 1–4 years, are the rates more favourable for girls or boys? In which age range is the gender gap widest? Or smallest? What could be the likely explanation for these differences?

Causes of death

SERIES A	Percentage distribution of deaths by major groups of causes and selected leading causes	
Formula	$$\frac{\text{Deaths to women (men) from each major cause group } i}{\text{Total deaths to women (men) from all causes}} \times 100$$	
SERIES B	Sex-distribution of deaths within major groups of causes and selected leading causes of death	
Formula	$$\frac{\text{Deaths to women (men) from each major cause group } i}{\text{Total deaths from cause group } i} \times 100$$	

Policy relevance

Information on cause of death is essential for planning, managing and evaluating the performance of health systems. In developing countries where a substantial number of deaths are due to avoidable causes, reliable statistics are required for identifying disadvantaged groups, targeting health interventions and assessing the cost-effectiveness of disease control strategies (Murray and Lopez, 1994). Understanding how underlying causes of death could be prevented can influence the distribution of resources and bring a better balance between curative and preventive health and thereby enhance the overall benefits for both women and men.

Data sources

Most data on cause of death come from registration but in developing countries registration remains limited. Data from hospitals, another usual source, tend to be biased towards causes of death experienced by those with access to hospitals—often urban, wealthy, more educated people.

Source table

Table 18.1. Number of deaths by major cause, sex and age group

Cause of death[a]	Age group													
	0–1		1–4		5–14		15–24		25–49		50+		Total	
	Girls	Boys	Girls	Boys	Girls	Boys	W	M	W	M	W	M	W	M
Diseases														
Respiratory tuberculosis														
Other respiratory diseases														
Infectious and parasitic diseases														
Diarrhoeal diseases														
Diseases of infancy														
Neoplasms														
Cardiovascular diseases														
Degenerative diseases														
Complications of pregnancy														
AIDS														
Subtotal														
External causes														
Motor vehicle accidents														
Suicide														
Homicide														
Cataclysms														
War														
Subtotal														
All other causes (residual)														
Total (all causes)														

Technical note: Respiratory diseases include tuberculosis, pneumonia, influenza and bronchitis. Other infectious and parasitic diseases include measles, malaria, dengue. Circulatory diseases include both cardiovascular diseases and degenerative diseases such as diabetes, liver cirrhosis, renal diseases and peptic ulcers. All others include protein-energy malnutrition (PEM), unspecified diagnoses, congenital malformations and senility. See WHO, *Manual of the International Statistical Classification of Diseases, Injuries and Causes of Death, 1975 Revision,* vol. 1 (Geneva, 1977), for a detailed list of causes.

Source: Give full citation for vital registration records or special surveys used. Indicate completeness of vital registration or standard error if sample household survey is used.

a. Adapted from table XIII.3, in Robert S. Northrup, "Decision-making for health care in developing countries", *Consequences of Mortality Trends and Differentials,* Population Studies, No. 95 (ST/ESA/SER.A/95).

Note: This table will have to be compiled separately for each year covered by the analysis.

Working table

Table 18.2. Percentage distribution of deaths by cause, sex and age group

| Cause of death[a] | Age group | | | | | | | | | | | | | |
| | 0–1 | | 1–4 | | 5–14 | | 15–24 | | 25–49 | | 50+ | | Total | |
	Girls	Boys	Girls	Boys	Girls	Boys	W	M	W	M	W	M	W	M
Diseases														
Respiratory tuberculosis														
Other respiratory diseases														
Infectious and parasitic diseases														
Diarrhoeal diseases														
Diseases of infancy														
Neoplasms														
Cardiovascular diseases														
Degenerative diseases														
Complications of pregnancy														
AIDS														
Subtotal														
External causes														
Motor vehicle accidents														
Suicide														
Homicide														
Cataclysms														
War														
Subtotal														
All other causes (residual)														
Total (all causes)	100	100	100	100	100	100	100	100	100	100	100	100	100	100

Technical note: Respiratory diseases include tuberculosis, pneumonia, influenza and bronchitis. Other infectious and parasitic diseases include measles, malaria, dengue. Circulatory diseases include both cardiovascular diseases and degenerative diseases such as diabetes, liver cirrhosis, renal diseases and peptic ulcers. All others include protein-energy malnutrition (PEM), unspecified diagnoses, congenital malformations and senility.

Source: Give full citation for vital registration records or special surveys used. Indicate completeness of vital registration or standard error, if sample household survey is used.

a. Adapted from table XIII.3, in Robert S. Northrup, "Decision-making for health care in developing countries" *Consequences of Mortality Trends and Differentials*, Population Studies, No. 95 (ST/ESA/SER.A/95).

Note: This table will have to be constructed separately for each year covered by the analysis.

Additional indicators or classifications

Percentage distribution of deaths of women and men from all causes combined may be presented by age groups and compared with age distribution of deaths for women and men from (a) diseases and (b) all external causes; or compared with the age distributions for specific disease groups and external causes. If detailed classifications of cause of death exist, select and rank the 10 or 20 most common causes of death and compare their proportions among women with those among men.

Likely problems

Death registration systems may not be well developed and therefore the statistics may be incomplete. Due to the medical training required, causes of death are usually reported by hospitals and less frequently by health centres. The figures may therefore exclude deaths occurring outside health centres or areas without hospital access. In many countries, coverage is incomplete and the population covered is not clearly defined. Another problem with the data relates to problems of classification, whereby a high proportion of deaths are attributed to ill-defined causes or no causes at all. A special effort should be made to ascertain the degree of coverage from studies that have evaluated the death registration system. In cases where coverage is limited to selected areas, the limitation should be carefully noted.

Interpretation

Sex differentials in mortality suggest social rather than biological factors with two fundamental exceptions: within the first month of life, boys have a biological disadvantage, and women of reproductive age have a biological disadvantage due to the risk of childbirth unless effective measures are taken to minimize this risk.

Deaths in the early years of life occur due to a combination of endogenous (biological) and exogenous (environmental or socio-economic) factors and are largely preventable, especially beyond the first month of life (Gómez, 1993).

Three quarters of deaths to children under age 5 in developing countries are due to infectious and parasitic diseases and another 30 per cent of deaths to this age group are from perinatal causes (WHO, 1992). In a study of excess female-male mortality in Latin America and the Caribbean it was found that proportionately more girls than boys died from causes that could have been avoided through immunization, proper nutrition, timely diagnosis and treatment. In developed countries, where nutrition and health care levels are adequate, boys experience higher mortality than girls from all causes during infancy and childhood (Gómez, 1993).

Higher mortality in men is often due to greater exposure to the risk of violent death or to voluntary but health-threatening behaviours such as drinking alcohol and smoking. Almost all countries report higher proportions of men compared to women dying from injuries and violence. In developed regions only 5-6 per cent of deaths to women and men are due to communicable diseases, compared to 70 per cent of deaths in sub-Saharan Africa (United Nations, 1995b). There are significant differences between women and men in deaths due to violence and injuries and in cardiovascular diseases (United Nations, 1995b). For example, in Latin America and the Caribbean the greatest difference between the sexes is in the external causes of death, and the death rates among adolescent boys are many times greater than for girls (PAHO, 1994).

At older ages deaths are mainly due to undiagnosed causes.

• For each age group and all ages combined, compare distributions for girls and boys/women and men.

• For infants, compare the relative proportions of death due to diseases of infancy (congenital problems, injuries during labour and low birth weight) with the relative proportions due to respiratory, infectious and diarrhoeal diseases, as well as with the residual category, to reflect differential care given to girls and boys.

• Evaluate the relative proportions of deaths due to respiratory, infectious and diarrhoeal diseases, and deaths in the residual category for boys and girls aged 1-4, which can indicate differential treatment.

• Differentials between girls and boys can give further insights into the treatment of the sexes. Which causes of death are more common among women and which among men? For which age groups is the cause of death structure similar for women and men?

Maternal mortality

SERIES A   Maternal mortality ratio (per 100,000 live births)

Formula $$\frac{\text{Deaths to women from pregnancy-related causes}}{\text{Total births}} \times 100,000$$

SERIES A   Percentage of maternal deaths due to abortion

Formula $$\frac{\text{Maternal deaths due to abortion}}{\text{Total maternal deaths}} \times 100$$

Policy relevance

Complications relating to pregnancy and childbirth still pose a threat to women's health and lives. In some countries maternal mortality remains a leading cause of death for women. In others, mortality risks have been reduced to insignificant proportions. Countries must expand the provision of maternal health services in the context of primary health care, including education on safe motherhood, prenatal care, adequate delivery assistance and provision for obstetric emergencies.

Data sources

Information on maternal mortality is based primarily on vital registration of deaths. However, death records are not very reliable in many developing countries and registration systems do not have complete coverage. When official statistics are not available, community surveys, evaluation studies and reports of consultants can be used, but with extreme caution. Some surveys, such as the Demographic and Health Surveys, also collect information on mortality.

Source table

Table 19.1. Number of live births and maternal deaths by cause and age of mother, for total, urban and rural areas

	Age group			
Cause of death	15–19	20–34	35–49	15–49
Total (urban and rural)				
Total live births				
Maternal deaths by cause				
Haemorrhage				
Infection (puerperal sepsis)				
Hypertensive disorders				
Obstructed labour				
Abortion				
Urban				
Same categories as above				
Rural				
Same categories as above				

Source: Pregnancy-related deaths for each age group are taken from table yy in (cite publication in full); births for the particular year are from vital registration (cite document if applicable).

Note: This table will have to be compiled separately for each year covered by the analysis.

Working table

Table 19.2. Maternal mortality ratio and percentage of maternal deaths due to abortion, for total, urban and rural areas

Age group	Maternal mortality ratio	Percentage of maternal deaths due to abortion
Total (urban and rural)		
15–19		
20–34		
35+		
All ages (15–49)		
Urban		
Same age groups as above		
Rural		
Same age groups as above		

Source: For each indicator, give full citations for vital statistics reports or demographic surveys used.

Note: This table will have to be constructed separately for each year covered by the analysis.

Additional indicators or classifications

Ratios are bound to vary significantly by region and between cities, small towns and villages in a given country. Thus to the extent possible, these ratios should be compiled for selected towns and other localities to show comparative health disadvantages based on areas of residence. Comparisons with neighbouring countries may also be presented to illustrate the differential in maternal mortality risks. Also important is the distribution of maternal deaths by cause.

Likely problems

The quality of data on maternal mortality are affected by such factors as limitations in the definition; under-registration of maternal deaths, which forms the numerator, and under-registration of births, the denominator. There are also problems of availability and accessibility of information since the data may not be tabulated. Classification of causes of death requires medical expertise and therefore deaths occurring outside the medical system may not be rightly identified by cause. It is necessary to evaluate the data used and to consult experts about the coverage and classification issues.

Interpretation

Most maternal deaths are avoidable. Yet, complications of pregnancy, childbirth and unsafe abortions are among the leading causes of death of women of reproductive age in developing regions. Maternal death is one of the five leading causes of death for women 15-49 years in 12 Latin American and Caribbean countries and is one of the 10 leading causes in most of the other countries in the region (PAHO, 1994).

WHO estimates for 1988 give maternal mortality ratios at 26 (per 100,000 live births) for developed regions. Rates vary substantially among developing regions—630 for Africa, 380 for Asia and 200 for Latin America and the Caribbean. Within the African region, ratios vary from 360 in northern Africa to 760 in western Africa. In eastern Asia, the average ratio is 120. In southern Asia, it is 570 (WHO, 1991). Within Latin America and the Caribbean, the ratio ranges from 26 (Costa Rica) to 340 per 100,000 births in Haiti (PAHO, 1994).

Each year, an estimated half million women die from pregnancy-related causes. Roughly 70,000 of these deaths (13 per cent) are due to unsafe abortions, most either self-induced or performed by unskilled providers under unsanitary conditions (United Nations, 1995b). Regions with particularly high proportions of maternal deaths due to unsafe abortion are South America (26 per cent), the Caribbean (24 per cent) and the former USSR (23 per cent) (World Health Organization, 1993a).

In the Latin American region, abortion accounts for about a third of maternal deaths in Argentina and Chile and about a quarter of the maternal deaths in Uruguay and Venezuela (FLACSO, 1995).

Some comparisons to consider include:

- Examine maternal mortality ratios for the country as a whole and compare with neighbouring countries or the average for countries in the region. How are the ratios changing over time?

- Does abortion account for a small or large proportion of maternal deaths? (A third, a quarter or less than one tenth?) Is the proportion changing over time?

- What is the magnitude of the difference in ratios and proportions between rural and urban areas? How are they changing over time?

Child-bearing in adolescence

Series A:	**Age-specific fertility rate for women aged 15–19**
Formula	$\dfrac{\text{Births to women aged 15–19}}{\text{Total number of women aged 15–19}} \times 100$
Series B:	**Percentage of women who have given birth by age 20**
Formula	$\dfrac{\text{Women aged 20 + who gave birth to their first child before reaching age 20}}{\text{Women aged 20 +}} \times 100$

Policy relevance

Motherhood at young ages (under 20 years) poses a higher than average risk of maternal mortality and children born to these mothers have higher rates of morbidity and death. Moreover, early child-bearing impedes advances for women's education and economic well-being. Policies must address the reproductive health needs of adolescents. Information and services should be made available to adolescents to help them understand their sexuality and protect them from unwanted pregnancies, sexually transmitted diseases and subsequent risk of infertility.

Data sources

The main sources of data on births by age of mother are national civil registration and demographic survey statistics. For some countries these data may also be available from population censuses and other types of household surveys. Data on births by age of mother are also available from demographic and health surveys.

Source table

Table 20.1. Births to women aged 15–49 by age group, for total, urban and rural areas, 1970–1990

Age of mother	1970	1980	1990
Total (urban and rural)			
15–19			
20–24			
25–29			
30–34			
35–39			
40–44			
45–49			
Total			
Urban			
Same age groups as above			
Rural			
Same age groups as above			

Technical note: Note the completeness of coverage of vital events and any changes in definitions made for the years in question.
Source: Give full citations for vital statistics reports or demographic surveys used.

Working table

Table 20.2. Percentage of births to women aged 15–19, for total, urban and rural areas, 1970–1990

	1970	1980	1990
Total			
Urban			
Rural			

Source: Births for the age group 15–19 are taken from table yy in (cite publication in full) and divided by the total births to women aged 15–49 to give the percentages of births to women aged 15–19.

Additional indicators or classifications

These proportions may be presented for different provinces, regions or selected cities. Cross tabulations with education of women can also be presented. Another important indicator of prevalence of early maternity is the age at birth of the first child.

To highlight the maternity risks for young mothers, further reference can be made to the differences between maternal mortality ratios for those under age 20 compared with those 20-34 years of age (discussed in the previous section).

Likely problems

In countries where registration systems are weak, the most likely sources of data are special inquiries carried out as part of the World Fertility Survey in the early and mid-1970s and the ongoing Demographic and Health Surveys that many developing countries are involved in. Survey data must rely on the sometimes inaccurate reporting of births and age of women.

Interpretation

The association between obstetric complications and early maternity has been documented in a number of studies. Adolescents under age 15 have five to seven times higher chances of dying during pregnancy and childbirth than women in their early twenties (PAHO, 1994).

The levels of adolescent fertility in Africa are among the highest. They are generally higher than in Asia and Latin America and are about four times the rates in Europe and northern America (United Nations, 1989).

Data from demographic and health surveys in 26 countries suggest that there are between 37 (Sri Lanka) and 210 (Mali) births per 1,000 women aged 15–19. The highest adolescent fertility rates are found in countries such as Liberia, Mali and Uganda with low female literacy (United Nations, 1995c).

In Latin America, the fertility rate of women aged 15–19 ranges from 61 (Uruguay) to 133 (Guatemala) per 1,000 (PAHO, 1994). High rates of adolescent fertility are generally observed in countries with high total fertility (PAHO, 1994).

• Compare the proportions of births occurring to women aged 15–19 (less than 20, and 35 and older) with the proportion to those aged 20–24, 25–29 and 30–34.

Pregnancy and childbirth

Series A: Percentage of births attended by trained personnel

Formula

$$\frac{\text{Births to mothers aged } (x, x + n) \text{ attended by trained personnel}}{\text{Total births to mothers aged } (x, x + n)} \times 100$$

Series B: Prevalence of anaemia among women aged 15–49

Formula

$$\frac{\text{Number of women aged 15–49 with anaemia}}{\text{Total number of women aged 15–49}} \times 100$$

Series C: Prevalence of anaemia among pregnant women aged 15–49

Formula

$$\frac{\text{Number of pregnant women aged 15–49 with anaemia}}{\text{Total number of pregnant women aged 15–49}} \times 100$$

Policy relevance

The risks of child-bearing are mitigated by proper prenatal and maternity care and by the mother's general health status. Fatalities from complications are greatly reduced when births are attended by trained personnel and when there is access to emergency obstetric care. Prenatal care provides an opportunity to screen for signs of illness or other complications that may occur during pregnancy, to treat diseases aggravated by pregnancy and to deliver preventive services, such as immunization against tetanus and treatment of anaemia. Malnourishment of mothers is often manifested in anaemia, increasing their susceptibility to infections and other illness, pregnancy complications and maternal death.

Data sources

Data on births attended by trained personnel may be obtained from administrative sources, such as statistics compiled by the health ministry, or from special fertility surveys, such as the Demographic and Health Surveys (DHS). The prevalence of anaemia can be estimated from various medical studies. For international comparisons, figures may be obtained from the World Health Organization compilation, *World Health Statistics Quarterly*, and similar publications.

Source tables

Table 21.1. Total births and births attended by trained personnel, by age of mother, for total, urban and rural areas, 1970–1990

Age of mother	1970		1980		1990	
	Total births	Births attended	Total births	Births attended	Total births	Births attended
Total (urban and rural)						
15–19						
20–24						
25–29						
30–34						
35–39						
40–44						
45–49						
15–49						
Urban						
Same categories as above						
Rural						
Same categories as above						

Technical note: Note definitions and limitations of data, such as completeness of coverage.
Source: Give full citations for reports or administrative records from which data were compiled.

Table 21.2. Total number of women and number of anaemic women aged 15–49 by pregnancy status, 1970–1990

Pregnancy status	1970		1980		1990	
	Women 15–49	Number anaemic	Women 15–49	Number anaemic	Women 15–49	Number anaemic
Pregnant						
Non-pregnant						
Total						

Technical note: Note definitions and limitations of data, such as completeness of coverage.
Source: Give full citations for reports or administrative records from which data were compiled.

Working tables

Table 21.3. Percentage of births attended by trained personnel, by age of mother, for total, urban and rural areas, 1970–1990

Age of mother	1970	1980	1990
Total (urban and rural)			
15–19			
20–24			
25–29			
30–34			
35–39			
40–44			
45–49			
15–49			
Urban			
Same age groups as above			
Rural			
Same age groups as above			

Technical note: Note definitions and limitatic ns of data,such as completeness of coverage.
Source: Give full citations for reports or administrative records from which data were compiled.

Table 21.4. Prevalence of anaemia among women aged 15–49 by pregnancy status, 1970–1990

Pregnancy status	1970	1980	1990
Pregnant			
Non-pregnant			
Total			

Technical note: Note definitions and limitations of data, such as completeness of coverage.
Source: Give full citations for reports or administrative records from which data were compiled.

Additional indicators or classifications

Access to adequate health care facilities is essential and can mitigate the devastating effects of anaemia and increase women's chances of survival during childbirth. In countries where special health surveys or studies have been conducted, further analysis could be done by comparing (a) the ratio of women aged 15-49 to health centres (hospitals, polyclinics, small clinics, etc.); (b) the ratio of women to trained midwives; (c) distance to the nearest health clinic and/or maternity centre; (d) percentage of women attending antenatal clinics; (e) percentage of women who have been immunized against tetanus. These series can be presented separately for rural and urban residence.

Likely problems

Data on trained birth attendants are not always readily available and, when they are, may not provide sufficient details to distinguish between categories of trained health-care providers, such as doctors, midwives and nurses. Available information on prevalence of anaemia is generally outdated and not representative. Since the determination of a condition of anaemia depends on clinical tests, the data are limited to prenatal clinic or hospital visits, ad hoc studies and special programmes.

Interpretation

Anaemia causes women to be less resistant to infection and diminishes their tolerance for haemorrhages during childbirth and abortion. It also impinges on the health status of the foetus and babies, posing serious mortality risks. Women's high requirements for iron during pregnancy and breast-feeding, cultural patterns of distribution and nutritional taboos also tend to aggravate their nutritional deficiencies (PAHO, 1994).

More than a third of the world's women suffer from anaemia during their reproductive years and about 50 per cent during pregnancy. The highest rates of anaemia are found among southern Asian women—58 per cent of women in that region and 75 per cent of pregnant women are affected. Fifty-three per cent of pregnant women in northern Africa, 51 per cent in sub-Saharan Africa and 63 per cent in south-eastern Asia are anaemic (United Nations, 1995b).

In developing regions overall, only about half of all births are attended by trained personnel, compared with 99 per cent in developed countries. Subregional data for 1993 show significant variations: only 35 per cent of births in eastern Africa are attended compared with 86 per cent in southern Africa; 31 per cent in southern Asia compared with 95 per cent in eastern Asia; and 76 per cent for tropical South America and 90 per cent in the Caribbean (WHO, 1993). In many developing communities, traditional birth attendants—usually local women untrained in modern medicine—are the only source of maternal health care or the only affordable alternative to clinics. A limited knowledge of hygiene among traditional birth attendants is compounded by the often unsanitary environments in which births take place.

- Which age groups are more susceptible to anaemia? How does their susceptibility change with pregnancy? What are the relative proportions of young and older mothers' use of trained personnel during childbirth? Is prevalence of attended births higher for women in high-risk age groups compared to other age groups (e.g., ages 20–29, 30–39, 40+)?

Family planning

Series A:	**Percentage of women using contraceptives by age group**
Formula	$\dfrac{\text{Non-pregnant women } (x, x + n) \text{ currently in a union using contraceptives}}{\text{Non-pregnant women } (x, x + n) \text{ currently in a union}} \times 100$
Series B:	**Percentage distribution of contraceptive users by method of contraception**
Formula	$\dfrac{\text{Women users of a specific method aged } (x, x + n)}{\text{Total women current users aged } (x, x + n)} \times 100$

Policy relevance

Using family planning methods to space or limit births improves the health of both mothers and children. Access to quality family planning services enables individuals to decide the number and spacing of their children, and allows women to bear children in a relatively risk-free pattern and prevent unwanted births. Priority should be given to meeting unfilled needs for fertility control and reducing the adverse effect of low prevalence of contraceptive use on maternal mortality (PAHO, 1994).

Data sources

Data on contraceptive use are provided by national surveys and other internationally coordinated surveys such as the World Fertility Survey, the Demographic and Health Surveys and the Contraceptive Prevalence Surveys. These data may be supplemented by records kept by organized family planning programmes and clinics.

Source tables

Table 22.1. Non-pregnant women aged 15–44 in a union who are using contraceptives by age group, for total, urban and rural areas

Age group	Total	Number using contraceptives
Total (urban and rural)		
15–19		
20–24		
25–29		
30–34		
35–39		
40–44		
45–49[a]		
15–44 or 15–49[a]		
Urban		
Same age groups as above		
Rural		
Same age groups as above		

Technical note: Note any coding decisions and sampling errors if sample survey data are used.

Source: Give full citations for fertility surveys or contraceptive prevalence surveys used.

a. The limit of 44 or 49 years depends on what the country defines as the end of the reproductive years.

Note: This table will have to be compiled separately for each year covered by the analysis.

Table 22.2. Distribution of women contraceptive users aged 15–44 by age group and method used, for total, urban and rural areas

Method used	Age group						
	All ages (15–44)	15–19	20–24	25–29	30–34	35–39	40–44
Total (urban and rural)							
Pill							
IUD							
Douche							
Condom							
Rhythm							
Withdrawal							
Abstinence							
Injection							
Female sterilization							
Male sterilization							
Other							
All methods							
Urban							
Same categories as above							
Rural							
Same categories as above							

Technical note: Note any coding decisions and sampling errors if sample survey data are used.

Source: Give full citations for publications used.

Note: This table will have to be compiled separately for each year covered by the analysis. The age range covered could also be 15–49, depending on what is defined as the reproductive years.

Working tables

Table 22.3. Prevalence of contraceptive use among non-pregnant women aged 15–44 in a union, by age group, for total, urban and rural areas

Age group	Contraceptive use (%)		
	Total	Urban	Rural
15–19			
20–24			
25–29			
30–34			
35–39			
40–44			
45–49[a]			
15–44 or 15–49[a]			

Technical note: Note any coding decisions and sampling errors if sample survey data are used.

Source: Give full citations for fertility surveys or contraceptive prevalence surveys used.

a. The limit of 44 or 49 years depends on what the country defines as the end of the reproductive years.

Note: This table will have to be constructed separately for each year covered by the analysis.

Table 22.4. Percentage distribution of women contraceptive users by method used and age group, for total, urban and rural areas

Method used	Age group						
	All ages (15–44)	15–19	20–24	25–29	30–34	35–39	40–44
Total (urban and rural)							
Pill							
IUD							
Douche							
Condom							
Rhythm							
Withdrawal							
Abstinence							
Injection							
Female sterilization							
Male sterilization							
Other							
All methods	100	100	100	100	100	100	100
Urban							
Same categories as above							
Rural							
Same categories as above							

Technical note: Note any coding decisions and of sampling errors sample survey data are used.

Source: Give full citations for publications used.

Note: This table will have to be constructed separately for each year covered by the analysis. The age range covered could also be 15–49, depending on what is defined as the reproductive years.

Additional indicators or classifications

Comparisons with neighbouring countries (or regional averages) can also be made. The age group corresponding to the reproductive ages should be consistent with that used in other sections of the publication. If the age group 15-49 has been used consistently, then the same age group should be used here, provided the data are available. If data are available, reasons for not using contraceptives should be analysed. Some studies collect data on contraceptive use by men as well. If such data are available, they should be presented in the same manner as those for women.

Initiatives have been undertaken to collect better information on topics related to the use of reproductive health services. Contraceptive prevalence surveys and demographic and health surveys are being redesigned to cover married and unmarried women and men, adolescents, knowledge of contraceptives and attitudes about family size. Quality-of-care surveys are collecting data on type and quality of services offered in family planning clinics. If any of these data are available, they should be included either by adjusting the main indicators in small tables or in the text or as material featured in sidebars.

Likely problems

Questions about current contraceptive use are usually asked of non-pregnant women currently in a union. Where lengthy post-partum abstinence is customary, there is a potential for overlap in reporting of contraceptive abstinence and post-partum abstinence. In countries where post-partum abstinence is included in the questionnaire, overlap between current practice of post-partum abstinence and contraception can be avoided by coding women who are abstaining post-partum as non-users of contraception.

Interpretation

In most developing countries with available data, national contraceptive prevalence rates rose considerably over the decade.
The proportion of women of reproductive age who use contraceptives increased from 14 per cent in 1960-1965 to approximately 57 per cent. Yet the gap between unmet needs and availability of contraceptives, especially for the unmarried and adolescents, remains large (WHO, 1995).

Studies show that in some regions a considerable proportion of women have more children than they desire. Yet not all of these women use contraceptives. The percentages of married women who want no more children but are not using contraceptives are 77 per cent for Africa, 57 per cent for Asia and the Middle East, and 43 per cent for Latin America (WHO, 1995).

The highest levels of contraceptive use among married women in 1990 were 79 per cent in eastern Asia and 72 per cent in the developed regions. Among other developing regions the next highest prevalence is in Latin American and the Caribbean, with 58 per cent, and the rest of Asia and the Pacific, with 42 per cent. Much lower rates are reported in Africa, only 18 per cent (United Nations, 1995b).

Sterilization is the form of contraception most widely used by women in the developing regions. In eastern Asia 33 per cent of women and 10 per cent of men chose it, accounting for nearly half of all contraceptive use. Traditional methods are most common in developed regions, where they account for nearly one third of total contraceptive use (United Nations, 1995b).

Concern about health complications is by far the most common reason why women stop using contraceptives—much more common than lack of access, husband disapproval, social pressures or religious belief (United Nations, 1995b).

An approach to analysing these statistics is to:

- Examine the differences in prevalence of contraceptive use across age groups. How is prevalence different between urban and rural areas? How is contraceptive use among women changing over time?

- Which methods are most popular among women overall? Among younger women? Among older women?

Timing of births

SERIES A   **Average interval between marriage and first birth**

Formula

$$\frac{\text{Sum (months between marriage and first birth)}}{\text{Number of women reporting interval}}$$

SERIES B   **Average interval and between first. second and subsequent births (in months)**

Formula

$$\frac{\text{Sum (months between } j^{th} \text{ and } (j + l)^{th} \text{ births}}{\text{Number of women reporting interval}}$$

Policy relevance

Short birth intervals have a debilitating effect on women's health and increase the risk of complications during subsequent childbirth. When intervals are reasonably long, say two years, the woman's body is allowed time to recover from the extra demands of pregnancy and lactation.

Data sources

The main sources of data for these indicators are fertility surveys, demographic and health surveys, or other household surveys that ask about births and intervals between births. The data collected from these surveys may be unpublished, and if so, will require some computation.

Source table

Table 23.1. Distribution of women married for at least two years and length of interval between first marriage and first birth and between subsequent births, for total, urban and rural areas

Interval (months)	Between first marriage and first birth	Between subsequent births					
		First & second	second & third	third & fourth	fourth & fifth	fifth & sixth	sixth & seventh
Total (urban and rural)							
0–7							
8–11							
12–23							
24–35							
36–47							
48–59							
60 or more							
Urban							
Same intervals as above							
Rural							
Same intervals as above							

Technical note: Note definitions and limitations of the sample.
Source: Give full citation for publication or survey and office responsible for the data used.
Note: This table will have to be compiled separately for each year covered by the analysis.

Working table

Table 23.2. Average interval between first marriage and first birth and between subsequent births, for total, urban and rural areas

	Average interval (months)		
	Total	Urban	Rural
First marriage to first birth			
First and second births			
Second and third births			
Third and fourth births			
Fourth and fifth births			
Fifth and sixth births			
Sixth and seventh births			

Technical note: Note definitions and limitations of the sample.
Source: Give full citation for publication or survey and office responsible for the data used.
Note: This table will have to be constructed separately for each year covered by the analysis.

Additional indicators or classifications

Birth intervals vary with birth order as well as with age. Average intervals between births could therefore be presented for specific age groups, for example for adolescents (15–19 years) and women in the late reproductive period (40–49 years). Comparing average intervals of young mothers with older mothers for the intervals between marriage and first child, and also between the first and second births could give an indication of trends towards shorter or longer birth intervals.

Likely problems

It is important to limit the calculation of marriage to first-birth intervals to women who have been married for a minimum number of years. Two years is often a culturally acceptable period for a couple to be childless and allows sufficient time for newly married women to be exposed to pregnancy, taking account of possible miscarriages or still births. Only those who have been married for at least the minimum number of years before the survey should be included in the calculations. Information on first births is subject to errors of omission and of accuracy of timing of births.

If there are no data on birth intervals between first and subsequent births, an average interval can be used. That is, for each woman the average birth interval can be expressed as the number of months between the first and last births over the total number of live births. These averages can then be summed over all women with non-zero intervals and divided by the total number of women with non-zero intervals. It should be noted that this can only be applied to women who have had at least two live births.

Interpretation

In many developing countries women give birth to too many children too close together and this increases the health risk to both mother and child. A reasonable length of time between pregnancies allows women to recuperate and to care for each child. Two to three years are deemed necessary for the body to recover completely from a pregnancy and to prepare itself for another, also allowing for breast-feeding of the infant (PAHO, 1994).

Of the 25 countries that have conducted Demographic and Health Surveys, nine recorded more than 40 per cent of births at intervals of less than two years; while six had fewer than 30 per cent of the births at intervals of less than two years (United Nations, 1994b).

In five demographic and health surveys conducted from 1990 to 1992, it was found that 50 per cent of the women had interbirth intervals below 27.6 months in north-eastern Brazil and below 33.0 months in Colombia (PAHO, 1994).

Repeated child-bearing in unsafe circumstances increases the lifetime risk of dying during pregnancy. African women face a 1 in 23 chance of dying from pregnancy-related causes in their lifetime. In contrast, the lifetime chance of dying in pregnancy in the United States is about 1 in 4,000 (United Nations, 1995b).

From the indicators presented determine:

- What the waiting period is between marriage and the first childbirth.
- How long a majority of women wait to have their first child.
- How the average birth interval changes with higher birth orders.

Threats to health (traditional practices, use of drugs, alcohol and cigarettes, AIDS and sexually transmitted diseases (STDs))

Series A: Prevalence of attribute i among women and men aged 15+

Formula

$$\frac{\text{Number of women (men) aged 15+ with attribute } i}{\text{Total women (men) aged 15+}} \times 100,000$$

Series B: Percentage women among persons with attribute i

Formula

$$\frac{\text{Number of women with attribute } i}{\text{Total number of women and men with attribute } i} \times 100$$

where attributes might include smoking, substance dependency or abuse, alcoholism, drug addiction, HIV infection, STD, etc.

Policy relevance

Various behavioural and traditional practices included in this section are significant threats to health and relate to gender, but national data on their prevalence and effects are scarce. Female genital mutilation still exists in certain countries and international and regional recommendations have called for measures to eliminate such practices harmful to the health of girls and women. Smoking, alcohol and drug abuse are a threat to the health of women as well as men, although they are generally seen as male and not female problems. Policies also need to recognize the incidence of HIV and AIDS among women as well as men. The number of women contracting HIV is growing faster than the number of men, and young women are most susceptible.

Data sources

Sources of data on threats to health are national surveys, disease intelligence reports from health departments or ministries, and special studies.

Source table

Table 24.1. Population aged 15 and over with selected attributes related to particular health risks, by sex, for two selected years

Attribute	Year 1				Year 2		
	Total	Women	Men		Total	Women	Men
Population 15+							
Lifestyle-related health risks							
Smoking							
Alcohol consumption							
Drug addiction							
Disease							
HIV-infected							
STD							
Occupational hazards							
Injuries							
Work-related diseases							
Work-related deaths							
Harmful traditional practices							
Female circumcision							
Initiation rites							

Technical note: Specify population covered and concepts and definitions used.

Source: For each attribute, give full citation for national health or other surveys used.

Working tables

Table 24.2. Percentage of population aged 15 and over with selected attributes related to particular health risks, by sex, for two selected years

Attribute	Year 1			Year 2		
	Percentage of population 15+ exhibiting given attribute			Percentage of population 15+ exhibiting given attribute		
	Women	Men		Women	Men	
Lifestyle-related health risks						
Smoking						
Alcohol consumption						
Drug abuse						
Disease						
HIV-infected						
STD						
Occupational hazards						
Injuries						
Work-related diseases						
Work-related deaths						
Harmful traditional practices						
Female circumcision						
Initiation rites						

Technical note: Specify population covered and concepts and definitions used.
Source: For each attribute, give full citation for national health or other surveys used.

Table 24.3. Percentage of females among persons with selected attributes related to particular health risks, for two selected years

Attribute	Year 1	Year 2
Lifestyle-related health risks		
Smoking		
Alcohol consumption		
Drug abuse		
Disease		
HIV-infected		
STD		
Occupational hazards		
Injuries		
Work-related diseases		
Work-related deaths		
Harmful traditional practices		
Female circumcision		
Initiation rites		

Technical note: Specify population covered and concepts and definitions used.
Source: For each attribute, give full citation for national health or other surveys used.

Additional indicators or classifications

The indicators may also be compiled for specific age groups such as under 15, 15–19, (20–24, 24+) or 20+, or other groupings depending on the specific indicators and the cultural norms related to the issue being considered. Other health hazards and specific traditional practices may be included as well.

Likely problems

Countries vary in the accuracy and completeness with which they report AIDS and STD cases, smoking, alcoholism, substance abuse and traditional practices. Available data are subject to an unknown degree of under-reporting, so estimates are not reliable. Surveys designed to yield national estimates of HIV prevalence, for example, have encountered immense logistical and design problems. There are hardly any data from surveys or administrative sources on prevalence on female circumcision.

In the case of female circumcision, data collection is bound to be difficult if the practice is illegal. The only potentially reliable source is surveys, but incomplete information can also be obtained from hospital records on complications from this practice.

Interpretation

Female genital mutilation is among the many practices that negatively impact on women's health and well-being. Other practices include dowry and bride price, marriage of girls before they have reached maturity and nutritional taboos. Female genital mutilation occurs mostly in Africa but also in Asia and among immigrant populations in some developed countries. Its prevalence is estimated to be as high as 70 per cent in countries such as Burkina Faso, Djibouti, Eritrea, Ethiopia, Mali, Sierra Leone, Somalia and the Sudan. Between 5 and 10 per cent prevalence rates are found in Uganda, the United Republic of Tanzania and Zaire (United Nations, 1995b).

One of the most important lifestyle choices from the point of view of health is tobacco smoking. At least a quarter of adult women smoke in most developed and developing regions outside of Africa. Africa has the lowest proportion of women smokers (14 per cent). In Latin America and the Caribbean, three out of every ten women smoke (United Nations, 1991b).

Excessive alcohol consumption also has serious deleterious effects, inducing cirrhosis of the liver and other digestive system diseases, mental disorders, certain cardiovascular diseases and violence. Women have a greater potential to become addicted to alcohol within a shorter period of time and are more vulnerable to cirrhosis of the liver than men are. Studies on prevalence of alcoholism in Costa Rica found a ratio of 2.3 men to 1 woman among heavy drinkers and 16 men to 1 woman among alcoholics (PAHO, 1994). Substance abuse has led to a rise in mental disorders, violence, susceptibility to infections and respiratory disease and the risk of HIV and AIDS.

WHO estimates that more than 16 million adults and 1 million children have been infected with HIV. By mid-1994 approximately 40 per cent of estimated cases of HIV infection were women (United Nations 1995b). In some major cities of North and South America, western Europe and sub-Saharan Africa, AIDS is now the leading cause of death among women aged 20–40 (United Nations, 1991b). As heterosexual transmission becomes an increasingly dominant route of HIV infection, proportionately more women and more poor people will be among those to suffer.

Sexually transmitted diseases are increasing rapidly among low-income populations in the United States, although they have generally declined in other industrial countries due to effective prevention and treatment. STDs tend to affect women of reproductive age and account for 0.5 to 1 per cent of maternal deaths in sub-Saharan Africa and for 20 per cent in the United States, where overall maternal mortality rates are much lower (United Nations, 1991b). Women face greater health threats from STDs than men do. Infected pregnant women are at higher risk of maternal and infant illness and death. Some reproductive tract infections increase the risk of contracting HIV. In many developing countries, STDs are rife with stigmas, taboos and the threat of social ostracism. Fear of rejection, reinforced by illiteracy and low self-esteem, prevents many women from reporting or discussing symptoms that might lead to prompt identification and treatment.

References and further reading

FLACSO (1995). *Latin American Women: Compared Figures.* Santiago: Instituto de la Mujer.

Gómez, Elsa G. (1994). Sex discrimination and excess female mortality in childhood, in *Health Conditions in the Americas,* vol. I. Scientific Publication No. 549. Washington, D.C.: Pan American Health Organization.

Heligman, L. (1983). Patterns in sex differentials in mortality in less developed countries, in *Sex Differentials in Mortality,* A. D. López and L.T. Ruzicka, eds. Miscellaneous Indicators No. 4. Canberra: Australian National University, Department of Demography.

Hosken, Fran (1993). *The Hosken Report: Genital and Sexual Mutilation of Females.* Lexington, Massachusetts: Women's International Network News.

Murray, C. J. L. and A. D. López (1994). Global and regional cause-of death patterns in 1990. *WHO Bulletin,* vol. 72, No. 3.

Pan American Health Organization (1993). *Gender, Women and Health in the Americas.* Scientific Publication No. 541. Washington, D.C.

_____ (1994). *Health Conditions in the Americas* vol. I. Scientific Publication No. 549. Washington, D.C.

Tinker, Anne, and Marjorie A. Koblinsky (1993). *Making Motherhood Safe.* World Bank Discussion Papers No. 202. Washington, D.C.

United Nations (1981). *Model Life Tables for Developing Countries,* Population Studies No. 77. Sales No. E.81.XIII.7.

_____ (1986). *Consequences of Mortality Trends and Differentials.* Population Studies No. 95. Sales No. E.85.XIII.3.

_____ (1989). *Levels and Trends of Contraceptive Use as Assessed in 1988.* Sales No. E.89.XIII.4.

_____ (1991a). *The AIDS Epidemic and Its Demographic Consequences. Proceedings of the United Nations/World Health Organization Workshop on Modeling the Demographic Impact of the AIDS Epidemic in Pattern II Countries: Progress to Date and Policies for the Future. New York, 13–15 December 1989.* Sales No. E.91.XIII.5.

_____ (1991b). *The World's Women 1970–1990: Trends and Statistics.* Sales No. E.90.XVII.3.

_____ (1992). *Child Mortality Since the 1960s: A Database for Developing Countries.* Sales No. E.92.XIII.10.

_____ (1994a). *Report of the International Conference on Population and Development. Cairo, 5–13 September 1994*. Sales No. E.95.XIII.18.

_____ (1994b). *The Health Rationale for Family Planning: Timing of Births and Child Survival*. Sales No. E.95.XIII.3.

_____ (1994c). *World Contraceptive Use 1994*. Wall chart.

_____ (1995a). *World Population Prospects: The 1994 Revision*. Sales No. E.95.XIII.16.

_____ (1995b). *The World's Women 1995: Trends and Statistics*. Sales No. E.95.XVII.2.

_____ (1995c). *Women's Education and Fertility Behaviour: Recent Evidence from the Demographic and Health Surveys*. Sales No. E.95.XIII.23.

United Nations Children's Fund (1996). *The State of the World's Children 1996*. New York: Oxford University Press.

World Health Organization (1977). *Manual of International Statistical Classification of Diseases, Injuries and Causes of Death: 1975 Review, vol. 1*. Geneva.

_____ (1989). *Preventing Maternal Deaths*, Erica Royston and Sue Armstrong, eds. Geneva.

_____ (1991). *Maternal Mortality: A Global Fact Book*. WHO/MCH/MSM/91.3. Geneva.

_____ (1992). *Global Health Situation and Projections: Estimates*. WHO/HST/92.1. Geneva.

_____ (1993a). *Abortion: A Tabulation of Available Data on the Frequency and Mortality of Unsafe Abortion, second edition*. HWO/FHE/MSM/93.13. Geneva.

_____ (1993b). *Coverage of Maternity Care: A Tabulation of Available Information, third edition*. Maternal Health and Safe Motherhood Programme. WHO/MCH/MSH/93.7. Geneva.

_____ (1995). "Women's health". WHO Position Paper, Fourth World Conference on Women, Beijing, China, 4–15 September 1995. WHO/FHE/95.8. Geneva.

HOUSING, HUMAN SETTLEMENTS AND ENVIRONMENT

Growth and distribution of rural and urban populations

Series A: Percentage of population urban and rural, by sex

Formula

$$\frac{\text{Number of women (men) in urban areas}}{\text{Total women (men)}} \times 100$$

$$\frac{\text{Number of women (men) in rural areas}}{\text{Total women (men)}} \times 100$$

Series B: Women to men ratio in urban and rural areas, by age group

Formula

$$\frac{\text{Population of women aged } (x, x + n) \text{ in urban (rural) areas}}{\text{Population of men aged } (x, x + n) \text{ in urban(rural) areas}} \times 100$$

Policy relevance

Differences in the quality of life between rural and urban areas exist in the standard of housing, health and other social services. Differences also exist in the level of economic activity and the economic returns from such activity. These factors affect how women and men participate in economic and social development processes and the outcomes, both positive and negative for them.

Data sources

Population censuses are the main source of data but demographic and household surveys and other special inquiries may be used if censuses are unavailable.

Source table

Table 25.1. Total, urban and rural population by sex and age group

Age group	Total		Urban		Rural	
	Women	Men	Women	Men	Women	Men
0–9						
10–14						
15–19						
20–24						
.						
.						
.						
75–79						
80+						
All ages						

Source: Give full citation for census report used.

Note: This table will have to be compiled separately for each year covered by

Working tables

Table 25.2. Percentage distribution of population by urban and rural residence, for each sex

	Total	Women	Men
Urban			
Rural			
Total	100	100	100

Source: Give full citation for census report used.
Note: This table will have to be constructed separately for each year covered by the analysis.

Table 25.3. Females per 100 males in urban and rural areas by age group

Age group	Urban	Rural
0– 9		
10–14		
15–19		
20–24		
.		
.		
.		
75–79		
80+		
All ages		

Source: Give full citation for census report used.
Note: This table will have to be constructed separately for each year covered by the analysis.

Additional indicators or classifications

As a context for understanding changes in the situation of women and men, the change in rural and urban populations between two periods should also be presented, computed either as a simple arithmetic rate or an exponential rate. Urban population can be further divided into capital city, other cities, and towns and villages, or classified by size of localities (e.g., 1 million or more; 500,000 to 999,999; 200,000 to 499,999; 100,000 to 199,999, etc.).

Age distributions of the urban and rural populations should also be analysed. High rural to urban migration tends to reduce the proportion of young adults, who are typically the most migratory, in rural areas.

This section can also summarize the rural-urban differences shown under other topics in the publication.

Likely problems

There are no internationally agreed-on definitions of urban and rural as such, and measurements are based on the practices in the particular country. These may change over time. The lack of consensus poses a difficulty in making comparisons between countries and between periods in a given country. This problem can be circumvented by presenting data by population size of locality.

Interpretation

In the mid-1980s, over two fifths of the world's population lived in urban areas. On the basis of 1994 population estimates, the United Nations projects the urban proportion to reach 50 per cent by 2010. The most urbanized developing region, Latin America and the Caribbean, is estimated to have 74 per cent of its population in urban areas. In the other developing regions, the proportion is 34 per cent for Africa and 33 per cent for Asia (United Nations, 1995a).

In some areas of the world, the ratio of women to men is much higher in urban areas that in rural areas. In developed regions, excluding eastern Europe, women outnumber men in urban areas by 106 to 100, while the ratio of rural women to men is about 96. In Latin America there are 106 women per 100 men in urban areas while the corresponding ratio in rural areas is 90. In sub-Saharan Africa there are fewer women than men in urban areas (95/100) but 106 women to every 100 men in rural areas. The comparative ratios for southern Asia are 88/100 and 97/100 respectively, and 90/100 and 96/100 in western Asia (United Nations, 1995b).

Examples of questions to be addressed are:

- How does the concentration of women compare to men's. Are women concentrated in urban or rural areas compared to men?

- How have the patterns of concentration changed over the years?

- Is the ratio of women to men increasing faster in rural or in urban areas? And in which areas is it decreasing relative to men?

- How does the women to men ratio in each age group compare with the ratio in the population as a whole? At which ages are the ratios higher in rural areas and in which are they higher in urban areas relative to the national age-specific ratios?

Internal migration

Series A: **Percentage distribution of the population by area of residence and origin**

Formula $\dfrac{\text{Number of women (men) residing in area } i \text{ who migrated from area } j}{\text{Total population of women (men)}} \times 100$

where areas i and j present the following combinations of origin and destination respectively: rural-rural, rural-urban, urban-rural, urban-urban.

Series B: **Percentage distribution of the population by duration of stay in current area of residence**

Formula $\dfrac{\text{Number of women (men) residing in area of residence for } (x, x + n) \text{ years}}{\text{Total population of women (men)}} \times 100$

Series C: **Sex composition of each category of population by migrant status and area of residence and origin**

Formula $\dfrac{\text{Women (men) residing in area } i \text{ who migrated from area } j}{\text{Total residing in area } i \text{ who migrated from area } j} \times 100$

Series D: **Sex composition of each category of population by duration of stay in area of residence**

Formula $\dfrac{\text{Women (men) residing in area of residence for } (x, x + n) \text{ years}}{\text{Total residing in area of residence for } (x, x + n) \text{ years}} \times 100$

Policy relevance

A major component of urban growth is internal migration, mainly from rural areas and for economic reasons. Migration exposes women and men to different kinds of experiences, many of which may cause significant changes in their lives. Although not all these experiences are positive, migration is a means of enhancing status and increasing social and economic opportunities.

Data sources

Censuses and sample surveys are the most important sources of migration data in developing countries. Information on migration and the place of origin of migrants is derived from cross-classification of information on past and current residence, such as place of birth, place of previous residence, place of current residence and duration of stay. Population registers are an additional source of data but mainly in developed countries. In most developing countries the registration systems are not sufficiently developed to provide reliable information for migration studies.

Source table

Table 26.1. Distribution of the population by migrant status and type of migration stream and by duration of stay in area of residence, by sex, for three selected years

	Year 1		Year 2		Year 3	
	Women	Men	Women	Men	Women	Men
Migrant status and migration stream						
Never migrated						
Rural to urban						
Rural to rural						
Urban to rural						
Urban to urban						
Duration of stay in area of residence						
Since birth						
Less than 1 year						
1 to less than 5 years						
5 to less than 10 years						
10 to less than 15 years						
15 or more years						
Total population						

Technical note: Note any differences in the definitions between years.
Source: Give full citation for census and survey reports used.

Working tables

Table 26.2. Percentage distribution of the population by migrant status and type of migration stream and by duration of stay in area of residence, by sex, for three selected years

	Year 1		Year 2		Year 3	
	Women	Men	Women	Men	Women	Men
Migrant status and migration stream						
Never migrated						
Rural to urban						
Rural to rural						
Urban to rural						
Urban to urban						
Total	100	100	100	100	100	100
Duration of stay in area of residence						
Since birth						
Less than 1 year						
1 to less than 5 years						
5 to less than 10 years						
10 to less than 15 years						
15 or more years						
Total	100	100	100	100	100	100

Technical note: Note any differences in the definitions between years.
Source: Give full citations for census reports used.

Table 26.3. Sex composition within each category of migration stream and by duration of stay in area of residence, for three selected years *(percentage)*

	Year 1		Year 2		Year 3	
	women	men	women	men	women	men
Migration stream						
Never migrated						
Rural to urban						
Rural to rural						
Urban to rural						
Urban to urban						
Duration of stay in area of residence						
Since birth						
Less than 1 year						
1 to less than 5 years						
5 to less than 10 years						
10 to less than 15 years						
15 or more years						
Total population						

Technical note: Note any differences in the definitions between years.
Source: Give full citations for census reports used.

Additional indicators or classifications

The indicators may be compiled for broad age categories such as children under age 15, working age population and older non-working age population. The classification may be disaggregated by distinguishing further the cities, medium-sized and small urban localities or specific towns of destination and/or origin. The duration of stay can be presented separately for rural and urban residents. The reasons for migration have important policy implications and should be covered if data are available.

Likely problems

The concept of migration may refer to lifetime (that is, in relation to place of birth) or be period specific (that is, in relation to previous residence at a given earlier period). It might also be defined with respect to the province (or region within the country) of previous residence. A careful review is necessary to ascertain which of these concepts apply to the data and ensure comparability between different sources of data. Population censuses do not provide data in sufficient depth for the study of determinants of migration and often the concepts have to be adjusted to be usable with the available data. The rates of migration vary according to the boundaries used, whether towns or villages, districts, provinces or states, or other types of administrative and geographical boundaries.

Interpretation

The importance of each type of migration stream differs from one country to another, as does the role of women and men in each. In countries such as India (1971, 1981), Malaysia (1970) and Thailand (1980), rural to rural migration constitutes the dominant stream for both women and men; in some, urban to urban migration is the dominant stream for both women and men, such as Egypt (1976), Pakistan (1973) and Brazil (1970). In the Philippines (1973) and the Republic of Korea (1966, 1970, 1975), the rural to urban stream was the most dominant. The urban to rural stream, though present, did not dominate migration in any of the 12 data sources from 9 countries in one study. Nevertheless, among this group of migrants women constituted more than 50 per cent in 7 of the 12 data sources. The highest share of women in any stream was in rural to rural migration in Egypt, India and Pakistan, rural to urban in the Philippines, the Republic of Korea, Thailand and Honduras, and urban to urban in Brazil (United Nations, 1993a).

With respect to duration of stay, proportionately more women and men migrants had been in their current place of residence for 10 or more years compared to shorter durations of stay in several countries, including Bangladesh (1974), Egypt (1976) and India (1981). In some countries, women constitute a higher proportion of all internal migrants than men (e.g., India, 1981; Nepal, 1981; Panama, 1980; Trinidad and Tobago, 1980; and Venezuela, 1981). Also, in most of the 12 countries, there is a slightly higher percentage of women among longer-term migrants (i.e., 5–9 years and 10 or more years stay) than among the shorter-term migrants (United Nations, 1993a).

Comparisons of national data may address the following questions:

- Are there proportionately more women than men in any of the specific streams of migrants?

- Which of these streams do women dominate and which do men dominate?

- How are the migration streams changing over the years for women as well as for men?

- Which of the sexes predominate among the long-term and short-term migrants?

International migration and refugees

Series A: Rate of immigration of women and men by age group

Formula
$$\frac{\text{Number of immigrant women (men) aged } (x, x + n)}{\text{Population of women (men) in country of destination aged } (x, x + n)} \times 1{,}000$$

Series B: Percentage distribution of women and men immigrants by international migration category (overseas workers, permanent immigrants, refugees)

Formula
$$\frac{\text{Number of women (men) immigrants of category } i}{\text{Total number of women (men) immigrants}} \times 100$$

Series C: Sex composition of immigrants by international migration category

Formula
$$\frac{\text{Number of women (men) immigrants of category } i}{\text{Total number of immigrants of category } i} \times 100$$

Policy relevance

International migration tends to affect women and men differently. The mobility of women and their subsequent adaptation to or integration in the host society, especially their participation in the labour force, are more intimately linked than the mobility and adaptation of men to the family structure and social forces defining the sexual division of labour in both countries of origin and countries of destination.

International migration policies may differentiate between migrants on the basis of gender, ethnicity or country of origin. Thus, such policies have an impact on the status of female migrants whether they be temporary labour migrants, permanent immigrants or refugees.

Data sources

The most comprehensive sources of data on migrant population by sex are the national population censuses and special surveys, which provide data on persons born outside the country. Administrative records are obtained through completed entry/exit forms at national frontiers, international airports and seaports. However, these data tend not to be tabulated, published or otherwise disseminated or classified by sex. Refugee-receiving countries have administrative data on refugees admitted into the country; however, these generally are not disaggregated by sex.

Source table

Table 27.1. Immigrants by sex, age group and migration category

	Immigrants				Population		
	Women	Men	Total		Women	Men	Total
Age group							
0–14							
15–24							
25–49							
50–64							
65+							
Total							
Migration category							
Overseas workers							
Permanent immigrants							
Refugees							
Total							

Technical note: State if all foreign-born are classified as immigrants.
Source: Give full citations for population censuses used.
Note: This table will have to be compiled separately for each year covered by the analysis.

Working tables

Table 27.2. Immigration rates by sex and age group

Age group	Women	Men	Total
0–14			
15–24			
25–49			
50–64			
65+			
Total			

Technical note: State if all foreign-born are classified as immigrants.
Source: Give full citations for population censuses used.
Note: This table will have to be constructed separately for each year covered by the analysis.

Table 27.3. Percentage distribution of immigrants by sex, age group and migration category

	Women	Men	Total
Age group			
0–14			
15–24			
25–49			
50–64			
65+			
Total	100	100	100
Migration category			
Overseas workers			
Permanent immigrants			
Refugees			
Total	100	100	100

Technical note: State if all foreign-born are classified as immigrants.
Source: Give full citations for population censuses used.
Note: This table will have to be constructed separately for each year covered by the analysis.

Table 27.4. Sex composition of immigrants by sex, age group and migration category *(percentage)*

	women	men
Age group		
0–14		
15–24		
25–49		
50–64		
65+		
Total		
Migration category		
Overseas workers		
Permanent immigrants		
Refugees		
Total		

Technical note: State if all foreign-born are classified as immigrants.
Source: Give full citations for population censuses used.
Note: This table will have to be constructed separately for each year covered by the analysis.

Additional indicators or classifications

Analysis of foreign-born women and men could also examine the age, marital status and economic activity status of migrants. Percentage distribution of immigrants according to duration of stay may also be presented.

Likely problems

Where census or survey data do not provide data specifically on international migration, the data may be derived from information on place of birth by defining all foreign-born as immigrants. This definition only captures lifetime migration but not return migrants. The data on refugees are provided mainly by governments of asylum countries based on their own records and methods of estimation but may generally not be disaggregated by sex.

Interpretation

International migration has acquired increasing importance with the widening gaps in demographic growth and economic progress among countries. Census information for the 1970s and early 1980s indicates that women accounted for almost half (48 per cent) of all lifetime international migrants. Yet considerable variations exist in women's share at national levels. The percentage of women among international migrants varied from 25 per cent in Bahrain to 69 per cent in Nepal (United Nations, 1994).

Women are outnumbered by men in international migration in developing regions — the sex ratio in the immigrant population is 80 women per 100 men. The ratio of women to men among the immigrant population tends to be low in labour-importing countries and is lowest in western Asia and northern Africa, where there are 65 women per 100 men. In South Africa, which has had a long history of importing labour, women accounted for as little as 35 per cent of all international immigrants living in the country in 1985 (United Nations, 1995b).

Worldwide, there are estimated to be 91 women per 100 men refugees. In Africa there are more women refugees than men; in other regions there are fewer women (United Nations, 1995b). The United Nations High Commissioner for Refugees (UNHCR) programme report on refugee populations by sex shows that women outnumbered men in three of twelve countries for which data are available; they almost equalled men in three other countries and were less numerous in the remaining six countries (United Nations High Commissioner for Refugees, 1994). Recent registration efforts in Kenya, Rwanda and Sri Lanka show the significant dominance in proportions of either sex in the refugee population. Women are slightly outnumbered by men in three refugee camps in Kenya, with 49 per cent of refugees being women. In Rwanda, 52 per cent of the refugees of 25 camps are women, and in Sri Lanka 51 per cent of refugees in six camps are women (special report of UNHCR).

Analysis of the data might attempt to discern:

- What category of people are dominant among the immigrant population?

- Among which age groups is immigration most popular among women and men?

- Are immigrants predominantly women or men?

- What are the relative proportions of women and men among refugees? Among overseas workers?

Access to water, sanitation and electricity

Series A: **Percentage of households with (or without) access to specific types of water, sanitation, light and cooking fuel, total and by sex of household head, for urban and rural areas**

Formula

$$\frac{\text{Number of urban (rural) households with access to facility } i}{\text{Total number of urban (rural) households}} \times 100$$

$$\frac{\begin{array}{c}\text{Number of urban (rural) households headed} \\ \text{by women (men) with access to facility } i\end{array}}{\text{Total number of urban (rural) households headed by women (men)}} \times 100$$

Series B: **Percentage of women-headed among urban (rural) households with (or without) access to specific types of water, sanitation, light and cooking fuel**

Formula

$$\frac{\begin{array}{c}\text{Number of urban (rural) households} \\ \text{with facility } i \text{ headed by women}\end{array}}{\text{Total number of urban (rural) households with facility } i} \times 100$$

Series C: **Percentage of urban (rural) household population of either sex with (or without) access to specific types of water, sanitation, light and cooking fuel**

Formula

$$\frac{\text{Women (men) living in urban (rural) households with facility } i}{\text{Total population of urban (rural) women (men)}} \times 100$$

Policy relevance

Women in developing regions face extra hardships and burdens unknown to women in developed areas, who take for granted their access to safe water, sanitation and electricity. Populations in the developed regions had universal access to safe water and sanitation facilities by the late 1960s. By contrast, developing regions face enormous problems in the availability of basic services. While urban households are more likely than rural to have basic services, substantial numbers of urban households still lack access. It is women who often must cope more directly with the unsafe conditions created by these problems.

Data sources

Population and housing censuses and household surveys are the major sources of information on the services available to household members. In some countries, the housing census may be supplemented by special studies. The degree of detail varies from country to country, depending on the significance placed on the need for such information.

Source table

Table 28.1. Number of households and household population by sex, access to water, sanitation and electricity and types of facilities, for urban and rural areas

Amenity	Number of households			Household population		
	Women-headed	Men-headed	Total	Women	Men	Total
Urban						
Access to water						
With piped water inside house						
With piped water within 100 metres of house						
Without piped water within 100 metres of house						
Total						
Access to sanitation						
With own toilet						
Without own toilet						
Total						
Main source of lighting						
Electricity						
Other						
Total						
Main source of cooking fuel						
Electricity						
Gas						
Kerosene						
Wood						
Other						
Total						
Rural						
Same categories as above						

Technical note: Piped water means that water is provided to the living quarters by pipes from a community-wide system or an individual installation, such as a pressure tank or pump. Piped water outside is intended to mean where the tap is within 100 metres of the door. A toilet is defined as an installation for the disposal of human excreta and indicates the availability of proper sanitation facilities. Whether it is situated inside or outside the living quarters is of varying significance according to the type being considered.

Source: Give full citation for population and housing census or household survey used.

Note: This table will have to be compiled separately for each year covered by the analysis.

Working tables

Table 28.2. Percentage distribution of women-headed, men-headed and all households by access to water, sanitation and electricity and types of facilities, for urban and rural areas

Amenity	Urban households			Rural households		
	Women-headed	Men-headed	All	Women-headed	Men-headed	All
Access to water						
With piped water inside house						
With piped water within 100 metres of house						
Without piped water within 100 metres of house						
Total	100	100	100	100	100	100
Access to sanitation						
With own toilet						
Without own toilet						
Total	100	100	100	100	100	100
Main source of lighting						
Electricity						
Other						
Total	100	100	100	100	100	100
Main source of cooking fuel						
Electricity						
Gas						
Kerosene						
Wood						
Other						
Total	100	100	100	100	100	100

Technical note: Note definitions for access to each amenity.

Source: Give full citation for population and housing census or household survey used.

Note: This table will have to be constructed separately for each year covered by the analysis.

Table 28.3. Percentage distribution of female, male and total household population by access to water, sanitation and electricity and types of facilities, for urban and rural areas

Amenity	Urban population			Rural population		
	Female	Male	Total	Female	Male	Total
Access to water						
With piped water inside house						
With piped water within 100 metres of house						
Without piped water within 100 metres of house						
Total	100	100	100	100	100	100
Access to sanitation						
With own toilet						
Without own toilet						
Total	100	100	100	100	100	100
Main source of lighting						
Electricity						
Other						
Total	100	100	100	100	100	100
Main source of cooking fuel						
Electricity						
Gas						
Kerosene						
Wood						
Other						
Total	100	100	100	100	100	100

Technical note: Note definitions for access to each amenity.

Source: Give full citation for population and housing census or household survey used.

Note: This table will have to be constructed separately for each year covered by the analysis.

Table 28.4. Percentage of women-headed households among those with and without access to water, sanitation and electricity, for urban and rural areas

Amenity	Urban	Rural
Access to water		
With piped water inside house		
With piped water within 100 metres of house		
Without piped water within 100 metres of house		
Total		
Access to sanitation		
With own toilet		
Without own toilet		
Total		
Main source of lighting		
Electricity		
Other		
Total		
Main source of cooking fuel		
Electricity		
Gas		
Kerosene		
Wood		
Other		
Total		

Technical note: Note definitions for access to each amenity.

Source: Give full citation for population and housing census or household survey used.

Note: This table will have to be constructed separately for each year covered by the analysis.

Additional indicators or classifications

For water supply several distance categories can be introduced or types of water sources other than piped (such as well, bore-hole, river). Similarly, toilet facilities can be categorized by the variety of types available in the country (e.g., water-closet, manually disposed, pit-latrine).

Likely problems

Although the information may have been collected in a survey or census inquiry about housing conditions, it may not have been tabulated according to the above format. Even if the information by household is available, already tabulated, it may not be disaggregated by sex of household head. Data may be presented in the publication without this breakdown if no additional tabulations can be obtained. It is generally assumed that women have the primary responsibility in these three areas and are more likely to be burdened by the absence of adequate water supply and sanitation.

Interpretation

Expanding access to adequate sanitation has generally been much slower than to piped water. Nearly 3 billion people still live without adequate sanitation. About a third of the developing world's population had access to proper sanitation facilities in the latter half of the 1980s. Rural-urban disparities remained wide. The coverage of sanitation facilities in urban and rural areas of developing countries was 74 per cent and 42 per cent, respectively, in 1990. In Africa 68 per cent of the urban population had adequate sanitation while only 22 per cent of the rural population did. The coverage was even lower in south-eastern Asia, where 50 per cent of urban and 12 per cent of rural populations had adequate sanitation (World Health Organization, 1992).

Coverage levels for safe drinking water were relatively higher. In Latin America, 85 per cent of the urban and 62 per cent of the rural population had piped water by the end of 1990. The corresponding proportions were 79 per cent and 32 per cent in Africa; 73 per cent and 64 per cent for south-eastern Asia; 71 per cent and 64 per cent in the western Pacific (World Health Organization, 1992).

The following types of comparisons can be made:

- Compare proportions of rural and urban households/population with specific kinds of basic facilities, such as safe drinking water, adequate sanitation, electricity as a source of light, woodfuel, etc.

- Differences in percentage distribution of women- and men-headed households with basic water and sanitation facilities.

• Differences in the presence of basic facilities between women-headed households in urban and rural areas; and between men-headed households in urban and rural areas.

• Are the gaps in the presence of basic facilities between women- and men-headed households wider or smaller in urban relative to rural areas?

Similarly for total populations, comparisons may be made between women's and men's access to adequate water and sanitation facilities by analysing:

• Differences between the distributions of women and men with the various types of facilities in the households in which they live, in urban and rural areas or in the country as a whole.

• Differences between distributions of urban and rural women, and between urban and rural men.

References and further reading

United Nations (1980). *Patterns of Urban and Rural Population Growth.* Sales No. E.79.XIII.9.

_____ (1991). *The World's Women 1970–1990: Trends and Statistics.* Sales No. E.90.XVII.3.

_____ (1993a). *Internal Migration of Women in Developing Countries. Proceedings of the United Nations Expert Group Meeting on the Feminization of Internal Migration. Aguascalientes, Mexico, 22–25 October 1991.* Sales No. E.94.XIII.3.

_____ (1993b). *World Population Monitoring, 1993—With a Special Report on Refugees.* Sales No. E.95.XIII.8.

_____ (1993c). World Urbanization Prospects: The 1992 Revision Sales No. E.92.XIII.11.

_____ (1994). *International Migration Policies and the Status of Female Migrants. Proceedings of the United Nations Expert Group Meeting on International Migration Policies and the Status of Female Migration. San Maniato, Italy, 28–31 March 1990.* Sales No. **E.95.XIII.10.**

_____ (1995a). *World Urbanization Prospects: The 1994 Revision.* Sales No. E.95.XIII.12.

_____ (1995b). *The World's Women 1995: Trends and Statistics.* Sales No. E.95.XVII.2.

_____ Economic Commission for Africa (1994). *Patterns, Causes and Consequences for Development Planning of Female Migration in Selected ECA Member States.* ECA/POP/TP/94(3b)/2.

United Nations High Commissioner for Refugees (1994). *Populations of Concern to UNHCR: A Statistical Overview 1994.* Geneva.

World Health Organization (1981). *Drinking Water and Sanitation, 1981–1990: A Way to Health (As at December 1985).* Geneva.

_____ (1992). *The International Drinking Water Supply and Sanitation Decade: End of Decade Review (As at December 1990).* Geneva.

WORK AND THE ECONOMY

Time use

Series A:	**Average hours spent by women and men in economic activities; unpaid housework**
Formula	$$\frac{\text{Total hours spent by women (men) on activities in category } i}{\text{Total number of women (men) counted}}$$
Series B:	**Women's and men's share of hours worked in economic activities; unpaid housework**
Formula	$$\frac{\text{Hours spent by women (men) on activity } i}{\text{Total hours spent by women and men on activity } i} \times 100$$

Broad groups of activities are used, such as economic activities—market production and non-market production; unpaid housework—meal preparation, child care, shopping, house maintenance (repairs, cleaning, laundry, gardening), other household chores, volunteer services, personal care and free time.

Policy relevance

The work of women contributes substantially to the well-being of families, communities and the nation and needs to be recognized in policies for credit, income and family security. However, much of the work of women is done within the household and is inadequately measured, even when it is economic. Time-use statistics provide a way to assess the different activities of women and men without being forced into the economic/non-economic dichotomy of national accounting.

Data sources

The main source of time-use statistics is generally special surveys designed for the purpose of collecting this type of data. An increasing number of developed countries are conducting time-use surveys as part of the official statistics. In developing countries, these statistics are not generally available in official statistics, though some time-use studies have been done mainly at the community level. Although limited, the studies that have been done show clearly the importance of these data in understanding women's and men's daily lives and work.

Source table

Table 29.1. Time spent by women and men in selected activities (hours per week), for total, urban and rural areas

Activity	Total		Urban		Rural	
	Women	Men	Women	Men	Women	Men
Economic activities						
Market production						
Non-market production						
Non-economic activities						
Preparing meals						
Child care						
Shopping						
House maintenance						
Other household chores						
Volunteer work						
Other (non-work activities)						
Personal care						
Free time						
Total number of hours						
Total number of persons surveyed						

Technical note: See International Labour Organization, *Surveys of the Economically Active Population, Employment and Underemployment: An ILO Manual on Concepts and Methods* (Geneva, 1990), chap. 1, for an explanation of the economic activity framework in the context of the system of national accounts (SNA); and John Wilson, *Time Use Pilot Survey, Sydney, May–June 1987*, Information Paper, Catalogue No. 4111.1 (Sydney, Australian Bureau of Statistics, 1987), for an example of an activities classification scheme.

Source: Give full citations for national reports and studies used.

Note: This table will have to be compiled separately for each year covered by the analysis.

Working tables

Table 29.2. Average time spent by women and men in selected activities (hours per week), for total, urban and rural areas

	Total		Urban		Rural	
Activity	Women	Men	Women	Men	Women	Men
Economic activities						
Market production						
Non-market production						
Non-economic activities						
Preparing meals						
Child care						
Shopping						
House maintenance						
Other household chores						
Volunteer work						
Other (non-work) activities						
Personal care						
Free time						

Technical note: See International Labour Organization, *Surveys of the Economically Active Population, Employment and Underemployment: An ILO Manual on Concepts and Methods* (Geneva, 1990), chap. 1, for an explanation of the economic activity framework in the context of the system of national accounts (SNA).

Source: Give full citations for national reports and studies used.

Note: This table will have to be constructed separately for each year covered by the analysis.

Table 29.3. Percentage distribution of time spent (hours per week) by sex and type of activity, for total, urban and rural areas

Activity	Total		Urban		Rural	
	Women	Men	Women	Men	Women	Men
Economic activities						
Market production						
Non-market production						
Non-economic activities						
Preparing meals						
Child care						
Shopping						
House maintenance						
Other household chores						
Volunteer work						
Other (non-work) activities						
Personal care						
Free time						
Total	100	100	100	100	100	100

Technical note: See International Labour Organization, *Surveys of the Economically Active Population, Employment and Underemployment: An ILO Manual on Concepts and Methods* (Geneva, 1990), chap. 1, for an explanation of the economic activity framework in the context of the system of national accounts (SNA).
Source: Give full citations for national reports and studies used.
Note: This table will have to be constructed separately for each year covered by the analysis.

Table 29.4. Women's and men's share of hours worked in selected activities, for total, urban and rural areas *(percentage)*

Activity	Total		Urban		Rural	
	Women	Men	Women	Men	Women	Men
Economic activities						
Market production						
Non-market production						
Non-economic activities						
Preparing meals						
Child care						
Shopping						
House maintenance						
Other household chores						
Volunteer work						
Other (non-work) activities						
Personal care						
Free time						

Technical note: See International Labour Organization, *Surveys of the Economically Active Population, Employment and Underemployment: An ILO Manual on Concepts and Methods* (Geneva, 1990), chap. 1, for an explanation of the economic activity framework in the context of the system of national accounts (SNA).
Source: Give full citations for national reports and studies used.
Note: This table will have to be constructed separately for each year covered by the analysis.

Additional indicators or classifications

In developing countries, time-use indicators should be compiled for urban and rural areas separately. Comparisons between women's and men's shares and average time allocations for different activities are a useful way of analysing changes in the sex division of roles in society and in the household.

The percentage distribution of time allocated to the different activities could also be presented separately for employed and non-economically active women and men, or for different age groups of the young and adult populations. In developed countries time-use studies are often carried out at 10-year intervals, thus making it possible to analyse trends.

Likely problems

If time-use studies are not available in official statistics, priority should be placed on locating any relevant data in academic and research institutions. Since data from developing countries tend to be from small local studies, particular attention should be given to documentation of the characteristics of the population studied (the number studied, age groups, place of residence, etc.), as they affect the interpretation of the data and comparability of different survey results. The unit of measurement may be either hours per day or hours per week.

There is often some confusion about the meaning of the term "unpaid work". It has been variously used to refer to (a) work done for members of the household or family, such as housework, child care and family-related services not recognized in national accounting as economic activity; (b) subsistence and other non-market activities such as volunteer work; (c) work in family enterprises for the market. To avoid confusion, the term "unpaid housework" should be used only to refer to the first category of unpaid work described above. Source documentation should always be reviewed carefully to ascertain the actual terms and their definition used in a given data set. (See United Nations, 1990b, for further discussion on time-use studies.)

Interpretation

Studies for selected countries, mainly in developed countries, show total hours worked by women exceed men's by at least two hours per week, and often 5–10 hours per week; and in a few countries women and men work almost the same number of hours (United Nations, 1991, pp. 81–82, and 1995a, pp. 105–106). There has been a decline in the share of time devoted to total work (paid and unpaid) by economically active women and men over the 1961–1992 period. During this period, the share of time devoted to paid work decreased for those employed full-time, while time allocated by women to unpaid work decreased whether or not they were employed, but increased significantly for employed men (United Nations, 1995a, p. 106).

Paid work dominates men's time in all countries for which data are available, while unpaid household work dominates women's time everywhere except Finland and some of the Baltic and eastern European countries. In most countries women spend almost twice as much time as men on unpaid housework and nine times as much in Japan (United Nations, 1995a, p. 106).

In many poor developing areas, women and girls spend three to five more hours per week than men in unpaid subsistence activities such as carrying water and wood, and growing and processing primary agricultural products for their families. In addition, they spend 20 to 30 more hours per week than men on unpaid housework (United Nations, 1995a, pp. 108-109).

The notion that women have a double burden may be tested by examining the differences between the total of women's and men's time allocated to work (economic and non-economic activities):

- What is the relative proportion of time spent by women and men in non-market compared with market activities? How does this differ from urban to rural areas?

- What are the differences between men and women in the time spent in economic activity and unpaid housework?

- What are women's and men's share in unpaid house work? How do relative shares in activities such as preparing meals, child care, shopping and other types of housework differ?

Economic participation and unemployment

Series A: Economic activity rates of women and men, by age group

Formula
$$\frac{\text{Economically active women (men) aged } (x, x + n)}{\text{Population of women (men) aged } (x, x + n)} \times 100$$

Series B: Share of women and men among the economically active population, by age group

Formula
$$\frac{\text{Economically active women (men) aged } (x, x + n)}{\text{Economically active population aged } (x, x + n)} \times 100$$

Series C: Unemployment rate by age group

Formula
$$\frac{\text{Unemployed women (men) aged } (x, x + n)}{\text{Economically active women (men) aged } (x, x + n)} \times 100$$

Policy relevance

Economic activity and unemployment rates are needed to monitor the extent to which women and men are engaged in production, to explore and interpret underlying differences in participation rates of women and men and to project the size of the labour force, based on the estimated size and composition of the population. Access to paid work is crucial to achieving self-reliance and ensuring the well-being of dependent family members.

Data sources

In nearly all countries, population censuses and household surveys are the usual sources of statistics on the economically and non-economically active population. However, in some developing countries comprehensive household survey data are unlikely to be available in sufficient detail except from one or two inter-censal surveys.

Source table

Table 30.1. Economically active, non-economically active and total population aged 15 and over by sex and age group, for total, urban and rural areas

| Age group | Economically active | | | | Non-economically active | | Total population | |
| | Employed | | Unemployed | | | | | |
	Women	Men	Women	Men	Women	Men	Women	Men
Total (urban and rural)								
15–19								
20–24								
25–29								
30–34								
35–39								
40–44								
45–49								
50–54								
55–59								
60–64								
65+								
15+								
Urban								
Same age groups as above								
Rural								
Same age groups as above								

Source: Give full citations for population censuses or household surveys used.

Note: This table will have to be compiled separately for each year covered by the analysis.

Working tables

Table 30.2. Economic activity rates of women and men by age group, for total, urban and rural areas (*percentage*)

Age group	Total		Urban		Rural	
	Women	Men	Women	Men	Women	Men
15–19						
20–24						
25–29						
30–34						
35–39						
40–44						
45–49						
50–54						
55–59						
60–64						
65+						
15+						

Source: Compiled from table yy in (cite publication in full).
Note: This table will have to be constructed separately for each year covered by the analysis.

Table 30.3. Women's share of the economically active population aged 15 and over by age group, for total, urban and rural areas (*percentage*)

Age group	Total	Urban	Rural
15–19			
20–24			
25–29			
30–34			
35–39			
40–44			
45–49			
50–54			
55–59			
60–64			
65+			
15+			

Source: Give full citations for population censuses or household surveys used.
Note: This table will have to be constructed separately for each year covered by the analysis.

Table 30.4. Unemployment rates of women and men by age group, for total, urban and rural areas (*percentage*)

Age group	Total		Urban		Rural	
	Women	Men	Women	Men	Women	Men
15–19						
20–24						
25–29						
30–34						
35–39						
40–44						
45–49						
50–54						
55–59						
60–64						
65+						
15+						

Source: Compiled from table yy in (cite publication in full).

Note: This table will have to be constructed separately for each year covered by the analysis.

Additional indicators or classifications

Presentation of data by five-year age groups makes for a clear but relatively detailed line graph. If this is not possible, the charts can be produced with 10-year age groupings. Broad groups, corresponding, for example, to youth (15–24), reproductive ages (15–44 or 49), 45–59, and the elderly (60+), may also be used if the purpose is to study these particular or other age groups. The age distributions of economically active and unemployed women and men may also be computed. The participation rates among those under age 15 and those 60–64 and 65–70 may also be of interest.

Likely problems

The concept of "economically active population" covers several disparate components such as employed and unemployed, paid and unpaid workers, full-time and part-time, regular, seasonal and casual workers (United Nations, 1993). The definition used may be different from one survey or census period to the next, and therefore reports and other relevant documentation on the surveys, such as questionnaires and interviewer's manuals, should be reviewed.

There are difficulties in identifying economically active women, and these tend to be more pronounced in rural areas, where most households are engaged in agriculture. The activities of women and girls as unpaid family workers in agriculture are easily overlooked. Difficulties also occur in urban areas where modern labour force conditions are changing the traditional roles of women and informal sector activities are predominant. In countries where these situations apply, it is important to call attention to the potential underestimation of women's labour force participation.

Unemployment is difficult to define and measure among poor urban and rural populations, especially for those heavily dependent on subsistence agriculture. Few data are available for the poorer countries of Africa and Asia. In many of these countries the measurement of unemployment still excludes people who, though available for work, may not be seeking work for a variety of reasons, either because they believe none is available or do not have easy access to formal job-search channels (United Nations, 1995a). Because this affects women more than men, this way of measuring unemployment works against enumerating women as unemployed and the International Labour Organization (ILO) has recommended that the criterion concerning those seeking employment be relaxed.

Interpretation

Urban growth is providing new economic opportunities for women in Latin America and the Caribbean. The recorded economic participation rates for urban women are twice those for rural women. By contrast, more limited urban growth and development in Africa and much of Asia over the past two decades has not offered women greater opportunities in the wage labour market. Urban employment opportunities have been primarily reserved for men. Many development policies have favoured men's production and jobs over those of women. Most Asian and African women remain and work in rural areas.

According to estimates made by the ILO, adult women's economic activity rates for 1994 ranged from 8 per cent in Algeria to 78 per cent in the Niger; men's rates were between 61 per cent in Samoa and 93 per cent in Burkina Faso, Burundi, the Niger and Rwanda. While the proportion of economically active men has declined everywhere, the gaps between women's and men's recorded participation remain wide. These gaps are widest in northern Africa, where women's economic activity rate averaged 21 per cent as against men's 75 per cent; western Asia, 30 per cent for women versus 77 per cent for men; and Latin America, 34 per cent for women compared with 82 per cent for men (United Nations, 1995a).

The age pattern of men's economic participation is almost universal. It increases sharply between ages 15 and 25 (or 30), stabilizes until around age 50 (or later in some countries) and declines thereafter. The age pattern of women's economic activity is more varied, reflecting how changes in the life cycle affect women's participation. Some countries have an early peak around age 20 with a decline thereafter, some have a late peak around age 50, and others have a plateau between ages 25 and 50 (United Nations, 1995a).

To analyse differences and similarities between women's and men's economic activity status:

- Compare activity rates of women and men for ages 15+ to see the gap between the sexes. How does the gap differ between urban and rural areas? How has it changed over time?

- Is women's share of the economically active population close to 50 per cent (i.e., between 45 and 55 per cent)?

- Examine the age patterns of participation for women and men. At what ages do the activity rates for women and men peak and when do they decline?

- In what ways are the age patterns and activity levels changing for women and men?

- Are the age patterns changing over time? Are they more similar or more differentiated?

- What are some of the plausible explanations for these differences and trends?

Non-economically active

Series A: **Percentages of women and men not economically active, by age group.**

Formula

$$\frac{\text{Non-economically active women (men) aged } (x, x+n)}{\text{Women (men) aged } (x, x+n)} \times 100$$

Series B: **Percentages of non-economically active women and men for selected age groups, by functional category**

Formula

$$\frac{\text{Number of women (men) aged } (x, x+n) \text{ non-active for reason } i}{\text{Number of non-economically active women (men) aged } (x, x+n)} \times 100$$

Series C: **Sex composition within the functional categories of non-economic activity**

Formula

$$\frac{\text{Women (men) aged } (x, x+n) \text{ non-active for reason } i}{\text{Women and men aged } (x, x+n) \text{ non-active in functional category } i} \times 100$$

Functional categories of non-activity may include home-making, studying, income recipient, etc.

Policy relevance

The numbers and proportions of non-economically active women and men may be used to identify population categories that are of concern for social policies with respect to employment, education, social assistance and other programmes.

Data sources

In nearly all countries, population censuses and household surveys are the usual sources of statistics on the economically and non-economically active populations. In some developing countries, however, comprehensive household survey data are unlikely to be available in sufficient detail except from one or two inter-censal surveys.

Source table

Table 31.1. Total population and non-economically active population by functional category, age group and sex, for total, urban and rural areas

Category of non-economically active	15+		15–19		20–24		25–49		50–59		60+	
	W	M	W	M	W	M	W	M	W	M	W	M
Total (urban and rural)												
Population												
Not economically active												
Home-making												
Studying												
Receiving income												
Other												
Total												
Urban												
Same categories as above												
Rural												
Same categories as above												

Source: Give full citations for population censuses or household surveys used.

Note: This table will have to be compiled separately for each year covered by the analysis.

Working tables

Table 31.2. Economically non-active rates by sex and age group, for total, urban and rural areas
(*percentage*)

Age group	Total		Urban		Rural	
	Women	Men	Women	Men	Women	Men
15–19						
20–24						
25–49						
50–59						
60+						
Total (15+)						

Source: Give full citations for population censuses or household surveys used.

Note: This table will have to be constructed separately for each year covered by the analysis.

Table 31.3. Percentage distribution of the non-economically active population by functional category of non-activity, sex and age group, for total, urban and rural areas

Category of non-activity	15+		15–19		20–24		25–49		50–59		60+	
	W	M	W	M	W	M	W	M	W	M	W	M
Total (urban and rural)												
Home-making												
Studying												
Receiving income												
Other												
Total	100	100	100	100	100	100	100	100	100	100	100	100
Urban												
Same categories as above												
Rural												
Same categories as above												

Source: Give full citations for population censuses or household surveys used.

Note: This table will have to be constructed separately for each year covered by the analysis.

Table 31.4. Percentage of women among the non-economically active population by functional category of non-activity and age group, for total, urban and rural areas

Category of non-activity	15+	15–19	20–24	25–49	50–59	60+
Total (urban and rural)						
Home-making						
Studying						
Receiving income						
Other						
Total						
Urban						
Same categories as above						
Rural						
Same categories as above						

Source: Give full citations for population censuses or household surveys used.

Note: This table will have to be constructed separately for each year covered by the analysis.

Additional indicators or classifications

Family structure, defined by a combination of presence of children and/or spouse, affects women's participation or non-participation in economic activity. Cross-classifications with the number and presence of children under school-going age might provide some explanation for the relatively low economic participation rates of women compared to men.

Likely problems

Statistical definitions, the language used, the order of questions and the time-reference period of the population census or household survey affect responses to inquiries concerning economic activity. Where women's economic activity is less regular than men's, a short reference period tends to exclude the former from being counted in the labour force.

The functional categories of the non-economically active population provide useful information for establishing dependency within households and are particularly relevant when examining the composition of households.

Interpretation

Data on the activity status of women and men in Sweden show that in 1994 about 20 per cent of women and 16 per cent of men aged 20–64 were not economically active (Statistics Sweden, 1995). The Botswana Labour Force Survey 1984/85 found that 18 per cent of women and 20 per cent of men were not economically active, and that half of the non-economically active women compared to two thirds of non-economically active men were students. In urban areas 35 per cent of women and 24 per cent of men were not working or not available for work; in rural areas, 37 and 32 per cent. Home duties claimed 38 and 44 per cent of the non-economically active women in urban and rural areas, respectively, as contrasted with 17 and 44 per cent of the men (United Nations, 1990b).

Women homemakers outnumbered economically active women in Lesotho, and 3 per cent of all homemakers were men (Lesotho, Bureau of Statistics, 1993). In some developing countries, there are no men classified as homemakers, for example in Morocco and Paraguay (1982), the Congo (1984), Kuwait and Turkey (1985) and Qatar (1986), as well as in some developed countries, including Denmark, Greece and Italy (1981) (United Nations, 1990a, table 37).

In Chile almost all non-economically active women aged 25–54 are homemakers, while at younger ages the main functional category is studying. In contrast, homemakers form a very small proportion of the non-economically active men of any age category, while for the age group 15–19 studying is the main functional category among the non-economically active (Chile, National Statistics Institute, 1995).

- At what ages is studying a major category of the non-economically active in the labour market for women and men?

- What is the major category of the non-economically active for women in the reproductive period? How does this differ from men and for other age groups?

- Which sex outnumbers the other in the different categories? How does this vary from one age group to another?

- At what ages are more than a quarter, one third or half of non-economically active women and men out of the labour force due to (a) studying, (b) home-making?

Status in employment and branch of industrial activity

Series A: Percentages of the economically active population by status in employment, for each sex

Formula $$\frac{\text{Economically active women (men) employed in status } i}{\text{Economically active women (men)}} \times 100$$

Series B: Percentages of the economically active population by branch of activity, for each sex

Formula $$\frac{\text{Economically active women (men) employed in branch of activity } j}{\text{Economically active women (men)}} \times 100$$

Series C: Percentages of the economically active population by branch of activity and status in employment, for each sex

Formula $$\frac{\text{Economically active women (men) employed in status } i \text{ and branch of activity } j}{\text{Economically active women (men) in branch of activity } j} \times 100$$

Series D: Sex composition of the economically active population in agriculture, industry and services (branch), by status in employment

Formula $$\frac{\text{Economically active women (men) in status } i \text{ and branch of activity } j}{\text{Economically active persons in status } i \text{ and branch of activity } j} \times 100$$

where employment status i can be classified as employees, employers, own-account workers (or self-employed), unpaid family workers, or others; and branch of activity j can be classified as agriculture, industry or services.

Policy relevance

Information on type or kind of economic activity is needed to study the economic and social structure of the labour force. Status in employment provides a statistical basis for describing workers' behaviour and conditions of work and for defining individuals' social class or socio-economic group (ILO, 1992b). The branches of industrial activity and their relative proportions among the economically active show the extent of changes in economic structure and the opportunities for women and men.

Data sources

Statistics on numbers employed and their characteristics, such as employment status and branch of industrial activity, are generally available from population censuses and surveys, economic censuses and surveys, agricultural censuses and surveys, and household surveys.

Source table

Table 32.1. Economically active population aged15 and over by employment status, branch of economic activity and sex, for total, urban and rural areas

Employment status	Agriculture		Industry		Services		Total	
	Women	Men	Women	Men	Women	Men	Women	Men
Total (urban and rural)								
Employer								
Own-account worker								
Employee								
Unpaid family worker								
Other/not stated								
Total								
Urban								
Same categories as above								
Rural								
Same categories as above								

Technical note: Note changes in definitions used in different censuses.

Source: Give full citations for population and economic censuses and surveys used.

Note: This table will have to be compiled separately for each year covered by the analysis.

Working tables

Table 32.2. Percentage distribution of the economically active population aged 15 and over by employment status, sex and branch of economic activity, for total, urban and rural areas

Employment status	Agriculture		Industry		Services		Total	
	Women	Men	Women	Men	Women	Men	Women	Men
Total (urban and rural)								
Employer								
Own-account worker								
Employee								
Unpaid family worker								
Other/not stated								
Total	100	100	100	100	100	100	100	100
Urban								
Same categories as above								
Rural								
Same categories as above								

Technical note: Note changes in definitions used in different censuses.
Source: Give full citations for population and economic censuses and surveys used.
Note: This table will have to be constructed separately for each year covered by the analysis.

Table 32.3. Sex composition of the economically active population aged 15 and over in each employment status and branch of economic activity, for total, urban and rural areas *(percentage)*

Employment status	Agriculture		Industry		Services		Total	
	Women	Men	Women	Men	Women	Men	Women	Men
Total (urban and rural)								
Employer								
Own-account worker								
Employee								
Unpaid family worker								
Other/not stated								
Total								
Urban								
Same categories as above								
Rural								
Same categories as above								

Technical note: Note changes in definitions used in different censuses.
Source: Give full citations for population and economic censuses and surveys used.
Note: This table will have to be constructed separately for each year covered by the analysis.

Additional indicators or classifications

The percentages may also be compiled to give the sectoral distributions of all statuses combined and within each of the statuses of employment (e.g., the proportion of employees in agriculture, industry or services, or the proportion of own-account workers in agriculture, industry or services). Using a more detailed classification of branch of activity with nine major groups and minor categories within each group will show better the areas of concentration of women and men. The nine groups are agriculture, hunting, forestry and fishing; mining and quarrying; manufacturing; electricity, gas and water supply; construction; wholesale/retail trade, hotels and restaurants; transport, storage and communications; financing, insurance, real estate and business services; community, social and personal services (United Nations, 1990c). For aggregate analysis, the nine major divisions are grouped into agriculture, industry and service sectors. In this grouping "agriculture" also covers hunting, forestry and fishing. "Industry" covers mining and quarrying [including oil production]; manufacturing; electricity, gas and water; and construction. "Services" covers wholesale and retail trade and restaurants and hotels; transport, storage and communication; financing, insurance, real estate and business services; and community, social and personal services (United Nations, 1991).

Likely problems

Due to biased reporting and mis-classification of women's activities, substantial numbers of women are reported as unpaid family workers as opposed to self-employed/own account workers, especially when they are employed on family farms. Furthermore, women's work in subsistence agriculture is often under-reported since this is often considered an extension of their domestic responsibilities. The quality of data varies from one source to another depending on the type of questions asked and the depth of interviewing. Census data are therefore not directly comparable to survey data on the economically active and their characteristics.

Employment status and branch of activity classifications are quite often produced for those who are currently employed and those unemployed who were previously employed. Check the population used before developing the indicators and take account of the coverage of population in the table title. The populations covered in the status in employment and branch of activity classifications differ from country to country. Some countries present this classification for the employed only; others include the unemployed who were previously employed.

Interpretation

In all regions except sub-Saharan Africa and south-eastern and southern Asia, a majority of women and men in the labour force are employees. In the developed regions in eastern Asia, about 80 per cent of the economically active women and men are employees. In contrast, in sub-Saharan Africa, 30 per cent of women and 40 per cent of men in the labour force are employees, and self-employment is the principal form of employment in many developing countries. In sub-Saharan Africa, 35 per cent of women and 41 per cent of men in the labour force are employers and own-account workers (United Nations, 1995a).

According to ILO estimates for 1994, three out of four economically active women in sub-Saharan Africa and at least one in two in southern Asia are found in the agricultural sector. In contrast, only a small fraction, less than two in ten of the economically active women in Latin America and the Caribbean and in the developed regions, work in agriculture. The important sector for women's employment in Latin America and the Caribbean and the developed regions, excluding eastern Europe, is services, which absorb over seven in ten economically active women (United Nations, 1995a).

Unpaid work in the Asia and Pacific region is highly prevalent in rural areas, and women are more likely than men to be engaged in the labour force as unpaid family workers. Much of the unpaid work in rural areas is in agriculture. In Thailand, 75 per cent of rural women in the labour force and 31 per cent of the rural male labour force are unpaid (Asian Development Bank, Center for International Research, 1993).

In Austria, at least 90 per cent of the economically active men and women in industry/manufacturing and services are employees; but only 9 per cent of women and 20 per cent of men are employees in the industry and services sectors. In contrast, 49 per cent of women and 69 per cent of men are self-employed in the agricultural labour force, while 44 per cent of women and 11 per cent of men are unpaid agricultural workers (Gross and others, 1994).

For analyses of women's and men's branch of activity and employment status the following questions may be considered:

- How are women and men distributed across employment statuses? Do these differ in any way from one branch of activity to another (e.g., agricultural compared with industry and services; or services compared with industry)?

- In which sector do employees tend to concentrate and in which do the self-employed tend to concentrate? Are these tendencies different for women and men?

- In which branch of activity (agriculture, industry, services) do women outnumber men? Which employs the most women and which the most men? How does this compare with women's share as employees and own-account workers in the different branches?

Occupational segregation

Series A:	Percentage distribution of the economically active population aged 15+ by major occupational group
Formula	$$\frac{\text{Economically active women (men) aged 15+ in each occupational group}}{\text{Total economically active women (men) aged 15+}} \times 100$$
Series B:	Sex composition within major occupational group
Formula	$$\frac{\text{Economically active women (men) in occupational group } i}{\text{Total economically active population}} \times 100$$

where occupational groups are as follows: legislators, senior officials and managers; professionals; technicians and associate professionals; clerks; service workers and shop and market sales workers; skilled agricultural and fishery workers; craft and related workers; plant and machine operators and assemblers; elementary occupations; armed forces.

Policy relevance

Women's and men's occupations are very different and the specific differences vary among regions and over time. There is a strong relationship between job segregation and lower pay levels for women. As the level, prestige and pay rise in the occupational hierarchy, so do the numbers of men.

Data sources

The major sources of data on the economically active population by occupation are the population census, labour force surveys and general household surveys. The classification of occupations is based on the International Standard Classification of Occupations (ISCO).

Source table

Table 33.1. Economically active population aged 15 and over by sex and major occupational group, 1970–1990

Major occupational group	1970			1980			1990		
	Women	Men	Total	Women	Men	Total	Women	Men	Total
Legislators									
Professionals									
Technicians									
Clerks									
Service workers									
Agricultural/ fishery workers									
Craft workers									
Machinists									
Elementary occupations									
Armed forces									
Other									
Total economically active									

Source: Give full citations for population censuses or labour force surveys used.

Note: The above occupational groups are from the International Standard Classification of Occupations (ISCO) as revised in 1988. Country classifications may differ in some cases and it is useful to note these differences in national tables.

Working tables

Table 33.2. Percentage distribution of the economically active women and men aged 15 and over by occupational group, 1970–1990

Major occupational group	1970		1980		1990	
	Women	Men	Women	Men	Women	Men
Legislators						
Professionals						
Technicians						
Clerks						
Service workers						
Agricultural/ fishery workers						
Craft workers						
Machinists						
Elementary occupations						
Armed forces						
Other						
Total	100	100	100	100	100	100

Source: Give full citations for population censuses or labour force surveys used.

Note: The above occupational groups are from the International Standard Classification of Occupations (ISCO) as revised in 1988. Country classifications may differ in some cases and it is useful to note these differences in national tables.

Table 33.3. Sex composition of occupational groups, 1970–1990
(percentage)

Major occupational group	1970		1980		1990	
	women	men	women	men	women	men
Legislators						
Professionals						
Technicians						
Clerks						
Service workers						
Agricultural/ fishery workers						
Craft and related workers						
Machinists						
Elementary occupations						
Armed forces						
Other						
Total economically active						

Source: Give full citations for population censuses or labour force surveys used.

Note: The above occupational groups are from the International Standard Classification of Occupations (ISCO) as revised in 1988. Country classifications may differ in some cases and it is useful to note these differences in national tables.

Additional indicators or classifications

More detailed classifications can be used for some of the major occupational groups in which there are either large groups of women or men, such as agricultural and service workers, or which consist of very different categories of workers, such as professionals and technicians (combining nurses with doctors). It is also useful to cross-classify occupational groups by employment status, such as employees, self-employed and unpaid family workers.

Likely problems

Though many jobs that are important from the standpoint of women are included in ISCO, these often appear at a rather low level of the classification. A classification by major or even sub-major groups will thus obscure many important characteristics of the structure of women's occupations. Every effort should be made to obtain the details of those basic data that show a significant division by sex. Specialized studies and publications are a useful supplement to the information contained in censuses.

Interpretation

The workplace is segregated by sex almost everywhere. Women are far under-represented in administrative and managerial occupations as well as in production and transport-related jobs. There are occupations such as nursing, typing and housekeeping where more than nine out of ten employees are women. Women hold well over half of the clerical jobs in the developed regions and in Latin America and the Caribbean, and over a third in sub-Saharan Africa and in Asia and the Pacific. In sub-Saharan Africa, the Caribbean and south-eastern Asia as well as eastern Europe, women account for more than half of the sales workers (United Nations, 1995a).

Even where women have secured their position in the labour market, they still face discrimination in terms of occupational segregation, career opportunities and level of salaries (United Nations, 1995b). Within an occupational group, women tend to be in less prestigious jobs. For example in 1990, more than one third of the professional and technical jobs in almost all regions were held by women (more than 50 per cent in Europe and the Caribbean) and these are mostly in lower-paid professional and technical occupations such as teaching (United Nations, 1991 and 1995a).

Most occupational categories group together many different jobs. Even where an occupational category appears to be sex-neutral, there is in fact sex segregation within the more specific job titles that comprise it. One study of certain firms in the United States revealed that most women were in jobs with completely different titles from men's. Only one tenth of the workers studied were in jobs that included both women and men (United Nations, 1991).

Questions to be addressed in the analysis of the data are:

- How are women and men distributed occupationally?

- In which specific occupations in the professional category are women concentrated and in which are men concentrated?

- In which occupational groups are women more or less likely to be engaged compared with men?

- Which of the occupational groups contain less than a quarter, a third or half or more women or men?

- In which occupational groups is the share of women or men between 40 and 60 per cent? Are these occupations big or small with respect to their relative size in the labour market as a whole (i.e., having a high proportion of all employed in the specific occupation)?

- Assess the degree of segregation of occupations. Which of the following typical patterns describes the situation in the country (United Nations, 1995a)?
  —Most occupations are either strongly women-dominated or male-dominated;
  —There are several men-dominated and women-dominated occupations as well as occupations with a more equal mix of women and men;
  —Women-dominated occupations are few, with relatively more men-dominated occupations and occupations with both women and men;
  —Most women workers are found in occupations with a moderately high proportion of women.

Wages and salaries

| Series A: | Women's average earnings or wage rate as a percentage of men's for selected occupations or branch of activity |

Series A: **Women's average earnings or wage rate as a percentage of men's for selected occupations or branch of activity**

Formula

$$\frac{\text{Average wage rate (or earnings) of women in occupation or branch } i}{\text{Average wage rate (or earnings) of men in occupation or branch } i} \times 100$$

Series B: **Women's average hours worked as a percentage of men's for selected occupations or branches of activity**

Formula

$$\frac{\text{Average hours worked by women in occupation or branch } i}{\text{Average hours worked by men in occupation or branch } i} \times 100$$

Policy relevance

Differences in women's and men's pay persist despite the fact that most developed countries have had equal pay laws since the 1960s or 1970s. Where the labour market is highly segregated, equal pay legislation tends to have little effect on wage differences. Broader legislation concerning equal opportunities in all spheres of work, such as equal access to occupational training and advancement, are potentially more effective in reducing the gap (United Nations, 1995a).

Data sources

Wages and salaries data come from different types of sources. Sample surveys or censuses of establishments are usually the source of data on average earnings and hours of work. In some countries, minimum wages and normal hours of work are from collective agreements or arbitral awards, relevant laws or regulations. Administrative records of bodies such as social security agencies and income/revenue tax services, where developed, also provide some information.

Source table

Table 34.1. Average wages and salaries of workers and average number of hours worked, for selected occupational and industrial groups, by sex of worker, 1970–1990

	Average wages/salary						Average hours worked					
	1970		1980		1990		1970		1980		1990	
	W	M	W	M	W	M	W	M	W	M	W	M
Occupational group												
Legislators												
Professionals												
Clerks												
Service workers and shop/market sales workers												
Craft and related Trade workers												
Industrial group												
Agriculture												
Non-agriculture												
Manufacturing												

Source: Give full citations for household or labour force surveys used.

Note: The above occupational groups are from the International Standard Classification of Occupations (ISCO) as revised in 1988. Country classifications may differ in some cases and it is useful to note these differences in national tables.

Working tables

Table 34.2. Women's average wages and hours of work as a percentage of men's in selected occupational and industrial groups, 1970–1990

	Women's average wages/salary as a percentage of men's			Hours worked by women as a percentage of men's		
	1970	1980	1990	1970	1980	1990
Occupational group						
Legislators						
Professionals						
Technicians						
Clerks						
Service workers and shop/market sales workers						
Craft and related Trade workers						
Industrial group						
Agriculture						
Non-agriculture						
Manufacturing						

Source: Give full citations for household or labour force surveys used.

Note: The above occupational groups are from the International Standard Classification of Occupations (ISCO) as revised in 1988. Country classifications may differ in some cases and it is useful to note these differences in national tables.

Additional indicators or classifications

Indicators may be compiled for combined occupation and branch of activity, such as managers in the agricultural, manufacturing or services branches of activity. Tabulations can also be presented for other sectoral classifications such as the institutional sector: civil service, public enterprises and private sector corporations.

Likely problems

Data on wages and salaries differ from source to source in terms of coverage, definition and methods of compilation. Statistics on wages can be expressed as wage rates or as earnings. Wage rates are the rates paid for normal time of work, comprising basic wages and salaries, cost-of-living allowances and other guaranteed and regularly paid allowances, but excluding overtime payments, bonuses and gratuities, etc. (ILO, 1987a).

Earnings are the remuneration in cash and in kind paid to employees at regular intervals for time worked or work done, together with remuneration for time not worked, such as for annual vacation, other paid leave or holidays before deductions (for taxes, social security, etc.), and excluding employees' contributions (ILO, 1987a).

These definitions make data collection from surveys and censuses difficult and statistics from these sources less reliable than from administrative sources.

Interpretation

Women receive less pay than men everywhere. This is in part because women hold low-level, low-paying positions in female-dominated jobs. Moreover, men are more likely to have regular full-time work and receive greater seniority and benefits (United Nations, 1991).

A review of data from 37 countries shows that in five of them women's average earnings in manufacturing industries was less than 60 per cent of men's earnings. In the Nordic countries, Australia and Italy, and also a few developing countries, the ratios are closer to parity. In these countries women's wages are more than 80 per cent those of men. Although the ratios of women's wages in manufacturing to men's have been increasing over the years, in a few of the 37 countries, women's wages are still only about half those of men, and in several others they were around 75 per cent relative to men's in the early 1990s (United Nations, 1995a).

In countries such as Australia, Belgium, Denmark, El Salvador, Finland, France, Greece, Myanmar, the Netherlands, New Zealand, Norway, Sri Lanka and Sweden, women's wages in manufacturing are between 75 and 92 per cent of men's (United Nations, 1995a).

Examples of questions to be addressed in the analysis are:

- What percentage of men's wages/earnings do women earn? Which occupational or industrial sector shows the biggest and which shows the smallest wage disparity between women and men?

- Are the ratios of women's and men's wages/earnings higher, lower or comparable with the ratios of their hours of work?

- Which occupations/industries show the highest ratios or most parity between women and men in hours worked?

Informal sector employment

Series A: Percentages of economically active women and men employed in the informal sector, by branch of activity

Formula

$$\frac{\text{Women (men) employed in informal sector in branch } i}{\text{Economically active women (men) in branch } i} \times 100$$

Series B: Sex composition of informal sector workers by branch of activity

Formula

$$\frac{\text{Women (men) employed in informal sector branch } i}{\text{All employed in informal sector branch } i} \times 100$$

where branch refers to manufacturing, transport, services, other and total non-agriculture.

Policy relevance

The informal sector is usually the fallback position for women who are excluded from paid employment. It also plays an important role in building skills and preparing some individuals for either formal or informal sector employment. The dominant aspect of the informal sector is self-employment. It is an important source of livelihood for women in the developing world, especially in those areas where cultural norms bar them from work outside the home or where, because of conflict with household responsibilities, they cannot undertake regular employee working hours.

Data sources

The main sources of statistics on the economically active population and its characteristics are censuses and surveys of population, labour force surveys and other types of household surveys. When data from population censuses and general labour force surveys are used, the classification of informal sector workers can be estimated from status in employment. In view of the increasing recognition of the importance of the informal sector, developing countries are paying more attention to this sector. Surveys on the informal sector have been carried out in some countries and these provide direct estimates of employment in the sector.

Source table

Table 35.1. Economically active population aged 15 and over and number in the informal sector by branch of economic activity and sex, for total, urban and rural areas

Branch of economic activity	Total economically active population 15+			Number in the informal sector	
	Women	Men		Women	Men
Total (urban and rural)					
Agriculture					
Manufacturing					
Transport					
Services					
Total					
Urban					
Same categories as above					
Rural					
Same categories as above					

Technical note: Note changes in definitions used in different censuses.

Source: Give full citations for population and economic censuses and surveys used.

Note: This table will have to be compiled separately for each year covered by the analysis.

Working tables

Table 35.2. Percentage of the informal sector labour force by sex and branch of economic activity, for total, urban and rural areas

Branch of economic activity	Total		Urban		Rural	
	Women	Men	Women	Men	Women	Men
Manufacturing						
Transport						
Services						
Total						

Technical note: Note changes in definitions used in different censuses.

Source: Give full citations for population and economic censuses and surveys used.

Note: This table will have to be constructed separately for each year covered by the analysis.

Table 35.3. Percentage of the informal sector labour force that is female, by branch of economic activity, for total, urban and rural areas

Branch of economic activity	Total	Urban	Rural
Manufacturing			
Transport			
Services			
Total			

Technical note: Note changes in definitions used in different censuses.

Source: Give full citations for population and economic censuses and surveys used.

Note: This table will have to be constructed separately for each year covered by the analysis.

Additional indicators or classifications

Further disaggregation of branch of activity may be used, such as separating retail and wholesale trade from other services. The percentage distributions can be computed using non-agricultural informal as the base for the distribution of women and men. Distributions can also be presented by employment status of those involved (i.e., employers, own-account workers, employees, unpaid family workers), by occupations or by combined occupation/branch of activity groups.

Likely problems

The definition of the informal sector may vary from one source to another, especially when dealing with ad hoc surveys. Some definitions restrict coverage to non-agricultural enterprises; some include subsistence agriculture; others cover employers, self-employed and unpaid workers; while others include all categories of workers in enterprises that have specified characteristics, such as size as defined by maximum number of persons employed (see ILO, 1992b.) When data from special informal sector surveys are used, the definition should be carefully noted and comparisons between sources should be undertaken with care. When only population census and household/labour force survey data are available, the coverage may need to be restricted to self-employed and unpaid family workers unless, as is the case in some countries, the classification of status in employment allows for distinguishing employers and employees according to size of (number of persons employed in) the enterprise.

Interpretation

In many countries the informal sector provides women with the only opportunity for work in the face of limited access to formal sector wage employment. Yet, in this sector work is hard and far less secure and the pay is generally below the minimum wage (United Nations, 1995b).

However, women and men must turn to the informal sector when employment is scarce (United Nations, 1995a). Two thirds of urban women work in the informal sector in west Africa. Most women are in personal services and in a narrow range of occupations in the informal sector (United Nations, 1995b).

The informal sector is often essential for the economic survival of women. In particular, poor women engage in petty trading or in such home-based industries as beer-brewing, soap-making and tailoring. In Zambia, for example, a study found that the importance of women's informal sector earnings to total family income increased dramatically in the 1980s (United Nations, 1991).

More than a third of the economically active women in a number of countries of sub-Saharan Africa work in the non-agricultural informal sector, and as many as 72 per cent in

Zambia. The percentage varies widely in Asia, from as low as 7 per cent in the Syrian Arab Republic and Turkey to 65 per cent in Indonesia. In Honduras, Jamaica and Zambia there are more women than men in the informal sector outside agriculture, while in Egypt, Iraq, Qatar and Turkey women constitute 5 per cent or less of the non-agricultural informal sector (United Nations, 1995a).

The percentage of women in informal sector transport is extremely low in all 22 countries studied, the highest proportion being 11 per cent in Zambia. However, women outnumber men in informal sector services in Brazil, the Congo, the Gambia, Honduras, Indonesia, Jamaica, Thailand and Zambia and also in informal sector manufacturing in Honduras, Indonesia and Malaysia (United Nations, 1995a).

Some of the questions to be addressed are:

• In which branches of the informal sector do women and men predominate?

• What are the main differences in the branch distributions of informal sector women and men?

Wage and salary workers

Series A:	Employees as a percentage of those employed, by sex and occupational group
Formula	$$\frac{\text{Women (men) employees aged 15+ in occupational group } i}{\text{Total women (men) employed aged 15+ in occupational group } i} \times 100$$
Series B:	Employees as a percentage of employed, by sex and branch of activity
Formula	$$\frac{\text{Women (men) employees aged 15+ in branch } j}{\text{Total women (men) employed aged 15+ in branch } j} \times 100$$

Policy relevance

Wage employment is more stable and secure than self-employment. Yet with ongoing economic restructuring, regular wage employment is increasingly being lost to less secure forms of employment. The size and distribution of women and men in wage employment is needed to monitor the differential effect of job losses on women's and men's overall employment and the types of jobs that are retained.

Data sources

Statistics on the population and characteristics of the economically active are generally available from population censuses and labour force and other household-based surveys. Administrative records may also provide information on government workers or formal private sector establishments. Wage employment data are derived from tabulations dealing with status in employment.

Source table

Table 36.1. Number of employees and total employed workers aged 15 and over by major occupational and industrial group

	Employees aged 15+		Total employed aged 15+	
	Women	Men	Women	Men
Occupational group				
Legislators				
Professionals				
Technicians				
Clerks				
Service workers				
Agricultural, fishery workers				
Craft workers				
Machinists				
Elementary occupations				
Armed forces				
Industrial group				
Agriculture				
Industry				
Services				

Technical note: For countries that use their own occupational or industrial classifications, note how these differ from international recommendations.

Source: Give full citations for household or labour force surveys used.

Note: The above occupational groups follow the International Standard Classification of Occupations (ISCO) as revised in 1988. If other classifications are used in the country, change the occupational groups in the table as required. This table will have to be compiled separately for each year covered by the analysis.

Working table

Table 36.2. Employees as a percentage of all employed workers by major occupational and industrial group

	Women	Men
Occupational group		
Legislators		
Professionals		
Technicians		
Clerks		
Service workers		
Agricultural, fishery workers		
Craft workers		
Machinists		
Elementary occupations		
Armed forces		
Industrial group		
Agriculture		
Industry		
Services		

Technical note: For countries that use their own occupational or industrial classifications, note how these differ from international recommendations.
Source: Give full citations for household or labour force surveys used.
Note: The above occupational groups follow the International Standard Classification of Occupations (ISCO) as revised in 1988. If other classifications are used in the country, change the occupational groups in the table as required. This table will have to be compiled separately for each year covered by the analysis.

Additional indicators or classifications

The industrial classification may be further disaggregated to the nine major groups according to the International Standard Industrial Classification of All Economic Activities (ISIC). Some specific occupations within the occupational groups may also be presented. The percentage distribution of women and men employees by institutional sector of employment (e.g., general government, government enterprises, private, cooperative) can also be presented.

Likely problems

The employees category in the status in employment classification is not a homogeneous group. There are various types of workers, such as regular employees working full-time or part-time, casual workers and contractual workers. It is useful to present the data by these categories of employees if a classification exists. Definitions used in censuses and surveys may change from one period to another and should also be taken into account when comparisons are made with data from different sources. Survey instruments and reports should be reviewed to ascertain changes that may have been introduced.

Interpretation

Wage and salary employment for women does not usually carry the same wages and benefits as for men. In most developed countries and some developing countries, most of the economically active women are wage and salary earners working for someone else (USAID, 1992).

Among the developing regions, women in eastern Asia, western Asia and Latin America and the Caribbean have benefited the most from wage and salary employment. In 1990, economically active Latin American women were more likely than their male counterparts to be employed as wage earners—64 per cent as compared with 60 per cent. The corresponding figures for sub-Saharan Africa were only 29 per cent for women as compared with 37 per cent for men. In several African countries, less than one tenth of economically active women received wages or salaries (United Nations, 1991 and 1995a).

Women's wage employment is highest in the developed regions and in eastern Asia, where about 80 per cent of women or men in the labour force are employed by others (United Nations, 1995a).

Among the specific questions to be addressed are:

- Which sector offers the most opportunities for wage employment?

- Are the wage employment opportunities more accessible to women or to men in agriculture, industry or services?

- Which occupations are most likely to offer wage employment to women and men?

Gender and poverty

The persistent and increasing burden of poverty on women is identified as a critical area of concern in the Beijing Platform for Action [1] and the eradication of poverty as an ethical, social, political and economic imperative was adopted as Commitment 2 of the Copenhagen Declaration on Social Development.[2] However, as a statistical topic, poverty could not be included in this *Handbook*. The definition and measurement of poverty are quite complex and entail choices of concepts and methods that can only be made in each country according to its own social circumstances and policy concerns. Necessary data are also particularly limited in developing countries. The analysis of women's poverty raises additional problems, in large part because income and expenditures data are usually collected for households and are not easily disaggregated or analysed in terms of the individual members.

Three basic hypotheses that need to be tested in the measurement of poverty by sex are (i) resources are not equally allocated within the household; (ii) women-headed households are more often poor than are men-headed households; and (iii) there are more women than men in poor households. In a special study for *The World's Women 1995: Trends and Statistics*, the International Food Policy Research Institute (IFPRI) compiled and analysed survey data from 14 developing countries to investigate two of these hypotheses. The results generally indicate that there are more women than men in poor households in half of the data sets from Africa and two thirds of the data sets from Asia. The analysis also suggests strongly but not conclusively that women-headed households are poorer in more than half the countries examined in Asia and sub-Saharan Africa. An analysis such as this would be useful in a national publication, but given the limitations of available data and the absence of wide agreement on concepts and standards for quantifying and measuring poverty, it is beyond the feasible scope of the present study.

Recently, as a follow-up to the global conferences on social issues, the United Nations Statistical Commission established an expert group to identify statistical issues growing out of the policy concerns raised and to propose a programme of work.[3] The eradication of poverty was indicated as a key issue and some appropriate indicators were proposed. As this work proceeds, priority should be placed on the concepts and data required for obtaining data on gender as a factor in poverty.

---

1. *Report of the Fourth World Conference on Women, Beijing, 4–15 September 1995* (United Nations publication, Sales No. E.96.IV.13), chap.I, resolution 1, annex II, para.44.

2. *Report of the World Summit for Social Development, Copenhagen, 6–12 March 1995* (United Nations publication, Sales No. E.96.IV.8), chap.I, resolution 1, annex I, sect. C.

3. "Expert Group on the Statistical Implications of Recent Major United Nations Conferences" (E/CN.3/1997/16 and E/CN.3/AC.1/1996/R.4, annex).

References and further reading

Asian Development Bank, Center for International Research (1993). *Gender Indicators of Developing Asian and Pacific Countries.* Manila.

Chile, National Statistics Institute (1995). *Women and Men in Chile: Figures and Reality 1995.* Santiago.

Gross, Inge, Beatrix Wiedenhofer and Werner Vötsch (1994). *The Economic and Social Role of Women in Austria.* Vienna: Government of Austria, Federal Ministry of Labour and Social Statistics.

International Labour Organization (1985). *World Labour Report.* Geneva.

_____ (1987a). *Bulletin of Labour Statistics: October Inquiry Results, 1985 and 1986.* Geneva.

_____ (1987b). *Year Book of Labour Statistics.* Geneva.

_____ (1990). *Surveys of the Economically Active Population, Employment, Unemployment and Underemployment: An ILO Manual on Concepts and Methods.* Geneva.

_____ (1992a). Report I: Measurement of Employment in the Informal Sector. Meeting of Experts on Labour Statistics, Geneva, 28 January–6 February 1992.

_____ (1992b). Report II: Revision of the International Classification of Status in Employment. Meeting of Experts on Labour Statistics, Geneva, 28 January–6 February 1992.

_____ World Employment Programme (1991). *The Urban Informal Sector in Africa in Retrospect and Prospect: An Annotated Bibliography.* Geneva.

Lesotho, Bureau of Statistics (1993). *Basotho Women and Their Men: Statistics on Women and Men in Lesotho.* Maseru, Lesotho.

Nordic Council of Ministers (1994). *Women and Men in the Nordic Countries. Facts and Figures 1994.* No. 94.3. Copenhagen.

Organisation for Economic Cooperation and Development (1984a). *The Nature of Youth Unemployment: An Analysis for Policy-Makers.* Paris.

_____ (1984b). *The Employment and Unemployment of Women in OECD Countries.* Paris. Prepared by Liba Paukert.

Statistics Sweden (1995). *Women and Men in Sweden: Facts and Figures 1995.* Örebro: Statistics Sweden Publications Services.

United Nations (1990a). *Demographic Yearbook 1988*. Sales No. E.90.XIII.1.

_____ (1990b). *Methods of Measuring Women's Participation and Production in the Informal Sector*. Sales No. E.90.XVII.16.

_____ (1990c). *International Standard Industrial Classification of All Economic Activities*. Sales No. E.90.XVII.11.

_____ (1991). *The World's Women 1970–1990: Trends and Statistics*. Sales No. E.90.XVII.3.

_____ (1993). *Methods of Measuring Women's Economic Activity: Technical Report*. Sales No. E.93.XVII.6.

_____ (1995a). *The World's Women 1995: Trends and Statistics*. Sales No. E.95.XVII.2.

_____ (1995b). *Women in a Changing Global Economy: 1994 World Survey on the Role of Women in Development*. Sales No. E.95.IV.3.

_____, Economic Commission for Latin America and the Caribbean (1995). *Social Panorama of Latin America*. Sales No. E.95.II.G.17.

United States of America, Agency for International Development (1992). *Gender and Generation in the World's Labor Force. Module One: International and National Trends*. Washington, D.C.

Wilson, John (1987). *Time Use Pilot Survey, Sydney, May–June 1987*. Information Paper, Catalogue No. 4111.1. Sydney: Australian Bureau of Statistics.

4. Presenting data
and designing the layout

PRESENTING DATA

At this stage, all the data should be collected, processed and ready for interpretation. Since data are the crux of the book, special care must be taken in their presentation to ensure that they are accurate and that they will not be misinterpreted.

Messages

As soon as work begins on writing the book, main messages and supporting messages based on the analysis of data should be developed. Charts and tables will illustrate those messages with data. Each chart and table should make a point, much like a paragraph. Although it may be easy to come up with points that it would be desirable to have illustrated in charts, compiling valid data that confirm each point may be difficult.

Potential problems

Unavailable data

If an entire data set is unavailable, other related data can be available to meet the need. For example, if the point is to illustrate a relationship between birth rates and female literacy, ideally birth rates for all regions should be shown, or for one given over several years, with female literacy in those regions or for those years. If literacy rates are unavailable, however, other data indicators of literacy can be used, such as female secondary or tertiary enrolment, years of education.

Another approach may be to show data from another country with a similar population structure or demographic characteristics. Such data must be footnoted carefully.

Incomplete data

Missing data points can often be estimated by methods such as linear interpolation. The method used should always be explained in the notes to the data.

Where data are not available and estimates are not possible or appropriate, the data set is often best presented in a table, where empty cells can show two dots or a dash and explained in a footnote. This makes it possible to show the data that are available and perhaps explain why certain items are missing.

Discontinuities in data can result from changes in methods of collection or in definitions. This is a common problem and can be explained in footnotes. Data should not be discarded for this reason.

Outliers

Outliers may indicate a data entry error or a genuine break from the trend or pattern. If they are the result of an error, the source of error must be investigated and corrected. If there is evidence of a systematic problem, precautions must be taken during the data collection and data entry phases to control it. If there is a break in the series due to conceptual, definitional or other such changes, the reason for the break should be explained.

WAYS TO PRESENT DATA

Data can be presented in words, in lists, in charts or graphs, in tables, in sidebars and in boxes. Sometimes the most important messages will be presented in more than one form, for example in the text, in a chart and in an annex table. The most effective way or ways of presentation must be decided. Whatever is chosen, the presentation should make the point clearly so the reader will understand it.

Words

The most direct way of expressing data is in words—make a point and back it up with hard figures. Numbers in text should be kept simple, such as the change in one ratio over a period of years, one or two sets of statistics relating to no more than two regions or groups within a country. Parallel construction in making the comparison makes it easier for the reader to remember what is being compared and to see the pattern. Numbers in text should not be used excessively. Too many numbers can confuse the reader and make for dull reading. When there are many numbers to present—for example, infant mortality rates for several groups over a number of years—a chart, series of charts or table may be used instead of presenting the data in a paragraph. For example:

GOOD

In 1970 the average ratio of women to men in advanced studies in these fields was 1 to 10 in all developing regions. Women's representation improved significantly by 1984 in developed regions and in Latin America and the Caribbean, reaching about 1 to 2, but it lagged far behind in Africa and in Asia and the Pacific, where the ratio was still about 1 to 5 in 1984. (*The World's Women 1970–1990: Trends and Statistics,* United Nations publication, Sales No. E.90.XVII.3, p. 47)

In the first example, the same ratio is compared and expressed in a parallel construction. The paragraph is easy to read and the reader will remember what is being compared and see the pattern.

BAD

The range in female life expectancy across these countries exceeds 25 years, from 47 in Nepal to 73 in the Republic of Korea. Infant mortality ranges from a low of 25 per thousand live births in the Republic of Korea to a high of 130 in Nepal. There is an even larger difference in child mortality between these two countries. While Nepal's infant mortality rate is about five times Korea's, its child mortality rate is nearly 11 times Korea's. The total fertility rate ranges from 2.2 in the Republic of Korea to 5.9 in Nepal. (Charles C. Griffin, *Health Care in Asia: A Comparative Study of Cost and Financing,* World Bank, Washington D.C., 1992, p.9)

Although only two countries are being compared in the second example, the order in which they are expressed changes, making it hard to see a pattern. Moreover, so much data are given that the reader can not remember them. This paragraph would be much better expressed as a series of charts or a small table where the data are easily accessible and the pattern more visible.

Lists

A list is really a small table that shows only one variable. It is a good sidebar illustration (sidebars are explained below) because it is small and does not require much explanation. A list is a good way to highlight an important data set that does not merit a whole chart or that is too small to be a text table. Lists are often in ascending or descending order of the variable, rather than alphabetical order. Lists can be a good substitute for bar graphs with many data points. They take up much less space, are easy to read, and can present data of varying magnitude.

Where the rural population is still growing more than 2 per cent a year
Percentage increase in rural population per year, 1985–1990

Lesotho	2.0
Nepal	2.1
Gambia	2.2
Guatemala	2.2
Iran, Islamic Rep. of	2.2
Bangladesh	2.3
Cambodia	2.3
Madagascar	2.3
Botswana	2.4
Burundi	2.5
Comoros	2.5
Malawi	2.7
Mongolia	2.9
Pakistan	2.9
Oman	3.0
Rwanda	3.1
Kenya	3.3

Source: The World Women 1970–1990: Trends and Statistics (United Nations publication, Sales No. E.90.XVII.3), p. 72.

◀ GOOD
This list presents one variable in ascending order. It is clear and easy to read.

BAD ▶
This table is too complex, both in subject matter and in presentation, to be a list. The run-over stubs are hard to distinguish from the subcategories and the data appear cramped and hard to grasp. This would work better as a text table, run wide enough to keep all the stubs one line each.

Estimated percentage distribution of deaths by cause, 1990

	Women	Men
Northern Africa and Western Asia		
Communicable, maternal & perinatal	48.7	44.0
Noncommunicable	45.8	44.0
Malignant neoplasm	6.7	8.2
Cardiovascular diseases	24.2	21.3
Injuries	4.4	10.3
Sub-Saharan Africa		
Communicable, maternal & perinatal	69.3	67.3
Noncommunicable	26.0	..
Malignant neoplasm	3.8	3.9
Cardiovascular diseases	13.9	9.9
Injuries	4.7	10.7

.. Not available.
Extract of chart 3.11, *The World's Women 1995: Trends and Statistics* (United Nations publication, Sales No. E.95.XVII.2), p. 71.
Source: Adapted from C.J.L. Murray and A.D. Lopez, "Global and regional cause-of-death patterns in 1990", WHO Bulletin, Vol. 72, No. 3 (Geneva, 1994).

Tables

Tables are most appropriate for presenting data, when there is a lot of related information to present, and comparisons to be made between several indicators. They are a good way to present data that vary greatly in magnitude or that show different kinds of statistics (such as dates, percentages and nominal values). Tables are preferable to charts for presenting incomplete data, where empty cells can be indicated by a dash or two dots and footnoted. Two kinds of tables are widely used in statistical publications, text tables and annex tables.

Text tables are small tables (less than one page) and are referred to in and are part of the text. The data presented in a text table should be simple and easy to understand, and should cover only a few (one or two) indicators. Text tables are needed to make clear and specific points which are further clarified in the text. To maximize their effectiveness, text tables should be kept small in size, highlighting a major point which can be stated as the title of the table.

Annex tables are relatively large, generally page-length or longer, and may present information on several characteristics and indicators, covering several geographical areas or administrative divisions in a single table. Although annex tables may be referred to in the text, such references should be kept to a minimum since they are placed at the end of the publication or at the end of each chapter. A summary of the data needed to support a point made in the text may be presented as text table, to give more direct and easier access to information. (See, for example, *The World's Women 1995: Trends and Statistics* (United Nations publication, Sales No. E.95.XVII.2), where the annex tables are placed at the end of each chapter.)

BAD

These data make a bad text table, primarily because there is much more text than data. The key words "improvement" and "deterioration" are buried in the long stubs, obscuring the point. In this case, the data would be better presented as part of the text. ▼

Relation between agricultural growth and two measures of agricultural policy, 1981–1986 and 1987–1991

	Median change in average annual growth (%)
Producer prices and agricultural growth	
Countries with improvement in the real producer price of agricultural exports	1.8
Countries with deterioration in the real producer price of agricultural exports	–0.3
Taxation and agricultural growth	
Countries with large decrease in taxation of export crop producers	2.0
Countries with small decrease in taxation of export producers	–0.1
Countries with increase in taxation of export crop producers	–1.6

Source: ...

GOOD

Here, the data clearly support the point made in the title—that women's representation is falling rapidly—by setting the data for 1987 and 1990 next to each other for easy comparison. ▼

Women's parliamentary representation is now rapidly falling in eastern Europe and the USSR

	Women in parliament (%)	
	1987	1990
Bulgaria	21	9
Czechoslovakia	30	6
Germany		
former German Dem. Rep.	32	21
Hungary	21	7
Poland		
Senate	..	6
Lower House	20	4
Romania	34	4
USSR		
Congress of Peoples' Deputies	..	16
Soviet Nationalities	31	14
Supreme Soviet	35	14

.. Not available.

Source: The World's Women 1970–1990: Trends and Statistics (United Nations publication, Sales No. E.90.XVII.3), p. 33.

Charts

Charts depict further simplification of data, which may or may not have been presented in a table. Charts can be used to great effect in publications—to inspire the reader to continue reading, to illustrate and amplify the main messages which the publication is sending, and to broaden the readership. If done well, charts can make a much stronger point than words or tables because they draw a picture for the reader and make major differences or similarities more easily discernible. Charts are generally better understood and interpreted by the average reader, and therefore appeal to a wider audience. Moreover, they provide visual relief for the reader and break up the monotony of the text. Authors' strongest points should therefore be made in charts, if possible.

The table provides too much information and will tend to divert readers' attention from the points being made by the data and discussion in the text. Also, it would take a lot of words to give a comprehensive description of the levels and patterns of change over the life cycle.

Table A. Economic activity rate by age group and sex, Nigeria, 1987 *(percentage)*

Age group	Women	Men
10–14	1.8	4.0
15–19	13.8	31.5
20–24	27.0	62.0
25–29	33.3	92.0
30–34	36.5	97.8
35–39	47.5	98.9
40–44	52.0	98.7
45–49	62.2	99.2
50–54	64.1	97.5
55–59	58.4	97.9
60–64	42.0	79.4
65+	30.6	50.0

Source: Calculated from International Labour Office, *Year Book of Labour Statistics, 1993* (Geneva, 1993), table 1, p. 15.

The chart gives a vivid picture of differences between women's and men's economic activity. The reader immediately observes the gender gap in activity rates and variations between women and men across age groups. In this example, the effect of the chart is to reduce a lot of figures in a way that the mind can easily absorb and is thus a better choice for presenting these data.

Economic activity rate of women reaches its peak about 25 years later than men's

Percentage economically active

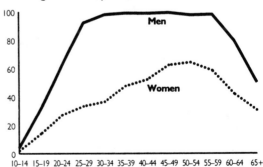

Source: Extract from *The World's Women 1995: Trends and Statistics* (United Nations publication, Sales No. E.95.XVII.2), p. 14.

Boxes

To elaborate on a point with a concrete example or to provide a technical description that would interrupt the flow of the argument in the text, consider the use of boxes—which get their name from the rule that surrounds them. Best when small, boxes sometimes extend to a full page or spread. They often use smaller type than does the text—and often are covered with a light screen of colour or black to distinguish them further.

Pull quotes

To provide visual relief and highlight important points, pulling a partial quotation from the text and displaying it in the outside margin—in a "pull quote"—can be part of the page design. Pull quotes usually appear in larger type than does the text. They need not be exact quotes, but they should appear on the same page or spread as the text they are pulled from.

Other marginal material

If the outside margin is not too narrow, it can also accommodate lists, definitions, smaller tables and charts, and even discussions of methodological issues, as in *The World's Women*.

TABLE DESIGN

Tables and charts display important information more economically than text can. There is, however, a tendency to overload them—a tendency to avoid.

Designing tables

The title describes the subject and coverage—or, better, spells out the message. Horizontal rules divide the body of rows and columns from the top and bottom matter. A straddle head describes the columns of numbers below it, with a straddle rule spanning (straddling) the columns so described in the subheads. A single column requires only a column head. And every column should have its unit of measure designated—with a unit designator.

Parts of the table
A. Title
B. Rules
C. Straddle head
D. Straddle rule
E. Subhead
F. Column head
G. Unit designator
H. Superscript letter
I. Stubs
J. Notes

Table B. Illiteracy, ages 15 and over, selected developing countries, 1990

	Illiteracy rate (%)			Number of illiterates (millions)	Per cent change 1970–90	Illiteracy rate, age 15–19 (per cent)
	Total	Women	Men			
Region A						
Country A	58.3	44.4	71.5	3.2	–7.2	..
Country B	91.1ᵃ	81.8	72.1	4.1	0.8	..
Country C	39.7	30.0	49.0	3.2	19.4	12.5
Country D	50.5	38.7	62.0	7.5	17.9	20.5
Region B						
Country E	86.1ᵇ	70.6	..	6.8	41.5	49.1
Country F	61.6	48.7	75.4	0.6	–0.9	..
Country G	51.8	38.2	66.3	280.7	26.8	34.4

Illustrative data.
Source: Give full citations for publications used.
.. Not available
a. 1989 data only.
b. 1988 data only.

Formatting tables

Depending on the technology available, it may or may not be possible to do much formatting of tables. With a typewriter, an excellent guide to formatting tables is in *The Chicago Manual of Style* (this is also a worthwhile guide to formatting tables in general). With a spreadsheet program such as Lotus 1-2-3 or Microsoft Excel, there are good options for larger tables using one or more pages, but it is difficult to integrate small tables with text on a well-designed page. For pages combining tables, charts and text, a good choice is a page layout program such as PageMaker or QuarkXPress. For large tables, "WYSIWYG" in Lotus 1-2-3 can be used very effectively.

The general rules for tables are as follows: each table must have a number and a title, all the columns must be labelled, every cell must contain data or a notation, all symbols must be explained and all notes must be presented and sources fully cited.

BAD

In this text table, the author has not edited the column heads for consistency or clarity. The heads have a haphazard appearance that is distracting and hard to understand and some notes are missing.

A. Title—*Table number is missing and title should indicate that these are selected countries.*

B. Case—*Avoid using all caps. Be consistent in the use of upper and lower case type. Treat each head under a straddle as a new head and capitalize.*

C. Units—*Where possible, make figures small by indicating units in the column heads. The unit for this column should be millions.*

D. Straddle rules—*Straddle rules should use a consistent amount of vertical space. Usually a whole blank line is allotted for the rule.*

E. Straddle heads—*Never use more than two stacked straddle heads. Information that straddles all the columns should be in the title. In this case, the information is redundant.*

F. Straddle heads—*Should always straddle two or more subheads.*

G. Vertical/horizontal alignment—*All heads should align at the bottom and be centred over the column.*

H. Empty cells—*A table should never have empty cells. If a cell is empty, indicate the reason with a symbol (such as two dots to indicate no data available).*

I. Rules—*Horizontal rules should be used to separate the column heads from the body of the table and the body of the table from the notes.*

J. Alignment—*Columns of data should align on the right. Round the figures to the first decimal place.*

K. Symbols—*All symbols should be defined in a common explanatory note at the beginning of the book and should be consistent throughout the book, including the annexes.*

L. Alignment—*These figures should align on the first decimal place with the superscript letters hanging over.*

M. Notes—*The notes are far too long and are redundant. Technical explanations of statistical methodology and the like should be given in a separate text. There is no explanation of the superscript letters in the table or the meaning of the double dots. Notes should be in a smaller type size than the body text.*

N. Order/clarity—*Reorder the countries alphabetically within each region. For clarity, put the region in bold and remove the indent before each country. Add an empty line between the regions.*

O. Legibility—*Avoid using abbreviations and symbols in column heads unless there is absolutely no room. Where possible, spell out.*

P. Source—*None provided.*

Table   Illiteracy in developing countries   [A]

	ILLITERATE POPULATION aged 15 and over			Number of illiterates [E]		Age 15–19 [F] Illiteracy rate (%) [G]
	Illiteracy rate (%) 1990 [C] [D]			[C] (000) 1990	[O] % change 1970–90 [I]	1990
	Total	Women	Men			
Region A						
Country B	91.1[a]	72.1	81.8	4.1	0.8	[H]
Country A [N]	58.3	71.5	44.4	3.2	−7.2	
Country D	50.5	62.0	38.7	7.5	17.9	20.5
Country C	39.7	49.0	30.0	3.2	19.4	12.5
Region B						
Country G	51.8	66.3	38.2	280.7	26.8	34.4
Country E	86.1[b] [L]	.. [K]	70.6	6.8	41.5	49.1
Country F	61.6	75.4	48.7	0.6	−0.91 [J]	..

[P]

Notes: Illiteracy rate is the number of adult illiterates (15 years and over) and those in the age group 15–19 expressed as percentages of the population in the corresponding age groups. Number of illiterates is the number of illiterates [M] in 1990, in thousands, and the percentage change in the number of adult illiterates between 1970 and 1990.

GOOD

After editing, the heads are much simpler and the title more informative. The text is consistent in case and all the heads are nicely centred above their columns. The straddle rule is centred vertically in the space provided and each column aligns to the right.

A. Column heads—*The heads are much simpler now that repeating information has been removed to the title.*
They are aligned at the bottom, centered over the columns and easier to read.
B. Straddle heads—*Straddle is centred vertically, in the horizontal space. It extends to the rightmost and leftmost ends of the subheads. The head is centred above the rule.*
C. Case/punctuation—*Case is consistent throughout the table. Every head and subhead is initial cap only. Punctuation reads normally.*
D. Legibility—*Spelling out per cent makes the table easier to read. In this case, it does not compromise spacing.*
E. Units—*Changing the unit to millions makes the numbers smaller and easier to understand.*

F. Empty cells—*The empty cell has been replaced by a "not available" symbol. The reader is not left wondering if there is something missing.*
G. Rounding—*Rounding to ensure consistent decimal places within the column looks cleaner and clearer.*
H. Alignment—*All the columns are aligned on the right. The figures that have superscript letters are aligned with the first decimal place. Letting the letter hang into the gutter draws attention to it without compromising orderliness.*
I. Notes—*The lengthy notes have been removed and replaced with a concise explanation of the double dots and the superscript letters. The type size is one point smaller than the text.*
J. Order/clarity—*The countries have been reordered alphabetically and aligned on the left. The hierarchy of region to country is clearer and the format is less busy.*

Table C. Illiteracy, ages 15 and over, selected developing countries, 1990

A	**B** Illiteracy rate (%)			**C** Number of illiterates (millions) **E**	**D** Per cent change 1970–90	Illiteracy rate, age 15–19 (per cent)
	Total	Women	Men			
Region A						
Country A	58.3	44.4	71.5	3.2	−7.2	**F** ..
Country B **J**	91.1[a]	81.8	72.1	4.1	0.8	..
Country C	39.7	30.0	49.0	3.2	19.4	12.5
Country D	50.5	38.7	62.0	7.5	17.9	20.5
Region B						
Country E	86.1[b] **H**	70.6	..	6.8	41.5	49.1
Country F	61.6	48.7	75.4	0.6	−0.9 **G**	..
Country G	51.8	38.2	66.3	280.7	26.8	34.4

Illustrative data.
Source: Give full citations for publications used.
.. Not available **I**
a. 1989 data only.
b. 1988 data only.

CHART DESIGN

As with tables, the title of a chart describes the subject and coverage—or, better, spells out the message.

Parts of the chart
A. Title
B. Unit designator, for the unit of measure of the y-axis.
C. Y-axis labels
D. Tick marks
E. Y-axis
F. Data point, given by height of bar
G. Source
H. Categories
I. X-axis
J. Legend

A More girls than boys die at a young age
B (Annual deaths per thousand children aged one to four, 1984–1990)

G *Source:* United Nations Development Programme, *Human Development Report 1995* (New York and Oxford, Oxford University Press, 1995); table 2.4.

Make the title a message

Every chart should make a point and that point should be given by the title. Titles that merely state what data are in the chart should be avoided—for example, "Years of schooling in rural and urban areas, 1974–1993". The reader can tell what the chart is about by the labelling on the axes. Instead, a conclusion should be presented—for example, "Rural children receive less education than urban children".

Label charts accurately and clearly

The most important element in a chart (after accurately plotting the data) is labelling. Without it, a chart makes no sense. The scale of each axis, the units, the categories and the years to which the data refer must always be indicated.

Units

The labels on the axes should be as small as possible in magnitude. That is, if one axis is in millions of US dollars, the axis should not be labelled 1,000,000, 2,000,000, 3,000,000 etc. Instead, the labels should read 1, 2, 3, and the unit indicator "million US$". Similarly, too many decimal places in labels should be avoided by reducing, where necessary, the unit indicator (from kilograms to grams, for example). Years should be written out with all four digits and do not need a unit indicator.

Scale

Each axis should always start at zero. If there is a compelling reason not to, a break in the axis before it reaches zero must be indicated. When comparing charts side by side, the same scale should be used. Two scales should never be used on the same axis for two different categories. If one value is much larger in magnitude than the others it should be indicated, for example, with a broken bar on a bar chart.

Categories

Where possible, categories should be labelled inside the chart and legends avoided. Legends slow the reader down because he or she must look back and forth to the chart. When labelling vertical bars, the text should be centred or flush left along the x-axis under each bar.

A note on colour

When designing charts with many categories of data, it is ideal to have a second colour to help distinguish the bars or lines. When only black is being used, bars may be distinguished by shades (densities) of grey and lines by grey values, where solid black is "100 per cent" density, dots or dashes, or some combination of these. When using shades of grey, they must not be too close in value. For example, 100 per cent, 60 per cent, 20 per cent and white are better than 100 per cent, 80 per cent, 60 per cent and 50 per cent. For lines, solid lines are preferable, with dots or dashes for no more than two categories. If categories are repeated in different line charts, the same kind of line for the same category should be used each time. This will help the reader identify the data.

GOOD▶
This chart is simple, clear and easy to understand. The message is stated in the title and the axes and lines are clearly labelled.

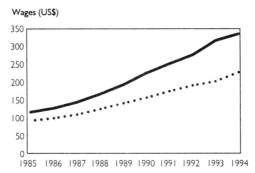

Women's manufacturing wages are increasing faster than men's—but still haven't caught up, Hong Kong 1985–1994

Wages (US$)

Source: Based on data from International Labour Office, *Year Book of Labour Statistics,* 1995 (Geneva, 1995), table 17A, p. 638.

PICKING THE RIGHT CHART

There are dozens of types of charts. The type of chart used depends on the kind of data used in the analysis and what point the authors wish to make. Choosing the correct chart can make the difference between providing the reader with a strong message and confusing the reader.

Line charts

Line charts require a continuous x-axis. Thus they are used to show data over time, over ages or age groups, school grades, incomes and other variables whose values fall conceptually in some order of regular progression and can be represented on the x-axis. Time-series data that are often shown in line charts are life expectancies at birth, infant mortality, labour force activity and literacy rates. Variables which are often shown by age or age group are rural and urban populations, labour force, employment and income.

Men and women are shown by different lines in the same chart or in separate charts if they are small.

More women than men are married below age 45, but for ages 45 and older, it is mainly men who remain married

Percentage currently married, 1990

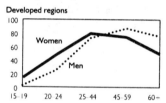

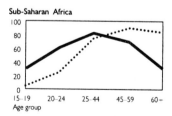

Age group

Extracted and adapted from chart 1.8, United Nations, *The World's Women 1970–1990: Trends and Statistics* (United Nations publication, Sales No. E.90.XVII.3); p. 15. *Source:* Prepared by the Statistical Office of the United Nations Secretariat from *Demographic Yearbook 1982* and *1987* (United Nations publications, Sales Nos. E/F.83.XIII.1 and E/F.88.XIII.1).

◀ **GOOD**

Age groups are appropriate data for a line chart. Though each line only has five points, by connecting them, the curve becomes obvious. In addition, the point at which the lines cross is also clear, which would not be the case in a bar chart.

BAD

This chart is confusing and cluttered. The title is not informative nor do the data impart any particular message. The data points are buried by the grid, the tick marks and the scale labels. This information would be better presented as a series of vertical bar charts, on spider web charts or as a text table. ▼

Development diamonds for Ghana, Thailand and Malaysia, 1989

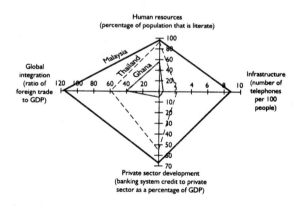

Extracted from box figure 1.2, World Bank, *Adjustment in Africa. Reforms. Results. and the Road Ahead* (Washington, DC, 1993), p. 40. *Source:* World Bank, "Ghana 2000 and Beyond—Setting the Stage for Accelerated Growth and Poverty Reduction", Economic Report 11486 (Washington, DC, 1993).

Vertical bar charts

Vertical bar charts can be used to illustrate data that do not vary in magnitude too greatly. They should not be used to illustrate a large number of data points, however, because the bars will be too thin. Another common error is to put too many categories in the same chart, making it hard to read. Vertical bars are often used for categories plotted in percentages or a ratio around one—for example, literacy rates, enrolment, the ratio of women to men, percentage of women in different occupations, and so on. A good use of a vertical bar chart is to choose one category, such as literacy rates, and present data from several countries or regions.

Men and women are shown as two sets of differently coloured or shaded bars side by side for each category or in separate charts. Where male and female add to 100 per cent, a stacked vertical bar chart may be considered.

GOOD▶

In this chart the bars for men and women are clearly distinguished. The grid is unobtrusive and does not obscure the data and the chart is big enough to accommodate the long region names.

The widest gaps in literacy between women and men are in Africa, western Asia and southern Asia

Percent illiterate, ages 20–24, 1990

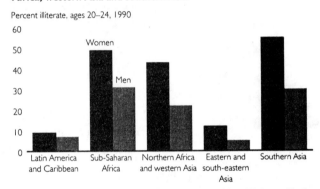

Source: The World's Women 1970–1990: Trends and Statistics (United Nations publication, Sales No. E90.XVII.3), p. 46.

Stacked bar charts

Stacked bar charts can be used for most kinds of data but they are most effective for categories adding to 100 per cent. A common problem with stacked bar charts is that one or more segments are too short to be visible on the scale. In this case, the data may be split into separate charts with different scales or lumped with the small values in another category. Stacked bars usually illustrate data such as rural and urban population, women and men in different occupations, percentage of the labour force in agriculture, industry and services, and other comprehensive categories.

Men and women are shown either on the x-axis with one stacked bar for each, or as different coloured segments of each bar with multiple values on the x-axis.

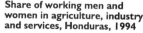

Share of working men and women in agriculture, industry and services, Honduras, 1994

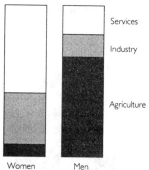

Services

Industry

Agriculture

Women   Men

Source: Based on data from *The World's Women 1995: Trends and Statistics* (United Nations publication, Sales No. E.95.XVII.2), table 12, p. 148.

◄ GOOD
The shares for women and men in different industrial sectors are clearly illustrated with a minimum of clutter. All the segments are large enough to be visible.

GOOD ►
In this chart, each bar represents an age group, with women and men as segments.

Women make up more than half of agricultural workers, especially among the very young and elderly, 1990

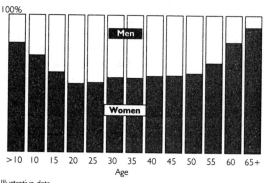

100%

Men

Women

>10 10 15 20 25 30 35 40 45 50 55 60 65+
Age

Illustrative data.
Source: Give full citations for publications used.

Horizontal bar charts

Horizontal bar charts have many of the same characteristics as vertical bar charts with one important difference: they should never be used to plot negative values with positive values, as a left-oriented bar will not necessarily imply a negative value. Vertical bar charts should be used for data that include negatives. Because they do not include negative values, horizontal bar charts are often used to plot two variables against each other, with two sets of bars originating from the y-axis. In addition, horizontal bars with one variable are often a good choice when the y-axis labels are long and more easily read horizontally.

Men and women are shown as two sets of different coloured bars side by side for each category or as two sets of bars originating at the y-axis and extending left and right. Where male and female add to 100 per cent, a stacked horizontal bar chart should be considered.

Fertility rate compared to contraceptive use, various countries, 1990

GOOD▶
One way to use a horizontal bar chart is to plot two variables against each other. To be effective, there should be a visible correlation between the two. Remember to label each set of bars accurately. In addition, one side should be in ascending or descending order.

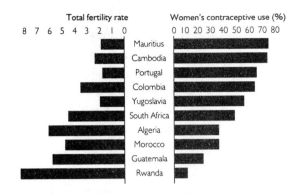

Source: Based on data from *The World's Women 1970–1990: Trends and Statistics* (United Nations publication, Sales No. E.90.XVII.3), table 5, pp. 67–70.

Age pyramids

Age pyramids plot the age composition of the populations of women and men as horizontal bars originating from the y-axis. The x-axis is usually either a nominal value or a percentage, where all bars add to 100 per cent. In these "age pyramids", each age group is shown in the centre of the y-axis with women and men on each side as horizontal bars. The age pyramid best illustrates at what ages most of the population is concentrated, rather than at what ages women and men are disproportionately represented, unless those differences are large.

Population by age groups in 1930 and 1980

GOOD▶
Age pyramids are best used with absolute values for the population or percentages expressed in relation to the total of all age groups and both sexes combined.

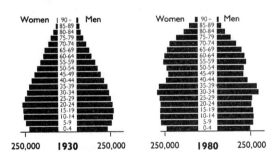

Source: *Women and Men in Sweden: Facts and Figures* (Statistics Sweden, 1985), p. 80.

261

Pie charts

Pie charts must always show shares that total to 100 per cent. A common error with pie charts is to show too many segments, resulting in labels that are hard to read and segments that are too narrow. In this case, however, since all data should be disaggregated by sex, there should be no need for labels other than "men" and "women". Pie charts are best for showing one segment as a percentage of the whole as it varies for different years or for different periods or categories. In such use, labelling is at a minimum and pies can be small. Data often illustrated in pie charts are population by region, population by occupation, disbursements to regions, share of aid received by regions, and so on.

Men and women are shown as the two segments of the pie or in separate pies.

Women perform the lion's share of unpaid housework in the UK, 1984

Preparing meals   Child care

Shopping   Other housework

Note: Shaded segments represent hours worked by women as a share of total hours worked by women and men in each task.
Source: Based on data from *The World's Women 1970–1990: Trends and Statistics* (United Nations publication, Sales No. E.90.XVII.3), p. 102.

◀ **GOOD**
Pie charts always show shares of 100 per cent, so it is not necessary to give the percentages. In this case, all the values are greater than 50 per cent, so the rest of the pie is implied.

Scatter charts

Scatter charts plot two variables against each other to show groupings around a trend line. They are often used to show outliers. A common error with scatter charts is to label all the data points in the chart, when only the outliers should be labelled. In general, scatter charts use more data points than can comfortably be shown in another kind of chart. They should be used cautiously as it is often difficult for the reader to see a pattern. Where a pattern is clear or not many data points are available, another type of chart, usually a horizontal bar chart, should be considered.

Men and women are shown using two kinds of markers in the same chart or in different charts.

Percentage of female teachers and female/male participation ratio in the first level of education, 1992

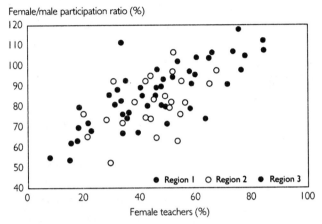

Female/male participation ratio (%)

● Region 1   ○ Region 2   ● Region 3

Female teachers (%)

Source: Adapted from United Nations Educational, Scientific and Cultural Organization, *World Education Report 1995* (Paris, UNESCO, 1995), p. 45.

Common design problems with charts and how to resolve them

Too many categories

This problem is especially common in pie charts and stacked bar charts. No more than four categories (or shares) should be used in these two types of charts. If there are more than four categories, a vertical bar chart may be tried. A good indicator that there are too many categories in a chart is if cross-hatching is necessary to distinguish bars in a graph. Black, white and perhaps two shades of grey in between (or colour, if it is being used) should suffice.

Too many lines

One of the most common problems with charts is the overuse of grids, ticks, frames and patterns. Both a horizontal and a vertical grid should not be used. One (usually the horizontal) will always suffice and often neither is necessary. Ticks (the short marks above or below the axes that denote units) are also often unnecessary. (They are essential, however, on an axis with a logarithmic scale.) Frames or boxes surrounding the data should always be used with scatter charts but are not necessary on most other kinds of charts.

Legends

Categories should be labelled inside the chart if possible rather than using a legend. Legends add visual clutter and force the reader to look back and forth to match the section of the chart to its label. In addition, where different shades of grey are used, or different types of lines, it may be difficult to tell which labels in a legend belong with which parts of the chart.

Labelling every value
Accurately labelled axes eliminate the need to label points in the chart; after all, a chart shows a pattern. If the exact points are important, they should be given in a text table. Labels inside a chart (other than category labels) are redundant and distracting.

Abbreviations
Abbreviations should be avoided in the text of a chart if they are not used in the book itself. If necessary, they should be standardized among all the charts and tables. Charts can also be made larger to accommodate the text or the text size reduced. Sans serif fonts, especially, can be legible at small sizes (6–8 points).

Too few data points/chart too big—A chart should never have more text than data. Charts that only illustrate two to four data points should remain part of the text. Similarly, charts should be kept as small as warranted by the number of data points and the amount of text.

Y-axis range too big for data—As the data are the most important part of the chart, they should occupy all the space allotted for them. If the highest point is only 530, for example, the y-axis should not extend to 1,000. One exception to this rule is in side-by-side charts, where data are being directly compared from chart to chart. In this case, changing the scale could be misleading.

Lines too thin, bars too skinny
The numbers should stand out with wide bars and heavy charts lines.

Misleading: two scales on one chart, scale not starting at zero, magnitude different in side-by-side charts
Two scales should not be combined on the same axis, even if they are on either side of the chart. The most common occurrence of this is a set of bars (representing nominal values) on one scale with a superimposed line (representing a percentage or average) on another. If the aim is to show a correlation between two variables, it is better to use a horizontal bar chart with two axes originating from zero.

In some cases, such as indexes (where the data are based on 100) and dates, one or both of the axes will not start at zero. In most other cases (percentages, nominal values, logarithms, etc.) the axis should start at zero. If all the data have values much higher than zero, a jump from zero to the lowest value on the scale should be indicated with a break in the axis line.

DESIGNING THE LAYOUT

The layout is the arrangement of words, numbers, symbols and graphic elements on the page. The goal of design is to support the messages and encourage readership though the use and arrangement of type and graphic elements. Therefore, design must follow the same standards as writing text and compiling data—it should be clear, concise and orderly without being intrusive.

Parts of the laid-out page

A. Left page (always even numbered)
B. Right page (always odd numbered)
C. Top margin
D. Outside margin
E. Gutter (between columns or pages)
F. Inside margin
G. Box (or sidebar) grid
H. Footers
I. Bottom margin
J. Chapter number
K. Chapter title
L. Pullquote. Short statement copied from text and highlighted in large type in the narrow column on the outside of the page
M. Body text (or body copy)
N. Page number (or folio)
O. Running feet (usually chapter or book title)
P. Box (or sidebar) title
Q. Box (or sidebar) text

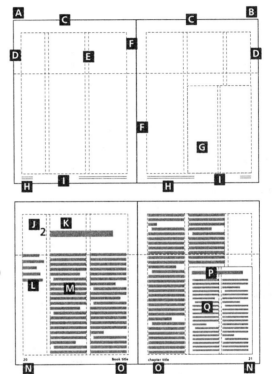

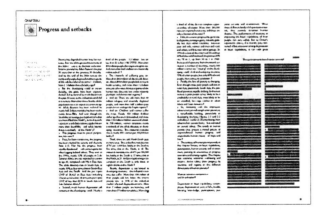

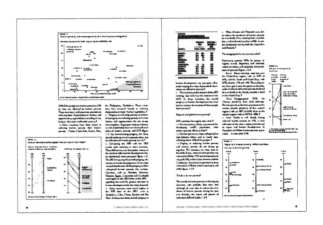

Establish a grid

A grid is a set of invisible lines on the page that set the boundaries for placing text and other elements. Elements include everything that is not text: boxes, charts, lists, pullquotes, photographs, maps, diagrams, summaries, footnotes, page numbers, headers and footers and graphic elements such as rules. The margins, columns, headers, footers and other items that appear on every page must be consistently placed throughout the book. Publications that do not use a grid appear sloppy and confused, which can lead the reader to question the authority of the publication and the accuracy of the research.

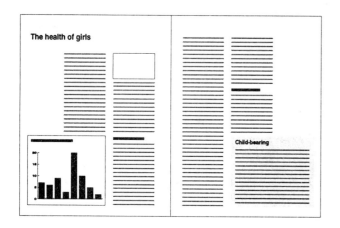

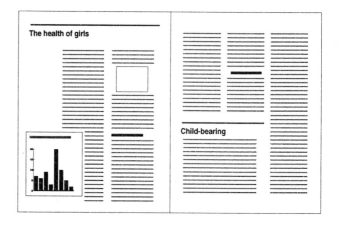

GOOD
In this layout, the grid determines the number and placement of the column (symmetrical on each side of the spread). Boxes line up with the text and are of standard width. Consistency and alignment harmonize the elements and make the page visually attractive.

BAD
This layout does not employ a grid: columns are of different widths and numbers and boxes are placed and sized at random. The lack of order and harmony makes for an unappealing look.

Vertical grid

The simpler the grid, the easier the layout and the fewer design decisions that must be made. If a grid is too simple, however, it will not be flexible enough to accommodate all the elements of a book, especially one containing tables and charts of various sizes.

On the facing page are grids appropriate for a statistical publication. In each case, the grid is symmetrical across two facing pages (or a "spread"). The inside margin (where the two pages meet) is usually larger than the outside margin to allow for binding. In mechanical drawings for preparing printer's films and photos, grids are drawn by hand on a pasteboard; in computer software, they appear as nonprinting rules.

Graphic elements are placed towards the outside of the page. This is because the reader's eye sees the outside of the pages first (especially if she or he is flipping through the book) and graphic elements are more likely to draw the reader in than text. When laying out pages, how the elements on both sides of a spread will interact visually should be considered.

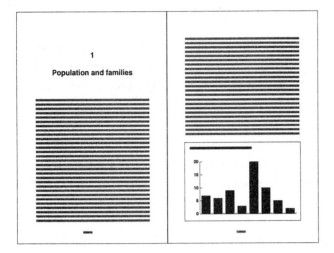

This is a sample of a one-column grid for a 6"X9" book. In this case, all the elements must be the same width—not a flexible enough grid for a statistical publication with many elements.

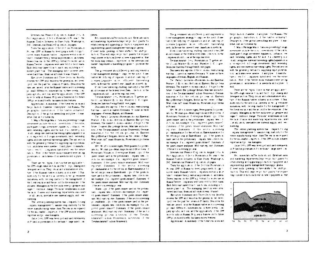

A common style for a statistics publication is a two-column grid on a letter-sized page. This grid uses two columns of the same width, centred horizontally on the page. All elements (such as boxes, tables, charts and pullquotes) must fit into one or both of the two columns.

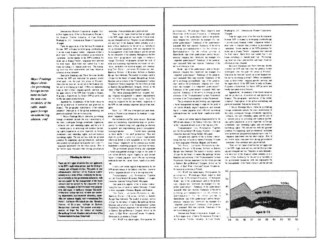

A more flexible and dynamic style is a two-and-a-half column grid. This off-centre grid uses two columns of the same width for the text, with a smaller column on the outside of each page that elements can spill into. Elements can fill any combination of columns. While this design is more flexible in preparing the first-proof layout, it is harder to make significant content changes after, as the half-size columns must be alternated consistently between left and right.

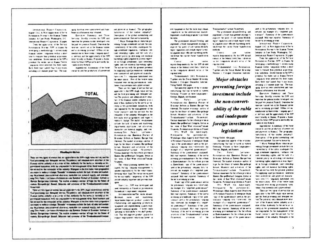

A three-column grid allows more text to fit on the page but reduces the flexibility of the layout. There is less white space on the page than with two columns, so the type chosen should be light and fairly small.

Horizontal grid

In addition to using the vertical grid that defines columns, the designer should be aware of the horizontal grid that is created by the type itself. The designer may also want to impose a horizontal grid for the placement of sidebars, page numbers, running heads or other repeating elements.

The first horizontal line to be aware of is the top margin. This is where the text starts on every page except for the opening page of each chapter, which usually has a different layout to accommodate the chapter number and title. The easiest treatment is to start every chapter at the same place on the page, low enough to accommodate the longest chapter title.

For vertical placement of boxes, tables and other elements, the designer should take into account the existing grid formed by the baselines of the columns of type. This is formed by the top and bottom of the "x-height" of the type. X-height refers to the height of a lower-case letter "x". When placing elements at the top of the page, the top of the element should align with the top of the x-height. Elements at the bottom of the page should align with the bottom of the x-height. Attending to these simple rules will give the design a clean, polished look.

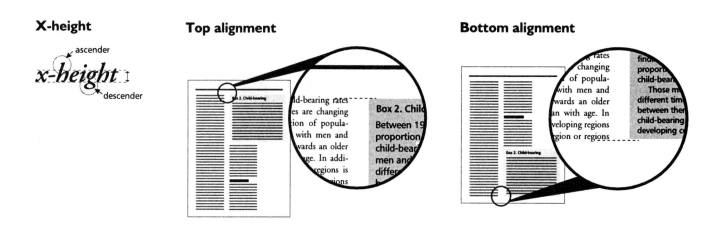

X-height

Top alignment

Bottom alignment

Standardize type styles

The choice of type is not as important as the consistent use of that type throughout the book. Consistent type visually reinforces the hierarchy of the messages and harmonizes the parts of the book.

Type comes in families that usually include roman (regular), italic, bold, bold italics and perhaps semibold or black. A good rule of thumb is to use no more than two type families in the same publication. A face with a large family that includes condensed or extended versions can be considered to give a wider range of choice.

There are two main categories of type: serif and sans serif. Stylistic and historical distinctions among serif faces limit which should be used together, whereas most serif faces may safely be used with most sans serif faces. Thus, a standard practice is to pick one serif and one sans serif face for a publication.

Commonly used serif typefaces:
Times, **Times bold,** *Times italic,* ***Times bold italic***
Palatino, **Palatino bold,** *Palatino italic,* ***Palatino bold italic***
Garamond, **Garamond bold,** *Garamond italic,* ***Garamond bold italic***

Commonly used sans serif faces:
Helvetica roman, **Helvetica bold,** *Helvetica italic*
Frutiger roman, **Frutiger bold,** *Frutiger italic*
Futura regular, **Futura bold,** *Futura italic*

An extended sans serif family:
Univers
Univers extended
Univers bold
Univers black extended
Univers black
Univers extra black extended
Univers light
Univers bold oblique
Univers condensed
Univers condensed bold

Times and Helvetica are probably the most widely used type faces for most purposes and in combination are always a safe choice. The United Nations Statistics Division chose Times and Univers condensed for *The World's Women: Trends and Statistics* as the latter is an elegant, simple face which is well suited to the space limitations commonly found in statistical tables and charts.

Type is traditionally measured in "points"—one twelfth of a pica. One inch is six picas or 72 points. Line spacing, or "leading", is also measured in points. Thus a type specification of "10 on 12-point Palatino" means 10-point Palatino type on 12-point leading. "Solid" leading means that the line spacing is equal to the size of the type—the letters practically touch from line to line. This book is set in 12-point Joanna on 15-point leading for the body text. Shorthand for picas is "p" and for points is "pt". So a measurement of 6p9 means "6 picas and 9 points", or six and three-quarter picas.

Type sizes and styles should be decided on for the different parts of the text and then implemented consistently. If 18 point Times bold left-aligned is chosen for chapter heads, for example, every chapter head must be set the same way.

Style name	Specifications
Body text	Times roman, 10/12, justified, 1 pica indent
Chapter head	Helvetica bold, 18/20, centred
Chapter number	Times extrabold, 30/30, left
A-head	Times bold, 10/12, left
B-head	Times italic, 10/12, left
Endnotes	Times roman, 8/10, justified, hanging indent of 1 pica
Table text	Times roman, 9/11, left
Table title	Times bold, 10/11, left
Table notes	Times roman, 7/9, left
Chart text	Helvetica roman, 7/8, left
Chart title	Helvetica bold, 8/10, left
Chart label	Helvetica bold, 7/8, left
Chart notes	Helvetica roman, 6/8, left

The designer must make a list of the different parts of the text and assign styles to each one before laying up the book. The sample list at left is a guide. Everyone involved in layout must have a copy. Variations in type with one style include bold, italic and different type sizes. Underlining, common in typewritten text, should never be used in published, typeset documents; italic should be used instead. Bold should be used very selectively in heads, never in text. In using desktop systems, shadow or outline styles should be avoided as these look unprofessional.

Create a visual hierarchy

Creating a visual hierarchy on the page involves type, grid and consistency. The choice of type should imply hierarchy: bigger, darker type for section heads and first subheads; smaller, lighter type for text and notes. The grid should reinforce that hierarchy—section heads and first subheads set off from the text by white space and/or rules, text evenly spaced and regular. The consistent application of the type and grid lets the exceptions stand out in a predictable way.

Every page must be consistent: the running head is the same distance from the top rule, the text starts at the same place on the page, the first subheads are consistently spaced between the text below and above them (more space above than below), and the text is indented the same amount on every page. In addition, text inside boxes should have a standard inset (no less than 6 points from the edge of the box).

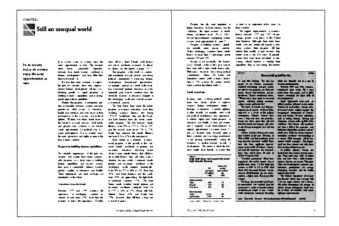

In the example at left, visual hierarchy is established through the use of rules, shading, placement, and type of style and size. The chapter title is large and set off by the small icon next to it as well as its placement over the outer margin. The first subhead is bold, the second is italic and both are set off from the text with an empty line above and below. The box and table also use text in decreasing weight and size, as its importance decreases. The box is set off by a shaded background and thin border. The table is set off by appropriate spacing and type that is smaller than the body text.

The table at right has a clear visual hierarchy. The title is the most prominent element in bold type, the text is a neutral, light type and the notes are smaller. Rules separate the title information from the column heads, the column heads from the body of the table and the body of the table from the notes.

Since 1975 both women and men have spent less time in total work in most of the developed regions

Time spent in work (hours per week)

	Economic activity		Unpaid housework	
	Female	Male	Female	Male
Northern America and Australia	18	44	36	10
Japan	28	56	31	3
Western Europe	15	41	35	8
Eastern Europe and USSR	36	52	39	15

Source: The World's Women 1970–1990: Trends and Statistics (United Nations publication, Sales No. E.90.XVII.3), p.82

References and further reading

Hedman, Birgitta, Francesca Perucci and Pehr Sundström (1996). *Engendering Statistics: A Tool for Change.* Örebro: Statistics Sweden Publications Services.

United Nations (1990). *Handbook for National Statistics Data Bases on Women and Development.* Sales No. E.89.XVII.9.

————— (1995). *The World's Women 1995: Trends and Statistics.* Sales No. E.95.XVII.2.

Wallgren, Anders, Britt Wallgren, Rolf Persson, Ulf Jorner and Jan-Aage Haaland (1996). *Graphing Statistics and Data.* London: SAGE Publications.

5. Producing and disseminating the book

PLANNING

Before the team begins writing, some fundamental issues of scope and organization should be decided. Specifically:

- How long the book will be (how many pages)
- What size the book will be (dimensions of the page)
- What the balance will be among text, charts and tables (for example, 65 per cent tables, 25 per cent text, 10 per cent charts)
- How the contents will be arranged (main messages, supporting messages, outline)

Decide on length

The factors that determine the length of any book are budget, content, audience, layout and how it is being printed.

Budget

The project managers should already have an idea of how many copies will be needed. Printing costs will vary significantly depending on the type of printing, how much can be done in-house, costs of paper and ink and so on. (See "Printing", below, for more details on printing options.) Within those constraints, however, fewer pages always means lower printing costs.

Content

Base the page estimate not on the amount of data accumulated but on how many points are going to be made (see "Messages", below). If there are one or two points for each indicator, decide how much will be written for each (two single-spaced pages, for example), then add a few pages for front matter (foreword, table of contents, copyright information), a preface or summary, bibliography—whatever additional material will be needed. Try to decide on an exact number of pages for each section since that will help guide the writing.

Placement of pages on a 16-page signature

Front

13	4	1	16
12	5	8	9

Back

15	2	3	14
10	7	6	11

Audience

Consider who will be reading the book when assigning a length to each indicator. How much time will they have? How technical can the writing be? If it is for politicians and leaders, for example, points should be made quickly—1,000 words (three typewritten pages) per indicator. If it is for fieldworkers and demographers, more detail is possible—2,500 words (seven typewritten pages) per indicator.

Layout

Manuscript length does not necessarily determine the length of the publication. A page that is typeset usually has more words per page than one that is typewritten or word-processed. A page of double-spaced typewritten text usually has about 350 words (in English). A two-column page typeset in 10-point type has about 700 words. Use a sample layout to determine the conversion between manuscript pages and typeset pages.

Printing

Try to think in multiples of 8 or 16 pages when setting a length for the book (if using offset printing). In offset printing, the pages are printed on both sides of a much larger sheet of paper, then folded down and cut. Each of those sheets is called a signature. The smallest possible signature is four pages (think of a greeting card: it has one fold and four sides that can be printed on), but generally a printer will use 16- or even 32-page signatures. If the book does not use all the pages in each signature, there will be blank pages at the end of the book. Remember to include front matter, which may be numbered separately, when doing the page count.

Decide on size

For a statistical manual with large tables, it is best to adopt the standard letter-size format— US letter, 8.5x11 inches, or A4, 21x29.7cm. Letter size is more flexible in terms of layout, but for the same reason it can be more difficult to lay out. A smaller size, such as 6x9 inches (15x23cm) or 4.25x5.5 inches (11x14cm), is simpler and can be more user-friendly but large tables are harder to fit.

Other possible dimensions are 7x10 inches, 7.5x9.25 inches and 10x10 inches. In general, however, unconventional page sizes are more expensive to print as there is more waste paper (from trimming).

Check with local print salespeople to find out the most economical sizes. Keep in mind that a smaller page size will mean fewer words per page and a longer book. In general, costs increase with page count rather than page size.

Parts of a book

These are all the possible components of a statistical publication. (Items in italics must be included.) The content of many of these components overlap and would not necessarily be used in the same publication—for example, the executive summary and the user's guide. Others can be combined to save space—for example, the foreword and the acknowledgements. A glossary of terms used will help the reader who may be unfamiliar with the terminology. It can be prepared by the writers. An index, on the other hand, where it is considered useful, should be prepared with specialized professional assistance. A list of abbreviations and acronyms is also recommended.

Parts of a book

Front cover
Inside cover
Title page
Copyright page
Acknowledgements
Foreword
Contents
List of tables and charts
Executive summary
Glossary of statistical terms
List of abbreviations, acronyms
User's guide or explanation of text
Chapters and tables
Annex tables
Text annexes
References
Bibliography (sources)
Index
Back cover

Decide on the balance of elements

Chapter 4 explains the different functions of tables, text and charts. The book should contain a mix of all three that is appropriate to the audience. For example, if mainly politicians and leaders are targeted, more text and fewer text tables but more charts may be appropriate. For a readership that is not as familiar with using statistical tables, the indicator tables should be grouped at the end of each chapter or in a statistical annex. For readers who do not need to refer to the basic data in tables, some of the more interesting numbers may be pulled out into smaller text tables.

A certain amount of the book will inevitably be large indicator tables. These are the crux of the publication and the foundation of all the messages and conclusions. However, the number of indicator tables can be limited by limiting the information included in each. It is not necessary to include data simply because they have been compiled. Choosing which data sets to include in the publication is just as important as choosing which points to make.

Most of the important points should be illustrated in a chart for three simple reasons:
- Readers (particularly laypeople) are more likely to look at a picture than a number.
- An illustration reinforces a point.
- Other media, such as journals, newspapers and magazines, are more likely to pick up and rebroadcast an interesting graphic than a table. If only a few charts are used, each should be made as valuable as possible.

Decide how to arrange the contents

To some degree, design considerations can shape the content of the book—certainly which aspects of the content will be highlighted. However, design should not interfere with content. With a rough idea of how the book will look—page size, words per page, room for figures and tables and so on—it is time to organize the content.

Chapter 3 gives a list of indicators to consider and is a good reference for indicator topics and order of presentation. Based on the project team's indicators and analysis, a provisional table of contents and estimate of the number of pages to be devoted to each chapter should be prepared. Chapters should be roughly equal in length, although there will almost certainly be more information for some than for others.

Here is a possibility:

Front matter (8 pages)—Title page, message from high-level, policy maker, preface, table of contents, list of abbreviations, Overview (6 pages)

Population, families and households (12 pages)

Public life and leadership (6 pages)

Education and training (10 pages)

Health and child-bearing (10 pages)

Housing, human settlements and environment (10 pages)

Work and the economy (6 pages)

Statistical sources and bibliography (4 pages)

Total: 72 pages plus cover (remember, the cover adds four more pages)

Make a dummy

It is often helpful to make a three-dimensional mock-up of the book to help to visualize the final product. For the cover, take two sheets of blank paper, staple them on the side and write in the text of the front and back covers and the inside covers.

Back cover Front cover

Inside front Inside back
cover   cover

Now take 36 sheets (or half the number of pages estimated), staple them on the side, number them 1 through 72 and write in what is planned on each page.

Working with the rough plan, decide which indicators will be presented in each chapter. For example, the 12-page chapter on education and training might have a two-page overview and 10 pages for indicators.

Do this for each chapter and then for the overview.

WRITING

In a gender statistics publication, the writing should fulfil two objectives. First, it should clearly and effectively convey the main messages based on the statistics. Second, it should express in simple yet lively terms the conclusions drawn from the sex-disaggregated data. These objectives will be reached if the writing is concise and limited to a central theme and supporting messages. Planning what to write before beginning will ensure this and make it possible to concentrate on content rather than form.

At the writing stage, the original goals, assumptions and hypotheses of the authors come up against the research findings themselves. Where the assumptions and hypotheses are borne out by the data, all that is required is to show the data and explain their significance. Where the data do not support the assumptions and hypotheses or contradict them, the authors must review the data and reconsider their conclusions.

Main message

The main message is the overall message of the publication, the single most important idea that the project team wants the reader to absorb. Determining the main message forces the writers to condense everything they know about the topic and everything they hope to achieve by writing about it into one statement. If they can not articulate it, then their reader certainly will not be able to. Use simple language and make the point at the start. (Most of the recommendations in this section on writing are drawn from the planning and drafting workbooks of Communications Development Incorporated, Washington, D.C.)

Examples:
For the first time, comprehensive data are available on women's economic, educational and health status.

Women's social, political and economic roles have been changing over the past 25 years—though only gradually in some areas.

After coming up with a provisional main message, ask:
• Does the message communicate the most important idea?
  NO→What is the most important idea? Rewrite.
• Is it longer than, say, 25 words?
  YES→Try to edit down.
• Could someone repeat the message word-for-word after one reading? (Try this on a colleague):
  NO→Use simpler language.

Supporting messages

After coming up with a good main message, think of a few supporting messages (usually three or four). In this case, there might be a supporting message for each of the indicator topics, for example, health and child-bearing, education and training, public life and leadership and so on. Unlike in other, less data-heavy publications, the indicators will direct the structure of the writing. Again, keep the supporting messages simple and clear.

Examples:
Government programmes targeted at pregnant women have resulted in lower infant mortality in all regions but women's health is still a problem in rural areas.

Though women now hold 23 per cent of municipal and regional elected offices, they still lag far behind men in national elected offices at only 8 per cent.

Subsections

Under each supporting message, think of three or four subsections. These will be the subheads for each chapter and will help organize the writers' points under similar topics.

Examples:
For the subsection that starts with the message: Government programmes targeted at pregnant women have resulted in lower infant mortality in all regions but women's health is still a problem in the poorest areas.
Subhead 1. Past successes
Subhead 2. Rural areas are the worst off
Subhead 3. Poor women's health status
Subhead 4. Projections

Put it together

The broad outline of the book is now complete. Think of the main message as the idea that ties the whole together and each supporting message as a chapter. On a fresh sheet of paper write the first supporting message (first chapter sentence) and subheads and list all the points to be made in that chapter under the appropriate subhead. Each of these points will become a paragraph. It may be helpful to note which data will be used to illustrate each point so the writers will have an idea of how many tables and charts there will be in the chapter.

Example:

Opening sentence: Women make up 51 per cent per cent of the population but hold only 11 per cent of elected political positions and make up only 3 per cent of heads of major companies.

Subhead 1. Women's representation still far from equal

Point 1: Over the past 30 years, women's representation at the local level has increased by only one-fifth percentage point a year on average.

Point 2: There has never been a woman head of State in this country nor in any of the surrounding countries.

Point 3: While women make up 51 per cent of the eligible electorate, they still hold only 11 per cent of all elected offices.

Point 4: Seventy per cent of all women in elected positions are involved in social, educational or health issues.

Point 5: Men hold 98 per cent of all policy, financial and executive offices.

Points that do not support the main message should be cut or the main message should be revised to include those points. Points that do not fit under any subhead should be cut or another subhead should be written to include them. When a final list of points is ready, check their order for continuity and flow. Do the same for all chapters of the book.

Overview, or summary

The opening chapter of the book is usually an overview or summary. Though similar in purpose, each performs a slightly different function. The ideal summary has as its opening paragraph the main message in 25–30 words and the three or four supporting messages, each in 25–30 words. The next three or four paragraphs elaborate on the supporting messages, followed by a short section on background and a somewhat longer section on issues and findings about those issues. Then follows a long section on what those findings mean for policy and what recommendations they suggest.

An overview, on the other hand, recapitulates the most important parts of the whole report, following the chapter structure. Executive summaries are more useful than overviews in that they do not merely reiterate the language of the chapters. For that reason, they are also harder to write.

PARAGRAPHS

The paragraph is the unit of composition for a piece of writing. Each paragraph should make one point with supporting details and examples. Try to think about a piece of writing in terms of paragraphs instead of pages. For example, a double-spaced typewritten page will usually contain between two and three paragraphs, so a 10-page report will have 25 paragraphs for a total of 25 points.

As paragraph topics are decided on, it will become clear that some will need to be expanded and that some can be compressed. This will help the writers rank their ideas by sections, subsections and points.

Paragraph contents

When the list of paragraphs is completed for each subsection, write the point of each paragraph on a fresh sheet of paper and list the examples and supporting details for that point. Where possible, refer to the data (table or chart) being used to make the point. The advantage of this technique is that ideas can be added under points as they occur to the writer, rather than on scraps of paper to be organized later.

Some points will have many examples while others may seem bare. In the first case, choose only the most pertinent examples or divide them into more than one point. In any event the examples must be explicit.

Writing a sentence that makes a strong point about the topic will help the author define the contents. Think about details or examples to be used to support the point. Then draft the paragraph, read it and rewrite it with any necessary improvements.

Paragraph drafts

With the contents of each paragraph spelled out, the material for each paragraph is clear. Writing the perfect paragraph will not be easy but it should be less difficult now that the order and content of the argument and paragraphs have been planned.

First, go back to the original point with its supporting details and examples. Some of these may have to be dropped and some added to develop the point more effectively. Next, decide on an order and place a corresponding number next to each detail and example that has been listed. Then write the paragraph.

Now ask:

- Do all the sentences pertain to the topic?
  NO→Delete if they are superfluous. If they introduce a new point, write a new paragraph based on that sentence.
- Does the point need to be rephrased?
  YES→Try stating out loud what point is to be made. This can help in choosing the right words.
- Is more than one point being made?
  YES→Divide the opening sentence into two new points and write a separate paragraph for each.
- Is there a logical flow to the sentences?
  NO→Rearrange until the flow seems right. Read the paragraph out loud to check flow.
- Can the language be simplified or superfluous words or constructions removed?
  YES→Do so.
- Is there unnecessary repetition?
  YES→Cut.
- Are there too may examples?
  YES→Cut the least interesting.

Two simple techniques can help the flow of the paragraph and give it more cadence. The first is to use words that coordinate the parts of the paragraph, for example:

First, ... Next, ... Last
One ... A second ... Yet a third
In addition ... Also ... However
Similarly ... Otherwise ... Consequently
Thus ... Therefore ... On the other hand

The second is to list items in a logical order: alphabetically, from smallest to largest (or largest to smallest), from worst to best (or best to worst) or from shortest to longest. For example:

Alphabetically

Women tend to outlive men everywhere except Bangladesh, Bhutan, Maldives and Nepal.

Smallest to largest

The largest increases in the proportions of women in urban areas were in Oceania (by 9 percentage points), Latin America and the Caribbean (by 14 percentage points), northern Africa (by 15 percentage points) and western Asia (by 18 percentage points).

Shortest to longest

Secrecy, insufficient evidence, and social and legal barriers continue to make it difficult to acquire data on domestic violence against women.

Section headings

Section headings are signposts for the reader and enable quick cross-referencing. They generally should be used for parts that are longer than two or three pages.

Although they do not present a complete idea, section headings should also be informative and interesting. Steer clear of such headings as "introduction", "summary", "background" and "conclusion", which are neither informative nor interesting.

Section head 1. Successes over the past 20 years

Section head 2. Where are the trouble spots and why?

Section head 3. Health status of the poorest women

Section head 4. The next 20 years—and beyond

Some pointers:
• Use the active voice
• Keep section heads in the same tense (usually the present tense)
• Keep heads short—no longer than two lines
• Avoid clichés and hackneyed phrases.

EDITING

It is recommended that a journalist or editor be contracted to edit the latter versions of the manuscript, but some general guidelines for editing early drafts of the book are given here.

Editing should fulfil two objectives. First, by eliminating unnecessary repetition, editing maintains clarity. Second, editing will help identify what information is missing from the text and encourage improvements to the publication's structure. Good editing emphasizes simplicity, clarity and the absence of jargon.

Editing tips

The first thing to do is analyse the structure of the text. To do this, make a paragraph plan which entails summarizing the meaning of the paragraph as briefly as possible. This allows the writer to check quickly the structure of the text and to determine what messages are either missing or repeated. The plan is also a useful tool for an editor who can easily grasp the main themes of the text without having to read the entire document.

The abbreviated list below gives editing tips that are fleshed out and more fully explained in any of the following books:

Bernstein, Theodore M. *The Careful Writer: A Modern Guide to English Usage*. New York: Atheneum, 1965.

The Chicago Manual of Style. 14th edition. Chicago: The University of Chicago Press, 1993.

Fowler, H.W. *A Dictionary of Modern English Usage*. 2d edition. Revised by Ernest Gowers. Oxford: Clarendon Press, 1987.

Ross-Larson, Bruce. *Edit Yourself*. New York: W.W. Norton & Co., 1982.

Strunk, William Jr. and E.B. White. *The Elements of Style*. 3rd edition. New York: Macmillan, 1979.

Words Into Type. 3rd edition. Englewood Cliffs, New Jersey: Prentice-Hall, 1974.

Construction

Fat

Writing is often larded with words that obscure the author's meaning rather than clarify it. Trim this fat off to direct the reader's attention to important words and ideas.
For example, reduce wordy constructions:

Wordy	*Better*
…provide a summary of…	…summarize the…
…have a tendency to…	…tend to…
It should be noted that women…	Women…
There are some regions that are…	Some regions are…
the reduction of debt	debt reduction

Pronoun references

Few things slow a reader down more than unclear pronoun references—signs of carelessness that quickly distract the reader from the author's meaning. Though the reader can usually divine what is meant, clarifying such references removes any doubt.

ORIGINAL

The Government has revised its social welfare policy and begun a programme of subsidizing school lunches in rural areas. *This* will encourage parents to enrol their children in school.

In many African countries nearly as many women as men are infected with HIV, and in some sub-Saharan cities, up to 40 per cent of *them* are infected.

REWRITTEN

The Government has revised its social welfare policy and begun a programme of subsidizing school lunches in rural areas. This *programme* will encourage parents to enrol their children in school.

In many African countries nearly as many women as men are infected with HIV, and in some sub-Saharan cities, up to 40 per cent of *women* are infected.

Dangling constructions

Danglers are phrases that are attached to the wrong subject. Often they appear at the beginning of a sentence. Danglers can be avoided by asking what the phrase refers to. If it refers to the wrong subject, the sentence should be rewritten.

ORIGINAL

After reviewing the latest unemployment figures, a policy change was announced by the President.

Widely available in urban Africa, 33 per cent of the rural population still lacks access to safe water.

REWRITTEN

After reviewing the latest unemployment figures, the President announced a policy change.

Widely available in urban Africa, safe water is accessible to only 33 per cent of the rural population.
or
Safe water is widely available in urban Africa, but 33 per cent of the rural population still lacks adequate access.

Abused relatives

That, which and who are often used as relative pronouns to introduce clauses that modify the nouns they follow. They are three of the most useful, and used, words in the English language.

That should be used to introduce a restrictive clause—a clause that restricts the definition or identity of the subject. Which introduces a clause that adds detail but does not limit or define the subject. Who is generally used for people and can introduce both types of clauses. Nonrestrictive clauses should be set off by commas, restrictive clauses should not.

As the following examples show, two sentences can mean entirely different things depending on whether a clause is restrictive or non-restrictive.

RESTRICTIVE

The coastal regions *that reported the lowest per capita income* had the highest infant mortality rates.
(Only those coastal regions with the lowest per capita income had the highest infant mortality rates. Coastal regions with higher incomes did not.)

The women in rural areas *who cooked over open stoves* had more respiratory infections than urban women did.
(Only those rural women who cooked over open stoves had more respiratory infections than urban women did.)

NON-RESTRICTIVE

The coastal regions, *which reported the lowest per capita income,* had the highest infant mortality rates.
(All coastal regions as a group had the highest infant mortality rates and they also reported the lowest income.)

The women in rural areas, *who cooked over open stoves,* had more respiratory infections than urban women did.
(All women in rural areas cooked over open stoves and they had more respiratory infections than urban women did.)

DISSEMINATING THE BOOK

Publishing is not the final step in the publication. Editors and authors must also take part in the dissemination process to promote the materials if their work is to make an impact on public policy. The promotion and marketing of the book may range from distributing leaflets to full-colour advertising, lecture tours, conferences and seminars, and electronic distribution.

The principal goals of publishing statistical studies on gender are to identify and make the readership aware of the socio-economic and political disparities between women and men, to set a standard for data collection in this area, and to back up or challenge existing theories or studies on gender disparity. As the scope and diversity of the readership increases the more likely it is that these biases will be remarked on, further studied and hopefully eradicated. Without effective marketing and dissemination techniques, reaching those goals will be almost impossible.

Marketing suggestions

Marketing and dissemination planning should begin while the book is still an idea. Funds for marketing and dissemination should be included in the project's overall budget. A well designed book with a large print run requires a large marketing budget to move the product and create a return on the resources invested in design and printing.

Evangelists

Turn all members of the work and advisory teams into evangelists who will personally bring the book's messages to the target audiences—cabinet ministers, members of parliament, editors of major publications, heads of research institutes, heads of interested non-governmental organizations and so on.

Flyers

One option is to produce flyers promoting the gender statistics book before it is published. These are called blads (usually two- to eight-page booklets with sample pages from the planned book, complete with cover and contents).

To make a blad requires real text, which means that the statistics group must create pages from whatever material is available and lay them up into a sample of the book. But most tasks are carried out after the study is complete and ready for publication. To save money, leaflets and circulars can be created and distributed by photocopying parts of the book to mail to universities, libraries and other potentially interested organizations. These circulars can also contain information about ordering the book through the mail or by telephone.

Journal articles

In many countries, new statistical publications are expected to be subject to a peer review before they are released to the general public. Before any statement is released to the press, an article summarizing the main conclusions and new data should be submitted to the appropriate national or international journals. The approval of the scientific and development community will carry weight with policy makers and heads of Government and will bolster the credibility of the findings.

Press releases

Like any product, the more able the producers are to pique interest in their product, the more successful they will be at dissemination. To this end, press releases about the contents and findings of the study are another inexpensive method of reaching the study's potential audience. Releases featuring news about the contents and publication of the study may be sent to print and broadcast media. Press releases are inexpensive to produce, requiring only a typewriter, media lists and postage. Any particularly dramatic charts should also be sent as part of the press release, as print and electronic media can easily pick up and broadcast such information. Make sure any charts distributed are clean and easy to understand.

Announcements with synopses

Synopses of the main messages and findings of the book should be forwarded to journals and periodicals that specialize in gender and related studies. These publications are eager to receive news and information concerning the outcome of gender-based studies and welcome abstractions of study contents—they might also print information on where to order or purchase the book.

Lectures and presentations

Although they reach a smaller audience, lectures or symposia can spread news of the study through word-of-mouth. A representative of the statistics group or publisher who visits governmental and non-governmental organizations and universities can deliver speeches and distribute materials related to the project. Conferences on women's or gender studies are effective for disseminating information about the project. The lecturer or representative can augment his presentation with audio-visual materials, pamphlets and circulars.

Electronic media

International computer networks such as the Internet can cover vast demographic areas for little money. Several Internet sites deal with gender, development and international issues and are excellent for sparking interest and debate. Electronic mail can also reach potential readers.

Using these dissemination methods, the gender statistics study should reach the intended audience.

GETTING FEEDBACK

An evaluation of the gender statistics publication project following its production and distribution helps determine its effectiveness. The publication's preparation and distribution should be examined first. However, the most important aspect of the evaluation is receiving feedback from the publication's users.

Interaction between the producers and the audience allows the producers to assess whether requirements were met and, thus, gauge the efficacy of the publication. Generally, the evaluation is carried out by the planners of the publication, by donors or by the national statistical service that generated the original data employed.

Help from readers

Factors to evaluate

Several relevant factors can be reviewed to evaluate the publication. Was the publication produced on time? Did the overall costs remain within the predetermined budget? These questions are easily answered and provide an immediate reference point for evaluation. The advisory group should be polled, since it provided guidance throughout the preparation and production of the publication.

The accuracy of the statistics themselves and the resulting conclusions should be examined. Errors in the original data can include inadequate coverage of the population (components not adequately covered or surveys that are incomplete), weaknesses in the responses gathered from surveys (questions not well formulated, interviewers not properly trained, respondents who are unclear, information processed incorrectly, analyses that are inadequate), or printing errors. If it is feasible, any inaccuracies or errors should be adjusted prior to the distribution of the publication (errata sheets are one solution). Of course, it is likely that an overall evaluation will occur only after the fact, in which case the results can be used to assist in the production of future publications.

Determine usefulness

Once the preparation of the publication has been evaluated, the publication's usefulness for its readers should be examined. An informal evaluation can establish which areas require detailed examination. If there are budget limitations, the available funds can be employed to evaluate those areas that most urgently require change. The objectives of the dissemination plan should be reviewed and the extent to which they were achieved should be established. Was the publication properly advertised? How was the press coverage?

An examination of the manner in which advocacy groups employ the publication is also helpful. If the publication is a tool that enables advocacy groups to engender changes in national policy, these groups should be addressed directly and surveyed.

Surveys

One way to obtain user feedback is to include a reader survey with the publication (see sample on facing page).

The results from a survey identify user groups and determine their priorities. Results can also distinguish if these priorities were adequately addressed, if they were omitted and which are irrelevant or obsolete.

People who are on mailing lists or received the publication for free can be surveyed by letter or telephone.

Meetings

Another, more direct method for communicating with readers and receiving feedback is to organize a meeting of known users to discuss the publication.

Results

The results of the evaluation are essential for formulating a plan for updating the publication or even for creating a different type of publication. The publication should be reassessed in light of the evaluation and updated or revamped accordingly.

Results of the evaluation should be written down so that participants in other projects can refer to them for help.

SAMPLE QUESTIONNAIRE FOR USERS

A. Respondent information

Name: _____

Organization: _____

Address: _____

_____

_____

Field

_____ Population

_____ Health

_____ Education

_____ Labour

_____ Agriculture

_____ Finance

_____ Urban planning

_____ Academia

_____ Media

_____ Other (specify):

Type of work or function:

_____ Researcher

_____ Planner

_____ Policy maker

_____ Programme designer

_____ Project formulation/implementation

_____ Statistician

_____ Other (specify):

B. How did you learn of this publication?

_____ Publicity in the media

_____ Articles in newspapers or magazines

_____ Through study/research

_____ Business sources

_____ Statistical office

_____ While working in a related field

_____ Through another government publication (specify):

_____ One or more requests by users

_____ Decision was made by others

_____ Familiarity with previous, related publications

_____ Suggestion by a superior/instructor

_____ Need for a source on gender statistics

_____ Other (specify):

C. Where did you purchase this publication?

_____ In a bookstore

_____ Through a government office

_____ Ordered directly from producer

Ordered directly from publisher

D. How did you use this publication?

Which areas did you consult?

(specify sub-category when possible)

_____ Population:

_____ Families and households:

_____ Labour:

_____ Political roles:

_____ Education:

_____ Health:

_____ Housing:

What are key areas that interest you?

(rank in order of importance)

_____ Population

_____ Families and households

_____ Labour

_____ Political roles

_____ Education

_____ Health

_____ Housing

What areas would you like to see investigated further?

(rank in order of importance)

_____ Population

_____ Families and households

_____ Labour

_____ Political roles

_____ Education

_____ Health

_____ Housing

_____ Other (specify):

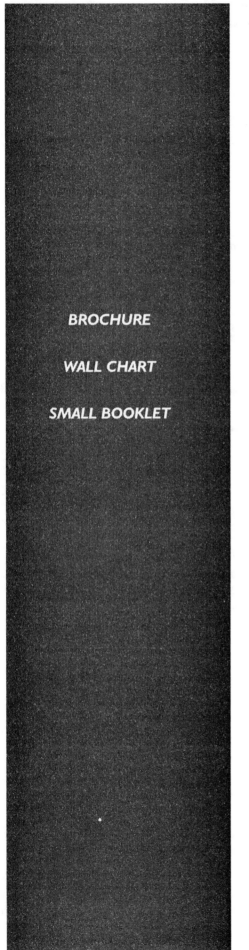

BROCHURE

WALL CHART

SMALL BOOKLET

ANNEX
Preparation of supplementary promotional materials

Although considerable energy and resources will be spent producing the book itself, the utility of brochures, wall charts and less elaborate publications, for example small booklets, must not be overlooked. These smaller pieces can go a long way towards promoting and disseminating the messages of the book or data on the situation of women and men in the country. Their size and brevity make them accessible and useful for most readers and handy for those who are interested in only a few illustrative numbers. In addition, their low cost allows them to be more widely distributed than the book itself.

BROCHURE

A brochure based on the book can serve many functions. Mainly, it will be used as a promotional piece to announce the existence and availability of the report. Since the physical dimensions of a brochure are small, there is not much room to go into detail or present large amounts of data. And since the goal of the brochure is to spark people's interest in the book itself, it would be inappropriate to try to include all the findings.

Dimensions

In general, a brochure is printed on both sides of one letter- or legal-size sheet, with one, two or three folds resulting in four, six or eight panels, respectively. Some thought should be given to the way the brochure is folded and the order in which the panels will be viewed. A clever design can get the reader's attention and lead him or her through the main messages in a logical and effortless way.

Illustration 1 shows the three most commonly used folds for brochures, with approximate dimensions for each panel of text. The designer should decide in advance which type of fold will be used, since it will greatly affect the design. Text should be inset from the left and right edges of the paper by at least a quarter of an inch.

Content

There is not much room in a brochure to make all the points that are supported in the book. Trying to squeeze in too much information inevitably results in columns of very small text, which is hard to read. It is better to pick the one or two main messages with one or two concrete examples in the form of charts, tables or numbers presented within the text.

The cover of the brochure will usually mimic the cover of the final book or could include a thumbnail of the report cover, if it is available. Another more commercial approach might be to take one of the more dramatic numbers among the findings and display it prominently on the cover panel, either with text alone or with a chart and some text.

Apart from the messages, the following information must be readily apparent: the name of the report, the date it will be available if it is not yet out, the name and address of the organization that has produced it, and an address and phone number from which the report may be ordered (if that is different). Other information that could be included might cover the members of the advisory board, agencies or bookstores where the report is being sold (or distributed), an order form for the report and collateral materials (a poster, more brochures, etc.) or a list of related publications from the same agency along with ordering information.

Illustration I. Paper sizes

Letter
8.5" x 11" or 66p x 51p

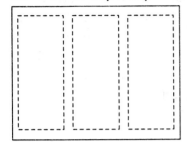

2 fold, 6 panels
Each panel is 18p wide and 43p high
with a 2p outside margin and a
4p gutter between each panel

A4
297mm x 210mm

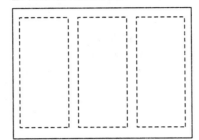

2 folds, 6 panels
Each panel is 79mm wide and
180mm high with a 10mm outside
margin and a 20mm gutter between
each panel

Legal
8.5" x 14" or 84p x 51p

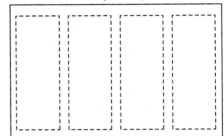

3 folds, 8 panels
Each panel is 17p wide and 43p high
with a 2p outside margin and a
4p gutter between each panel

Types of folds

Barrel fold

Gate fold

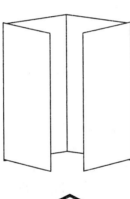

Accordion fold

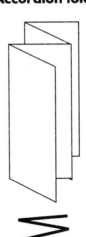

Distribution

Brochures are often part of a press kit or other promotional material. They are also used as direct mail pieces sent to organizations, academic and research institutions, individuals, and the like who may need the information presented in the book. In general, brochures do not need to be sent in an envelope. (When designing a self-mailer, remember to reserve one panel for the address label.) Because they are cheap to print, brochures make good hand-outs at conferences, lectures, social events and other gatherings.

Design and layout

Brochures are relatively inexpensive to print because they require little paper and many brochures can be printed from one sheet. When designing a brochure, it is important to limit the amount of text and also to think about the placement and size of the text. Because the width of each panel is small, body text in brochures must be small as well. However, small type size can be a deterrent to the reader. One way to lead the reader into the text is to use a larger type size for the heads or main messages. If these are sufficiently compelling, the reader will want to read on.

If there are any charts in the brochure, they should be very clear. Complicated charts should be reserved for other outputs—for example, a poster—where there is more room for explanations. Favour bar charts, line charts or pie charts, rather than scatter charts or area charts.

Illustration 2 provides a suggested template for the design of an accordion-fold brochure with six panels (three on each side) that would be a self-mailer. If the brochure is not a self-mailer, the back cover panel might be used for more information on the organization or a list of distributors of the book, for example. Or the designer might want to extend the inside story to three panels and move the order form to the back panel.

Printing

One way to attract the reader is by using colour. A two-colour brochure is still quite inexpensive and the second colour can be used to enliven and highlight the important points. In general, the two colours are black and another, brighter colour. But it is possible to use two colours without black, as long as one is dark enough for the text to be legible. In a two-colour brochure, the designer might want to apply a light shade behind the text on some or all of the panels for variety.

Although it is acceptable to use two colours for the brochure even if the report is only one colour, it is not advisable to deviate too much from the overall design and feel of the report. The designer should consider how all the pieces will look together, especially if they will be used in a press kit or bundled for distribution. The design should be appropriate to each piece, while still clearly belonging to a family of products.

Illustration 2. Sample brochure

Panel #1   Back cover   Front cover   Panel #2   Panel #3   Panel #4

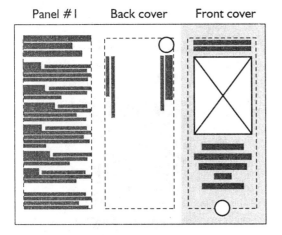
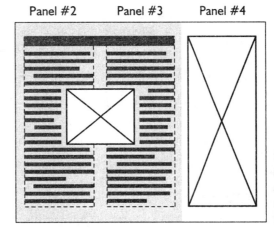

Shaded areas indicate where a second colour might be used in the background

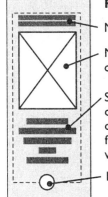

Front cover

Name of organization

Miniature cover of book

Short description of book or statement about status of women based on findings in book (15–25 words)

Logo of organization

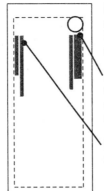

Back cover for self-mailer
Leave room for address and postage

Logo, name and address of organization (sideways)

Name of book (sideways)

Panel #1
Possible content:
• Contents of the book by section with the main message for each
• Reviews by policy makers and academicians
• The most important or intriguing findings and numbers, in bullet form

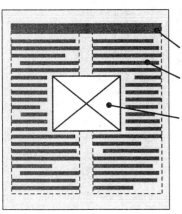

Panels #2 and #3

Name of book

Main message of book with some numbers

Graph or table illustrating the most important numbers or trend

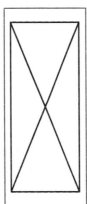

Panel #4
Order form
Should include:
• Payment options
• Number of copies to be ordered
• Cost per copy (including discounts for special groups)

May include:
• Other publications from the same organization
• Check box to be added to mailing list

Illustration 3. Brochure example

Contents

Overview

1. Population, households and families
Numbers of women—numbers of men; households and families; child-bearing and child-rearing

2. Population growth, distribution and environment
Where women and men live; migration; women and the rural environment in developing countries

3. Health
Life expectancy; the health of girls and boys; health risks; reproductive health; disability

4. Education and training
Literacy; enrolments; education and child-bearing; higher education

5. Work
Work and time use; women and men in the labour force; the informal sector; child labour; access to credit; unemployment; gender in the labour market

6. Power and influence
Top positions in politics and business; women in the United Nations—the first 50 years; women in the media; violence against women

Contributing agencies:
The World's Women 1995 was prepared by the Statistical Division, Department for Economic and Social Information and Policy Analysis of the United Nations Secretariat, as a collaborative effort with the United Nations Children's Fund (UNICEF), the United Nations Population Fund (UNFPA), the United Nations Development Programme (UNDP), the United Nations Development Fund for Women (UNIFEM) and the Division for the Advancement of Women and the Department of Public Information of the United Nations Secretariat. Additional support was provided by the International Research and Training Institute for the Advancement of Women (INSTRAW), the United Nations Educational, Scientific and Cultural Organization (UNESCO), the World Food Programme (WFP) and the World Health Organization (WHO).

The World's Women 1995
Trends and Statistics

United Nations Publications
Room DC2-853, Dept.D007
New York, NY 10017

Women and men too often live in different worlds— worlds that differ in access

The empowerment of women is an important end in itself. In addition, it is essential for the achievement of sustainable human development.

to education, in work opportunities, in health needs, in personal security and in leisure time.

The World's Women 1995 Trends and Statistics

The World's Women 1995: Trends and Statistics

With issues of gender equality moving to the top of the global development agenda, better understanding of women's and men's contributions to society is essential for speeding the movement from agenda to policy to practice. *The World's Women 1995: Trends and Statistics* provides information and analyses to highlight the economic, political and social differences that still separate women's and men's lives and how these differences are changing.

How different are women's and men's lives? Anecdote and misperception abound, in large part because good information has been lacking, leaving policy ill-informed, strategy unfounded, practice unquestioned. Fortunately, this is beginning to change. *The World's Women 1995: Trends and Statistics* presents statistical pictures of the changes that have taken place and the situation of women and men in the areas of health, schooling, family life, work and public life.

• Literacy rates for women have increased over the past few decades—to at least 75 per cent in most countries of Latin America and the Caribbean and eastern and south-eastern Asia. But high rates of illiteracy among women remain in much of Africa and in parts of Asia.

• Major obstacles still arise when women strive to translate their high-level education into social and economic advancement. In the world of business, for example, women rarely account for more than 1 or 2 per cent of senior management positions.

• In formal politics—as heads of state, ministers and members of parliament—women's participation remains the exception. At the end of 1994 only 10 women were heads of state or government.

• Many women are choosing to marry later and have fewer children. Those who wait have better access to education and greater opportunities to improve their lives.

• Women's increased access to education, to employment and to contraception, coupled with declining rates of infant mortality, have contributed to the worldwide decline in fertility.

• Too many women still have no access to reproductive health care. More than half a million women die each year in childbirth and millions more develop pregnancy-related health complications.

Chart 3.17
Estimated levels and trends in maternal mortality, 1983 and 1988

	Maternal deaths (thousands)		Maternal mortality per 100,000 live births	
	1983	1988	1983	1988
Developed regions	6	4	30	26
Africa				
Northern	24	17	500	360
Sub-Saharan Africa	126	151	670	600
Latin America and Caribbean				
Central America	9	8	240	160
South America	23	17	290	220
Caribbean	2	2	220	260
Asia and Pacific				
Eastern Asia	12	30	55	120
South-eastern Asia	52	42	420	340
Southern Asia	230	224	650	570
Western Asia	14	12	340	280
Oceania	2	1	300	600
Total	500	509		

Note: Figures for maternal deaths may not add to totals due to rounding.

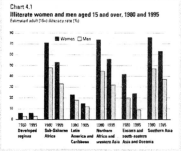

Chart 4.1
Illiterate women and men aged 15 and over, 1980 and 1995
Estimated adult (15+) illiteracy rate (%)

■ Women □ Men

1980 1995 Developed regions | 1980 1995 Sub-Saharan Africa | 1980 1995 Latin America and Caribbean | 1980 1995 Northern Africa and western Asia | 1980 1995 Eastern and south-eastern Asia and Oceania | 1980 1995 Southern Asia

• The number of women contracting HIV is growing faster than the number of men. Young women are most susceptible. In Uganda, reported AIDS cases among women aged 15–25 are twice those of men.

• Two thirds to three quarters of household work in developed regions is performed by women. In most countries studied women spend 30 hours or more on housework each week while men spend around 10 hours. Even when employed outside the home, women do most of the housework. Among household tasks the division of labour remains clear and definite in most countries.

The World's Women 1995: Trends and Statistics
E. 95.XVII.2 92-1-161372-8, 216 pp., $15.95
For information on how to purchase a copy of this or any other title, please see order form.

WALL CHART

A poster, or wall chart, can be produced in lieu of or in conjunction with the brochure. It can be used as a promotional item, an educational tool, or a professional resource—or a combination of the three. The main goal of the wall chart is that it be informative and appealing enough that people will want to hang it on their wall.

Dimensions

A wall chart can be created in a great range of sizes. To bring down the cost of printing, it is advisable to talk to the printer about what sizes are most efficient. However, an unusual size—say, taller or wider—can have a dramatic effect. Another consideration is the size of the wall chart when folded; it should be small enough to fit in a folder or press packet, or it may be shrink-wrapped with the report itself.

Illustration 4. Standard wall chart sizes

25 x 38 inches
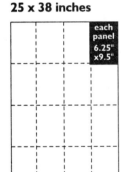

24 x 36 inches
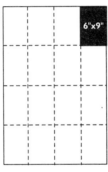

20 x 26 inches
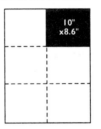

17 x 22 inches
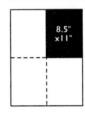

Standard sizes do not take into account bleeds. An extra quarter inch, at least, should be allowed on each edge with a bleed.

A0 (841mm x 1189mm)
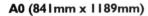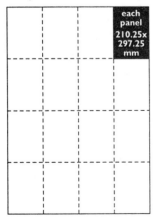

A1 (584mm x 841mm)
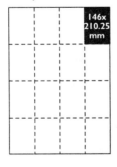

A2 (420mm x 594mm)
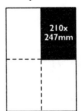

Content

Wall charts for statistical reports, unlike other kinds of posters, usually find their best use as quick reference material for schools and other institutions. Therefore, a large, easy-to-follow chart or table, rather than a strong photograph or illustration, is the most appropriate content.

The target audience and expected location of the wall chart must be considered when selecting topics and designing graphic presentations. In classrooms and meeting halls, wall charts with topical outlines and basic figures can guide lectures and provide a focus for discussion. In libraries and offices where data are frequently referenced for research papers and policy decisions, simple tables and graphs would be useful.

As in the brochure, the name of the report, the agency producing it, and an address and telephone number are all required. Unlike the brochure, however, the sources for the data on the wall chart should be clearly listed, since it will be used for reference. The sources will follow the same format as those in the report (see chapter 2, "Format of referencing sources of data").

Distribution

The poster may be mailed to schools, libraries, universities, government agencies, non-governmental organizations, and other research and policy agencies. It may be shrink-wrapped and included with the report. It will certainly be part of any press kit. When presenting the report at a press conference, lecture, convention or other public gathering, the poster should be prominently displayed.

Design and layout

A wall chart must be designed for clarity. Its primary objective is to communicate quickly, ideally within 10 to 30 seconds. Because it communicates both visually and literally, a wall chart should use large type and avoid many numbers, labels, notes and complicated keys. Well designed graphs or maps present a better means for attracting attention and for communicating the message quickly.

The poster will probably be printed on one side only. Therefore, some thought should be given to which panel will be the "cover" when the poster is folded, since all panels will be visible when it is unfolded. When the content of the poster is mostly numbers, presented in a large table, the designer might consider using a graphic such as a map or a screened-back photograph as a backdrop, as long as it does not obscure the text. It is essential that the numbers be easy to read across and down. Therefore, consider using rules, colour or shading to

Illustration 5. Sample wall chart

Text explaining main messages of book, the trends observed in the table.

Cover panel will be on top when wall chart is folded. Contains title of book and name of organization.

One or more tables listing the major indicators: fertility, mortality, income, employment, and so on.

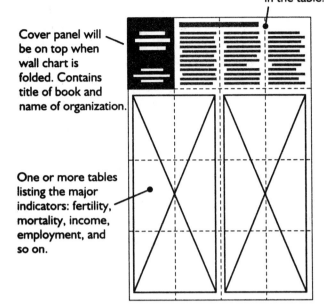

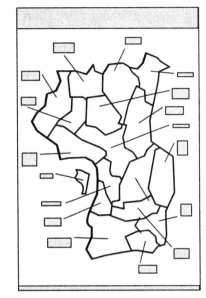

Back of poster may be blank or could include a large graphic, such as a map. In this case, the country is divided by province, with one or two indicators illustrated for each province.

aid the reader in finding the correct number. It should be noted, however, that presenting a large table of numbers on the wall chart limits its appeal and therefore its audience.

If a chart is the main element in the poster, it should be of sufficient sophistication to warrant using a poster-sized sheet, but not too complicated to follow.

The wall chart should generally present data on one topic graphically, with one central message. The main message could, however, be communicated by using more than one indicator. (See chapter 3 for a discussion on indicators relating to different topics, subtopics and their policy relevance.) The choice of focus for the wall chart should be guided by the intended audience and the type of response expected. The wall chart could be used to lend support to prevailing notions about the gender gap, to highlight unexpected findings generated by analysis of the data, or to further some policy initiatives.

If the wall chart is to be used to present mainly numbers, it is a good idea to use a grid to aid design (illustration 4). One possible grid is the lines on which the poster will be folded (usually quarters). The grid will help give the wall chart a sense of order and consistency, which is otherwise difficult to achieve when the wall chart is large and there is so much information that could be displayed.

The following are some points to remember when designing a wall chart.
- Title—The title should convey the message of the wall chart. It should state in clear terms what the chart is trying to say. The title should be large, legible from 10 feet away, and should contrast with the background—light letters on a dark background or dark letters on a light background. The title should span the width of the poster. The wall chart should include only enough specific data to support the title.

- *Visual element*—The visual element, which can take the form of a chart, a map or a drawing, should use data to illustrate the title of the poster. A subhead should be added to explain the element if the title does not.
- *Verbal elaboration*—Two or three short statements can be used to back up the message in the title and the graphic. The text should refer directly to the graphic or any other data or text in the poster. It is a good idea to repeat in the text some of the data presented in the chart to back up the message.

Use of colour

Unlike a brochure or booklet, colour is very important in a poster, especially for larger sizes. The reason for this is mostly aesthetic—a 24-by-36-inch white piece of paper with black text on it will be too stark to make an appealing poster. But there is also the issue of communication—when presenting a large amount of information, it is helpful to have a second or third colour to help organize the data and guide the reader's eye along the page. Light bars of colour behind alternating rows of table can be a great aid to finding the right number. Likewise, colour coding can greatly enhance a large map or chart.

On the other hand, too much colour can make the poster garish and an eyesore. Especially when two or more bright, vivid colours are combined. Save the bright colour for small icons or symbols. Use a lighter value of the colour behind text or numbers. Remember, the goal is to make the data as easy to read as possible.

Choice of paper

On the technical side, since the poster will, it is hoped, be hanging on a wall for some time, a durable, coated paper stock should be used. In addition, a flood (edge-to-edge) varnish will help against scuffing and fingerprints, especially on areas with heavy ink coverage. Varnishing both sides can prevent the poster from curling. Since the poster will probably be folded rather than rolled up in a tube, choose a paper that will not crack on the folds and avoid heavy ink coverage.

SMALL BOOKLET

A small booklet that presents data in a clear and simple format—without trying to analyse numbers in any detail or challenge policy—is a fast and low-cost way of providing unified and organized data for rapid dissemination. It can be a sound basis for discussions and decision-making—and a good starting point for broader, more analytical publications. The audience is typically government officials, policy makers, non-governmental organizations, academic and research institutions and advocates of gender equality.

The goal of such a booklet is to make basic gender statistics available to policy makers, advocates, the media and anyone else concerned with gender. The booklet should be easily understood by lay people, and should improve dialogue between users and producers of gender-specific statistics.

The booklet should cover the major topics or fields where data have been compiled and should present the data by using a comprehensive set of graphics and tables to convey the national situation of women in relation to men.

Dimensions

Many dimensions are possible and, again, it is worth consulting the printer about which will be most efficient and cost-effective. Pages must be large enough to fit at least one chart or small table, or both, large enough to be deciphered at a glance. A small but common size for a booklet is roughly 4.25" x 5.5" (11 cm x 23.5 cm), which is a fourth of the dimensions of the letter-size sheet, or any derivative of the standard sheet size in a country, to maximize

Illustration 6. Booklet sizes

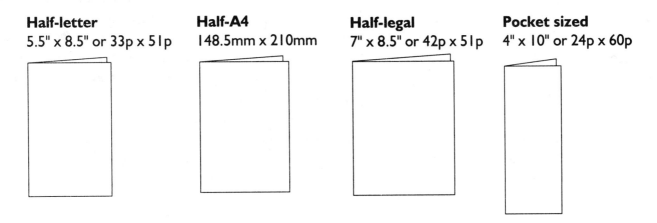

Half-letter	**Half-A4**	**Half-legal**	**Pocket sized**
5.5" x 8.5" or 33p x 51p	148.5mm x 210mm	7" x 8.5" or 42p x 51p	4" x 10" or 24p x 60p

portability and minimize paper waste. A small page size limits the amount of information and the type size that can be presented in the tables. A half-letter size is sometimes used.

For purposes of economy, the booklet should not have more than 72 pages in a format that can be easily saddle stitched (staple-bound).

Many of the national gender statistics booklets have used the quarter-letter or quarter-A4 dimensions. It is, however, easier to do the layout with the half-letter or half-A4, since this gives more space to fit charts and tables, especially wider or larger tables.

Content

The purpose of the booklet is to provide a quick reference to key indicators and messages in a simplified, condensed form. It may be the only report on gender statistics or be complementary to the book. It could in general be assumed that for many, this is the only comprehensive source of data on women and men. It should therefore be seen as an independent publication.

Because the booklet is attempting to present the data mainly in the form of small and simple tables and charts, the content is more straightforward. Analysis should be kept to a minimum. The text should be brief and specific to the data in the tables or charts being interpreted. It should clarify or highlight the main findings without resorting to explanation of the factors or background information.

The content of the booklet may vary according to the issues identified by those producing the booklet, but the following is one example of possible sections for such a booklet. See chapter 2 for some guidelines on identifying gender goals and issues.

Preface

A preface to the booklet, written by someone responsible for its production, should state the goals of the publication and make a general comment on gender statistics, women in development or other national concerns relevant to the material presented. The preface might also include information about sources of data, or acknowledgments for help in producing the publication.

The goal for women and men in development

Follow the preface with a general statement about the goals for women and men in development. This statement could be illustrated by presenting a national or international mandate for achieving those goals. It could include excerpts from a constitution or royal decree regarding the rights of individuals with respect to opportunity, or from a national or international plan for development. For example:

> The Platform for Action is an agenda for women's empowerment. It aims at accelerating the implementation of the Nairobi Forward-looking Strategies for the Advancement of Women and to removing all the obstacles to women's active participation in all spheres of public and private life through a full and equal share in economic, social, cultural and political decision-making.
>
> [*Report of the Fourth World Conference on Women*, Beijing, 4–15 September 1995 (United Nations publication, Sales No. E.96.IV.13), para. 1.]

The need for statistics on women and men

Why are such statistics needed and who benefits from them? What is the goal in collecting such data? Clear answers to these questions can go a long way towards raising support for producers of gender statistics. Spell out how statistics relate to development planning and programming. For example:

> Statistics influence knowledge and attitudes everywhere. They have an especially important role in policy development as a tool to:
> - Raise consciousness about the situation today and changes over time
> - Provide ideas for measures to be taken
> - Provide a sound base for policy
> - Evaluate the effects of measures that have been taken.
>
> (Hedman and others, 1996, p. 41.)

Glossary of terms and tips on how to read statistics

It should not be assumed that all users and potential users of statistics are familiar with the terms and symbols found in statistical publications. Provide the reader with a guide on how to read charts and a glossary of statistical and technical terms. For example, percentage (%) can indicate the proportion of all women or the proportion of all men with a specific characteristic, such as head of household, or it can indicate distribution within a specific group, such as the proportion of women to men among employees within an industry. Any statistical terms used in the booklet, such as formal and informal sector, should be defined.

Indicators and data

The booklet should aim to present data for each of the subject-matter fields discussed—for example, (a) population, families and households; (b) public life and leadership; (c) education and training; (d) health and child-bearing; (e) housing, human settlements and the environment; (f) work and the economy. The number of topics and indicators considered under each is related to the availability of adequate and timely data and the desired size of the overall book. (See chapter 2, "Listing indicators".)

What remains to be done?

At the end of the booklet, think about spelling out the long-term goals for women in development. Mention the importance of dialogue and cooperation between the users and producers of statistics. What problems in the collection and compilation of statistics need improvement and in what way? For example, underuse of existing data, data gaps, biased measures, concepts and classifications, and poor links between users and producers of gender-specific statistics.

Information about the national statistics office

Include areas of focus, contacts, phone numbers and addresses.

Design and printing

The elements of presentation used in the booklet will be text, tables, charts, and photographs or hand-drawn artwork if desired. Photographs or illustrations on title pages are a good way to identify the topics. Each topic could therefore start on a new page and the title page for each topic could have the drawing/picture that relates to the subject of the section. This makes the reader reflect on the gender issues and focus better on what the numbers that follow are saying about women, men and development.

Remember, the goals are simplicity and clarity. Check at every step to ensure the design is as simple as possible and cannot confuse the reader.

Make a list of all the chapters for the booklet and list the indicators to be illustrated beneath the appropriate headings. Then determine the number of pages it will take to display everything. In general, unless making a comparison of related indicators, try to limit a page to one or two indicators. If an indicator consists of a large amount of data that will make up a table, it might have to cover two facing pages.

Determine the typefaces to be used for text, figures, labels and heads. For information on type, refer to the section on design principles in chapter 4 of the Handbook. Whatever styles are chosen, they must remain consistent throughout the booklet.

Determine presentation

On the list of chapters and indicators, jot down next to each indicator a general statement about what the data explain. Is the number a percentage or a unit? Does it show a trend over time? Is there a comparison? How many things are being compared? For example:

> Indicator: labour force by occupation—in every occupation, the number of men and women participants is far from equal.

This process will help to indicate which data might have an interesting point that could be illustrated in a chart better than a table.

Present data as a table, a bar chart, a line chart or a pie chart. Data should not be presented in text, but perhaps summarized in a few words after a table to offer additional perspective. For example, after presenting the age at first marriage for women in six different age groups, summarize the data: "About two thirds of all married women married the first time before 20 years of age".

The booklet should aim to balance the presentation of data in different formats. Too much of one format, such as tables, becomes monotonous. But not all data are appropriate for charts. A diverse presentation will keep readers interested, increasing comprehension and retention of information. Text, no matter how brief, stating the main finding from the table or chart, also breaks the monotony in presentation.

Consistency should guide design and presentation. If population shares are plotted in a pie chart on one page, plot population shares in pie charts throughout the section or the booklet. If an item appears in a table as a column heading, do not make it a line item in another table. Label consistently—do not refer to "life expectancy at birth" in one table and "life expectancy" in another.

Constructing a table

When constructing a table, make sure no data are missing and that no cells are empty. Round all numbers to the nearest whole, unless the range is particularly small or detailed. Place data in columns with text left justified and numbers right justified so that the last number in the series is aligned with those beneath it. Use consistent symbols for "not available" or "not applicable" in the appropriate cells.

Make sure a table has the following elements: title, notes, defined symbols and source of data.

Present data in tables if:
- The goal is to deliver numerical values
- There are any missing data that would represent a break in a chart or line
- The range of data is very large, such as 0.1 to 1,000
- The data are too awkward for a chart—that is, the labels are too long, the range is too large, or the data are averages
- There is no discernable pattern
- The data are abstract—standard deviations, gini coefficients or regressions

For more detailed information about tables, refer to chapter 4, "Presenting statistics and indicators".

Constructing bar and line charts

First determine the elements of the chart and how to plot them. Time is always plotted on the x-axis. Unless the range is particularly small, always round numbers on the axis.

Hints:
- Do not mix horizontal and vertical bars on the same page
- If the data reflect negative values, plot bars on a horizontal axis (below the axis)
- If comparing two indicators, plot the bars on opposing sides of a vertical axis
- A line chart should never consist of more than three lines

Present data in a bar chart if:
- The subject measured is a discontinuous set—for example, regions, male and female, fertility rate and maternal mortality
- The goal is to present the relationship between two indicators
- There are two aspects of data, such as male/female, rural/urban, for one time

Present data in a line chart if :
- The subject measured is a continuous set—for example, relationships such as income versus access to sanitation, or time lines such as data from 1975 to 1990
- The data show a trend—a continuous trend, a particular trend or change—or in comparing trends
- Comparing three aspects of data

For more detailed information about bar charts and line charts, refer to chapter 4, "Presenting statistics and indicators".

Constructing a pie chart

First, determine the value or percentage being presented. Figure the angle of the pie piece and plot it on the circle starting upright at 12 o'clock and moving counter-clockwise. Label clearly both segments of the pie. Colour the larger segment of the pie black and the smaller segment white.

Present data in a pie chart if the objective is to illustrate one share compared with the whole—for example, the proportion of women versus the whole population, or the economic gains from subsistence farming versus the whole GDP

What to avoid in pie charts:
* Do not show the mix within a whole compared with the mix within another whole
* Do not show one share compared with another share

For more detailed information about pie charts, refer to chapter 4, "Presenting data and designing the layout".

Producing camera-ready art and printing the booklet

Refer to chapter 5, "Producing and disseminating the book", for instructions on producing camera-ready art and printing the booklet.

Distribution

A concerted effort should be made to ensure that the booklet, with or without the book itself, gets into the hands of all senior government officials, leaders of policy and social groups, religious leaders, newspaper editors and owners, local women's organizations, and anyone else who might be enlisted to promote or act on the messages of the report. The booklet is meant to have an accessibility and immediacy that spurs action, or at least reaction.

Design and printing

As the content is simple, so too should be the design. Given the small page size, no more than one or two type faces should be used and fewer rather than more colours are recommended. In fact, a black and white booklet can be just as effective as one using colour. The overall look should be clean, spare and functional, allowing easy recognition of the numbers and facts. A useful design element is navigational information, such as tabs and headers that direct the reader to each topic or indicator. If the piece is to be pocket-size, design the cover so that the title is clearly visible at the top.

Some thought should be given to the order in which the information is to be presented. The most logical choice is to follow the topics in the order they appear in the book itself. On the other hand, it may be appropriate to put the most commonly requested data first, for easier access.

References and further reading

Hedman, Birgitta, Francesca Perucci and Pehr Sundström (1996). *Engendering Statistics: A Tool for Change*. Örebro: Statistics Sweden Publications Services.

Wallgren, Anders , Britt Wallgren, Rolf Persson, Ulf Jorner and Jan-Aage Haaland (1996). *Graphing Statistics and Data*. London: SAGE Publications.

Illustration 6. Sample page layout

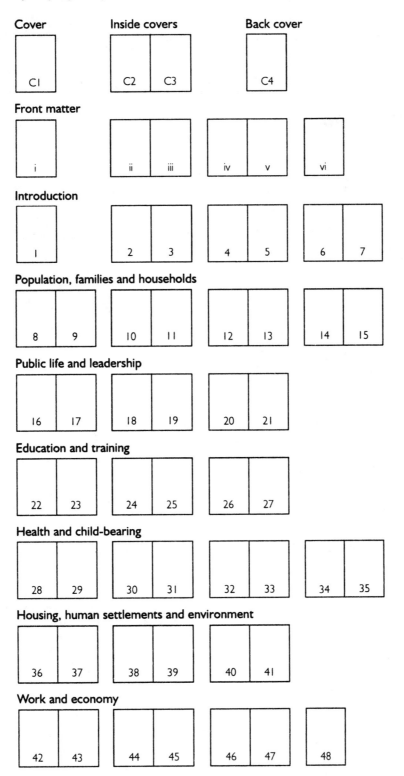

Botswana

Figure N. Teachers by level of school, 1988

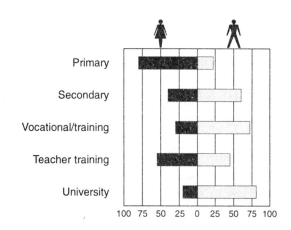

Source: Education Statistics, 1988, CSO - MFDP.

Women dominate at primary level as teachers but their representation decreases at higher levels, especially at the vocational, technical and university level. Women also number significantly more than men at teacher training colleges. Despite the predominance of women in the education system they are not well represented at management and decision-making levels.

WORK -

WHAT DO WE DO?

People are the most important resource in development. Furthermore, healthy people are more productive and can contribute more effectively in development. Health services and facilities have expanded in the last two decades. In the past five years substantial progress has been made in family planning and health in general. Improvements in this sector have had positive impacts on infant and child mortality rates.

Figure F. Infant and child mortality, 1973–88
Rate per thousand

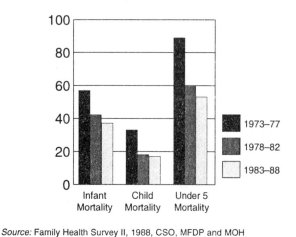

Source: Family Health Survey II, 1988, CSO, MFDP and MOH

Infant mortality rate	The number of deaths of infants, under 1 year of age, per 1000 live births in a given year
Child mortality rate	The number of deaths of children, under 5 years, per 1000 live births in a given year
Under-five mortality rate	The number of deaths of children, between birth and age 5, per 1000 live births in a given year

Table 10. Children aged 12–23 months immunized, as recorded or reported by mother, 1988

Immunization	% Urban	% Rural
DPT 1	99.5	97.4
DPT 2	99.5	96.1
DPT 3	97.5	92.7
Polio 1	99.5	98.3
Polio 2	99.5	97.0
Polio 3	96.6	90.6
Measles	94.6	91.8
BCG	99.5	98.3
Total	91.2	87.6

Source: Family Health Survey II, 1988, CSO - MFDP

Reprinted from Botswana, Central Statistics Office, *Women and Men in Botswana: Facts and Figures* (Gaborone, 1991).

United Republic of Tanzania

CHAPTER TWO. EDUCATION, INFORMATION AND COMMUNICATION

2.1. Primary education

Primary education that is both compulsory and universal aims at giving pupils a permanent ability in literacy and numeracy, with emphasis on reading, writing and arithmetic. It also intends to give pupils education that is complete in itself, inculcating a sense of commitment to the total community, and to help the pupils accept the values appropriate to Tanzania's future as well as preparing learners for further education. Primary education generally starts at the age of 7 and lasts for seven years; that is standard one to seven. Universal primary education was introduced in November 1977. Since then, all children aged 7 to 12 are eligible for enrolment. About 570,000 children enter primary school every year. The enrolment in primary schools is about 75 percent of the population in age group 7–13.

Table 2.1(a). Total enrolment in primary schools, 1988 and 1990
(Thousands)

	1988 W	1988 M	1990 W	1990 M
Level		Enrolment		
I	284	291	304	314
II	244	266	273	283
III	234	239	251	266
IV	295	283	267	274
V	177	176	205	203
VI	153	154	215	209
VII	187	180	157	156
Total I–VII	1574	1591	1674	1705
%	49.7	50.3	49.5	50.5

Source: Ministry of National Education.

CHAPTER THREE. EMPLOYMENT

3.1. Employment

Table 3.1(a). Population 15 years and above, 1988

Age group	Total	W	M
15–19	69	36	33
20–24	52	29	23
25–29	50	27	23
30–34	33	17	16
35–39	27	14	13
40–44	22	12	10
45–49	17	8	9
50–54	18	10	8
55–59	10	4	6
Total	298	157	141

Population (thousands)

Source: Population Census, 1988.

Table 3.1(b). Population 15 years and above, 1988

Place of work	Total (no.)	W (%)	M (%)
Govt. Ministries	21198	27	73
Parastatal	4985	20	80
Total	26183	26	74

Source: Dept. of Statistics, Zanzibar.

Table 3.1(c). Government employees by educational attainment, 1990

Educational level	Total (no.)	W (%)	M (%)
Masters + Post-graduate	149	15	85
BSc/BA	276	15	85
Diploma	474	14	86
Certificate	3853	44	56
Others	2748	40	60
Total	7500	39	61

Source: Dept. of Statistics, Zanzibar.

Reprinted from United Republic of Tanzania, Bureau of Statistics, *Women and Men in Tanzania* (Dar es Salaam, 1992).

People's Republic of China

Average age at first marriage for women aged 15–49 in urban and rural areas, 1949–92

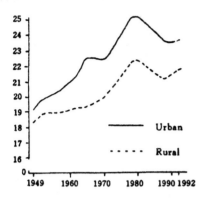

Source: Population Statistics, the State Statistical Bureau.

Note: Data for men are not available.

> Average age at first marriage for women of reproductive age: the average age of women aged 15–49 at first marriage occurring within a specific period of time (usually one year).

The average age at first marriage for the women at reproductive age is increasing, but is higher in urban than rural areas.

Marriage and divorce, 1978–93

(Million couples)

Source: Register of Marriage, Ministry of Civil Affairs.

The *New Marriage Law of the People's Republic of China,* promulgated in 1980, stipulated that the minimum marriage age is 22 years for men and 20 years for women. This revised the regulations of marriage age formulated during the "Cultural Revolution" (men 27 and women 25). The former regulation accounts for the rise in marriages in 1981.

Employed population by age in urban and rural areas, 1990

(Percentage distribution and sex distribution)

Area	Age	Percentage distribution Women	Percentage distribution Men	Sex distribution Women	Sex distribution Men
Urban					
	16–24	27	22	47	53
	25–34	36	33	46	54
	35–44	29	27	45	55
	45–54	11	15	36	64
	55–59		5		
	Total	100	100	43	57
Number (millions)		69	91		
Rural					
	16–24	36	31	49	51
	25–34	29	27	47	53
	35–44	23	22	46	54
	45–54	12	14	42	58
	55–59		5		
	Total	100	100	45	55
Number (millions)		201	241		

Source: 1990 Population Census.

Employment rate by age in urban and rural areas, 1990

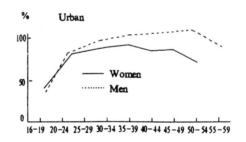

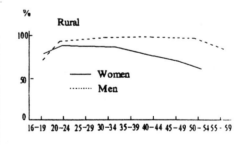

Source: 1990 Population Census.

Reprinted from People's Republic of China, State Statistical Bureau, *Women and Men in China: Facts and Figures 1995* (Beijing, 1995).

References and further reading

Hedman, Birgitta, Francesca Perucci and Pehr Sundström (1996). *Engendering Statistics: A Tool for Change*. Örebro: Statistics Sweden Publications Services.

Wallgren, Anders, Britt Wallgren, Rolf Persson, Ulf Jorner and Jan-Aage Haaland (1996). *Graphing Statistics and Data*. London: SAGE Publications.

Litho in United Nations, New York
15133—August 1997—4,530
ISBN 92-1-161394-9

United Nations publication
Sales No. E.97.XVII.10
ST/ESA/STAT/SER.K/14